"This volume brings together many anecdotes and intellectual highlights relating to the Rogatchover, the remarkable talmudic prodigy whose work fascinated so many of his successors, particularly in the Hasidic world, including the last Lubavitcher Rebbe."

—Shalom Carmy
Chair of Bible and Jewish Philosophy
Yeshiva University

"R. Yosef Rosen (the Rogatchover Gaon) was one of the towering figures of the early twentieth century revolution in conceptual Talmud study. He was also a major influence on another twentieth-century giant: R. Menahem Mendel Schneerson, the seventh Lubavitcher rebbe. Yet his challenging works are hardly known to the general public. R. Dovber Schwartz has now rendered this vast and deep corpus accessible, in clear, contemporary language, yet based on thorough and profound learning and for the first time in English! Both seasoned scholars and beginners will derive much benefit and enjoyment from this comprehensive introduction to an intellect of which one famous writer said one could carve out two Einsteins."

—Jonathan Garb
Gershom Scholem Professor of Kabbalah
Department of Jewish Thought - Hebrew University
Head of Amirim Honors Program in the Humanities

This excellent volume, "From Many One: A Glimpse into the Rogatchover's Universe" by Rabbi DovBer Schwartz, provides the English reader—in a superbly written fashion—with a glimpse of the brilliance of the Rogatchover in many different areas of halacha and hashkafa. It is well worth reading, and anyone who invests in studying this excellent work will gain enormously from it. The book clearly explains both the specific topics reviewed and the general methodology employed. The author is to be commended for engaging his subject so well.

—Rabbi Michael J. Broyde
Professor of Law, Emory University School of Law

"This long essay on the Rogachover marks one of only a few attempts to make Rabbi Rosen's contributions to the world of traditional Torah study accessible to a wide audience. Dovber Schwartz takes on the challenge with both enthusiasm and erudition. He synthesizes much of the existing scholarship that has been available until now only in Hebrew and offers his own conceptual reading of what makes the Rogachover one of the most creative and compelling of the modern halakhists."

—Prof Don Seeman
Emory University

D1329403

The Rogatchover Gaon

A Glimpse into

the Rogatchover's Universe

By R. DovBer Schwartz

The Rogatchover Gaon
A Glimpse into the Rogatchover's Universe

By R. DovBer Schwartz

ISBN: 978-1-304-43253-7

Cover painting by Rivka Siegel

Design, Layout, and Typesetting by Alexander Becker
www.alexanderbecker.net

Contents

Preface

When I was eighteen, I realized that I wanted to produce something concrete to show for all the exertion and time I was investing in learning, some unique achievement to add to the field I was studying. Perhaps it would be just a compilation or clarification of an issue—but something.

I started toying with different ideas. First I thought to write an analysis of the *Shulhan Arukh ha-Rav's Hilkhot Yom Tov*. It is written in an astounding way; from his subtle literary nuances, one can deduce incredible insights on the Talmudic source material. This is amply demonstrated by the Lubavitcher Rebbe in many places, and beautifully illustrated in *Migdal Or* (the essays on *birkhot ha-nehenin*) and various other books and pamphlets as well. I wanted to create a commentary on *Masekhet Betsah* culled from the implications and insights in *Shulhan Arukh ha-Rav*. I started researching and writing, but after half a year and several notebooks, I realized that I was not ready for the task.

I then thought of writing a book clarifying all the disputes between the Rambam and the Ramban, a theme the Lubavitcher

Rebbe develops in multiple places in *Likute Sihot*. I gave up on this as well; it was not for me.

My next idea was to write a commentary on the Talmud based on all the numerous places in *Likute Sihot* where the Lubavitcher Rebbe explains a *sugya* in the Talmud. In many places, he innovates original and rich approaches to central areas of Talmudic analysis, but the format of the content is not accessible to anyone outside of the clique of scholars who know precisely where, in all thirty-nine volumes, there is an analysis of a particular *sugya*. Besides finding all the material, the other challenge is that the content is presented in a didactic manner that is not always easy to digest.

I also realized that I was not comfortable writing a truly original work. I knew full well my intellectual deficiencies and how little of the vast literature of Talmud and rabbinics I had mastered. Contrasting this with the writings of the scholars that I studied, who had the entire Talmud at their fingertips, it seemed like a bad joke to think that I could add something of my own to the output of this vast network of giants. Instead I wanted to compile and clarify. I thought of myself as a facilitator, doing the grunt work and working in the trenches to bring to light different areas of fields in Torah that had not yet received full clarification. I started to notice the Lubavitcher Rebbe's fascination (there is no other word) with the Rogatchover Gaon. The richness and subtle nuance in his works attracted me and I started trying to learn his *sefarim*—with the emphasis on trying. It seemed impossible for reasons I will amply demonstrate in Chapter Two. I fondly remember one line of his that I spent several days trying to unpack.

The profound creativity and revolutionary thought of the Rogatchover is immensely attractive. It is razor-sharp and crystallizes many dense and overwhelming fields of Torah. Yet it is dense, cryptic, and written in short staccato bursts of terse information. I sought to open up his ideas to a larger audience. Nothing had been written in English, and in Hebrew, there were (and are) only two books that unpack his cryptic writings, *Mefaneah Tsfunot* and *Tsfunot ha-Rogatchovi,* which are themselves still very difficult and dense. An idea appeared in my mind to translate and analyze his works in English. This idea took shape over several years, culminating in the book you now hold in your hand.

I have tried to balance the book between an academic style and a relaxed and friendly yeshivah voice. It is my sincere hope that I have not alienated either cadre of readers by not being firmly ensconced in either natural and comfortable habitat. I did research independently, as well as in conjunction with several professors and Torah scholars who are knowledgeable on these topics. For the chapters on Hillel and Shammai and *kamut* and *ekhut*, I have primarily relied on the sources that the *Mefaneah Tsfunot* brings, although I have taken liberty in restructuring the order and often the thrust and theme of various sources. I have also relied on word searches, consultation with the few people well versed in *Tsafnat Paneah*, and cross-referencing from the *Klale ha-Torah ve-ha-Mitzvot*. The *Mefaneah Tsfunot* greatly reduces the workload of the researcher trying to unravel the works of the Rogatchover, but I have not bound myself to Kasher's understanding of the text. At times, after careful study of the source material, I have deviated from Kasher's understanding of a passage. His understanding is itself only implied by his ordering of the various sources from the *Tsafnat Paneah*, since his comments are sporadic and terse. The other chapters were built primarily from the original source of the *Tsafnat Paneah*.

The Hebrew terms in this book have been italicized and translated in parentheses the first time they appear. For example, the frst time I write sugya it appears as *sugya* (a topic in the Talmud). The next time, it is merely italicized as *sugya*.

In using personal pronouns, I have stuck to the time-tested method of using he, him and his. This is simply the easiest and least confusing way of doing it, and not a reflection of this book's intended audience.

This book is primarily an attempt to present the thoughts and writings of the Rogatchover to the public. I hope it will pave the way for future research by other scholars. It is not meant to be a biography. As an afterthought, I have included a short chapter on the Rogatchover's life as an introduction. Its stories are not exhaustive or rigorously sourced.

I was hesitant to publish this book, because the Rogatchover is a giant and I feared that it would not do him justice. However, my teacher, the Lubavitcher Rebbe, had this to say: "Each and every person has a personal responsibility to innovate in Torah, as the *Alter* Rebbe clarifies in *hilkhot talmud torah*... in earlier generations, they were very careful with *hidushim* in Torah, even when they were only theoretical and not halakhically actionable. This was true for speaking *hidushim* and even more so for writing and publicizing them. Only after a great many conditions were met was it considered acceptable for someone to write and publish his Torah.

In our generation, things have changed. While it is still true that tremendous precautions and scrutiny are required, on the other hand, because of *yeridat ha-dorot,* we need to find ways to increase the thirst for learning Torah. Therefore it is fitting and appropriate to encourage all those who are capable of writing Torah. Even if they are unsure whether their writings are in alignment with the Torah of truth, not only should they not refrain from writing, but quite the contrary, they should write and publish it. Not just for friends, but for the entire public at large. And the main reason is, as I just said, that we see when people have an outlet for their creativity in learning, their vibrancy and vitality in learning Torah is increased. And not just them but also their peers, in the spirit of 'kinat sofrim tarbeh hokhmah.' Additionally, it is the nature of man that when he shows his writings to the public, his ego itself will compel him to check and recheck his sources and logic, etc...." (*Sefer ha-Sihot* 1991, p. 560).

In keeping with his advice, I am going ahead and publishing this book, knowing full well that there may be errors and mistakes in it, perhaps even major ones. If you find any, or simply have a comment to make, email me at berryschwartz@gmail.com.

Acknowledgements

I have so many people to thank; people without whom this book would not have been possible. Contrary to popular custom (I love being contrary), I will thank my wife first.

Elisheva – my source of inspiration and resilience

George Rohr – without whom this book would be a dream waiting to happen. You're awesome.

My parents and siblings – you guys rock.

Pops and Mama B – your kindness and generosity doesn't stop.

Zalman Alpert – who was amazingly helpful with research

Mary Ann – for always having time to help with research

Dovid Olidort

Doobie Lisker and Yossi Krazniansky – a constant help in research

Michoel Seligson

Sarah Beck – a gifted editor

Fitz Rabin – for being there

Rivka Siegel – who painted the gorgeous cover illustration

The following people were really supportive and encouraging of my book throughout the process.

Professor Chaim Saiman

Professor Don Seeman

Professor Yonatan Garb

Alexander Becker – an outstanding publisher, formatter, typesetter and awesome Jew

My family and friends for being there.

Chapter One

1.1 Chronological Overview

Rabbi Yosef Rosen, known as the Rogatchover Gaon, was born in Rogatchov, Belarus, in 1858. His father, Ephraim Fishel Rosen, was a well-known and respected Lubavitcher hasid. At the tender age of five, his father took him to see the third Lubavitcher Rebbe, the *Tsemah Tsedek*, who instructed him to learn Tractate *Nazir*. The Rebbe placed his hand on his head and blessed him with becoming a great scholar. He then added that "it would be worthwhile for the boy to learn *Nazir*." Upon exiting the Rebbe's study, the young boy remarked to his father: "Why do you think the Rebbe told me to study *Nazir*? Is not one obligated to learn the whole Torah? It must be that he wants me to become a *nazir*! And perhaps the first part of his blessing, that I will become a great scholar, is dependent on the second part of his blessing, my being a *nazir*."

And so it was, from that day on, that the Rogatchover rarely let his hair be cut. (One who undertakes *nezirut* for life, a *nezir olam*, is allowed to cut his hair when it gets too heavy.) His wild and untended hair was his unique identifying mark.

Other theories are that he did not want to uncover his head since he would not be able to learn Torah, or that it hurt him to cut his hair. A strange explanation was offered by Rabbi Yissachar Tamar, who heard it from Yosef Friher, an attendant of the Rogatchover. Friher claimed that the Gaon had a condition in which his hair was so matted and bunched together that it was dangerous to cut.

My father heard from Shmuel Katz who was told by the Rogatchover that the reason he did not like to cut his hair was simply because it tickled him.

As the boy progressed in his studies, he soon outpaced all of his teachers, so his father undertook the education of the prodigy. It was a sight to see, father and son in the midst of a heated Talmudic debate, each one developing his side of the argument and becoming, for the moment, equals.

When he reached the age of bar mitzvah, his father sent him to Rabbi Yosef Dov Soloveitchik, the Rav of Slutzk and later Brisk, where he became a study partner of Rabbi Chaim Soloveitchik for a year, even though he was a full five years younger than Reb Chaim. The two geniuses took to studying the Rambam together with a special zeal. Their teacher, Rabbi Yosef Dov Soloveitchik, reportedly was none too happy about this, as he wanted the boys to immerse themselves more in the Talmud and its various commentaries. Both of them would later pen their masterpieces on the Rambam. The Rogatchover was known by the nickname of *ilui he-hatsuf,* the impish genius, due to his sharp wit and biting humor. It is interesting to note that his father, a prominent and devoted Lubavitcher hasid, sent him to study with Lithuanian scholars. Possibly this is because Lubavitch did not have a yeshivah until the year 1897. Or perhaps his father simply wanted him to benefit from the tutelage of the outstanding scholars of Slutzk and Brisk. Either way, there was a large amount of cross-pollination among the various sections of Jewry and the yeshivot in those days.

After this, the Rogatchover went to the city of Shklov, where he studied with Rabbi Yehoshua Leib Diskin. In the year 1876, he married, and was supported by his father-in-law for eight years in Warsaw. After much communal pressure, he agreed to act as the Rav there for a period of time.

In 1889, when the Rogatchover was 31, the Kapuster Rebbe[1], Rabbi Shlomo Zalman Schneersohn, appointed him to be the Rav of the hasidic community in Dvinsk. The Lithuanian Rav there was Rabbi Meir Simhah Ha-Kohen, the author of the *Or Sameah* and *Meshekh Hokhmah*, with whom he enjoyed good relations. The townspeople took great pride in their having such a great man as their leader and looked on the Rogatchover with much affection. Reportedly, the fifth Lubavitcher Rebbe was also involved, as he instructed his hasidim to travel to Warsaw to convince the Rogatchover to come to Dvinsk after the previous Rav had passed away. In 1914, he was forced to flee Dvinsk and move to Petersburg, later Leningrad, only returning a full ten years later, in 1924.

The Rogatchover Gaon passed away in Vienna on the 11th of Adar, 1936 (5696) at the age of 78, and was buried in Dvinsk. All three communities—Riga (his place of birth), Vienna (where he died), and Dvinsk (where he was the Rav)—fought for the honor of having this giant of a man be buried in their cities. After committing to all the financial burdens involved, the city of Dvinsk was chosen for his final resting place. His main work, a commentary on Maimonides, was published during his lifetime. The remainder of his surviving writings appeared in the United States many years after his death. All are titled *Tsafnat Paneah*, a title given to the Biblical Joseph by Pharaoh (Genesis 41:45).

His manuscripts were smuggled out of Latvia on microfilm during World War II by his successor, Rabbi Yisrael Alter Safran-Fuchs (1911–1942), who remained in Latvia to complete this task, and his daughter, who had come to Dvinsk from *Erets Yisrael* to help preserve her father's manuscripts. Both died at the hands of the Nazis as a result. A portion of these manuscripts was edited and published by Rabbi Menahem Kasher.

---

1   When the Tzemach Tzedek died, several of his sons became Rebbes in different towns. His youngest son, Rabbi Shmuel Schneersohn became the Rebbe in the city of Lubavitch. Another son, Rabbi Yehudah Leib Schneersohn became the Kapuster Rebbe. Yehudah Leib's oldest son Shlomo Zalman became the second Kapuster Rebbe on his death in 1866.

The only reason we have the works of the Rogatchover today is because of the incredible heroism of the Rogatchover's daughter, Rebbetzin Rochel Citron, and of the Rogatchover's successor in Dvinsk, Rabbi Yisrael Alter Safran-Fuchs. When the Rogatchover passed away, Reb Alter was chosen as his successor, although he was only twenty-five and still unmarried. From the moment of his acceptance until the last day of his life, he spent every moment in dedication to the writings of his great teacher. Amazingly, during the most difficult of times, the war years of 1940 and 1941, he managed to publish two volumes of responsa from the Rogatchover. During this desperate period, the Rogatchover's daughter, Rebbetzin Citron, by then widowed, left Palestine to help Rabbi Safran-Fuchs publish the Gaon's works.

But times got worse. The end was coming closer and the Nazis were nearing Dvinsk. Rabbi Safran-Fuchs and Rebbetzin Citron had many opportunities to escape to the United States, where they had relatives, but they remained in Dvinsk to save the writings of the Rogatchover. Thus began a race against time. For two years, Reb Alter and Rebbetzin Citron, against great and dangerous odds, made micro-photographs of the Rogatchover's writings—the glosses on the sides of his Gemarot, Humashim, and other *sefarim*—and sent them to Reb Alter's uncle in America, Rabbi Zvi Hirsch Safran. Every two weeks, Reb Alter faithfully mailed his precious cargo.

All in all, he miraculously managed to send one entire Gemara (*Makot*), twenty-five hundred pages of Talmudic glosses, fifteen hundred pages of commentary on the Rambam, and twelve hundred more pages covering assorted parts of the Torah. The last package was sent one week before the Nazis entered Dvinsk.

But the tale is not over. From June 1941, when the last package of the Rogatchover's Torah writings was sent to America, until June 1957, the tiny photographs lay abandoned and unread. Mrs. Yetta Leah Safran, to whom the writings had been entrusted, made a number of attempts to bring the manuscripts to public attention. The organizations with whom she spoke were largely uninterested and claimed that there was no way to sufficiently enlarge the miniscule prints. So the matter remained for sixteen years.

In 1957, the hand of God guided the interaction of a number of events to allow the Rogatchover's writings to finally emerge from obscurity. Rabbi Menahem Kasher found out about the manuscripts and, with the aid of several foundations, among them Yeshiva University, specifically Rabbi Dr. Samuel Belkin, obtained the funds to establish the *Makhon Tsafnat Paneah,* which published some writings of the Rogatchover. Rabbi Pinchas Teitz, the second president of the *Makhon Tsafnat Paneah,* was responsible for publishing seven volumes of the Rogatchover's writings after the passing of Rabbi Kasher, who directed the first publications. Rabbi Shlomo Torshansky, director of the Torah Department of the Claims Conference for the Jews of Germany, funded the various scholars involved in publishing the Rogatchover's writings. Among the honorary presidents of the foundation were such illustrious figures as Rabbi Moshe Feinstein, Rabbi Yosef Dov Soloveitchik, and Rabbi Pinchas Hirshprung. The Lubavitcher Rebbe sent several checks to the institute and was very supportive.[2]

1.2 Publications

His works include the following:

Tsafnat Paneah. His magnum opus, two volumes on the Rambam's *Mishneh Torah,* printed in 1903.

Hibur al Moreh Nevukhim. In the back of his Torah commentary.

Tsafnat Paneah al ha-Torah. A five-volume set on the Torah.

Tsafnat Paneah al ha-Shas. Four volumes covering Tractates *Bava Kama, Bava Metsia, Makot, Horayot,* and *Sanhedrin.*

Tsafnat Paneah Responsa. The Dvinsk edition contains two volumes, one printed in 1940, the second in 1941. The Warsaw edition contains three volumes, all printed in 1935.

Mikhteve Torah. A book of correspondence between the Rogatchover and Rabbi Mordechai Kalina, containing two hundred ninety letters from the years 1922 to 1926. The entire correspon-

---

2   *Learn Torah, Love Torah, Live Torah: HaRav Mordechai Pinchas Teitz, the Quintessential Rabbi,* by Dr. Rivkah Blau. Ktav, 2001 page 40.

dence started with one letter from Rabbi Mordechai Kalina, and the ensuing two hundred eighty-nine letters were all derivative concepts and debates arising from the first letter.

The books written on the Rogatchover's writings are few. The most extensive one is the *Mefaneah Tsfunot*, by Rabbi Menahem Kasher. The first part of the book contains several essays on the methodology and conceptual framework of the Rogatchover. The second part of the book is a compilation of sources from the Rogatchover on several key concepts. Unfortunately, this part of the book is essentially unintelligible without vast amounts of time spent unraveling the sources, because there is little explanatory or supplementary material provided.

Another book, *Tsfunot ha-Rogatchovi*, by Rabbi Moshe Grossberg,[3] is more conceptual and analytical then the *Mefaneah Tsfunot*. In it, the author provides background and context for several of the Rogatchover's core concepts. Rabbi Grossberg also annotates much of the responsa of the Rogatchover in his *Haamek Iyun*, adding background information on the sources cited in the letters.

Another source is an essay written by Rabbi Shlomo Yosef Zevin. In his book *Ishim ve-Sihot*, a methodological and conceptual analysis of several of the giants of Torah scholarship in the last century, he explains some of the central guiding principles behind the Rogatchover's system of Torah analysis.

Another source, and probably the most readily understandable and user-friendly one, is the *Pirke Mavo*, written by Rabbi Moshe Shlomo Kasher, the son of Rabbi Menahem Kasher. It is printed in the beginning of each volume of the *Tsafnat Paneah al ha-Torah*. Rabbi Moshe Shlomo Kasher also translated an article by Rabbi Chaim Sapir, "*Der Lebediker Shas*" ("The Living Talmud").

Another two scholars who added to this area are Rabbi Yehoshua Mundshein (*Paneah Raza*) and Rabbi M.M. Tenenbaum (*Shitat*

---

3   The Lubavitcher Rebbe sent a letter of support and encouragement in 1977 to Rabbi Grossberg which is printed in the beginning of *Haamek Iyun*. In the letter he praises his efforts to clarify the Rogatchover's writings. At the end of the letter he voices several concerns with two places in *Haamek Iyun* that he felt did not explain the Rogatchover's intent correctly.

Limudo shel ha-Rogatchovi). Rabbi Tenenbaum also published two volumes of correspondence between the Rogatchover and Rabbi Yehiel Ha-Kohen, *Kitve Rabi Yehiel*.

Recently two volumes of *Sheelot u-Teshuvot Tsafnat Paneah he-Hadashot* were published. They include responsa on *Orah Hayim* and *Yoreh Deah*, as well as glosses on the *Tur*. Many letters of the Rogatchover were reprinted there as well, with an accompanying translation.

Rabbi Shlomo Sabel published a volume of his correspondence with the Rogatchover, *Shalme Yosef*. Three volumes of explanatory material were recently published by Rabbi Yosef Ben-Shimon from Montreal on the Rogatchover's commentary on the Rambam. In 2005, a biography was published by Yair Buruchav.

This book is the first attempt to present this great man and his scholarship to the English-speaking public.

1.3 Unique Character and Scholarship

In this biographical chapter, I have tried to describe the character and personality of Rabbi Yosef Rosen. One who wants to describe a giant and master in his discipline will inevitably bump into the question of where the personality stops and the scholarship begins. For example, if one is writing a biography of Einstein's personality, how can one omit his innovations in physics? They are irrevocably linked to the man. He breathed and lived physics. The same problem applies here, *lehavdil*. So much of the Rogatchover's personality shines through his style and method of Torah study. This is even truer for him then for other Torah scholars because his model of Torah study is integrated into one harmonious worldview and lifestyle, as we see in Chapter Two. As a result, many legal rulings, comments on the Talmud or the Bible, responsa, and other passages indicative of the Rogatchover's personality are interwoven into this chapter.

The Rogatchover has an extraordinarily unique personality. He is a colorful and eccentric rabbinic figure without parallel. His behaviors, thought patterns, and interactions with people do not fit into the normative, conventional persona of a Torah scholar. Attempting to comprehend the world he inhabits and his persona is quite difficult. The Rogatchover is a complex man whose nuanced, subtle cognitive world is fully understood only by himself. Besides this, he is a saintly man and a world-class *talmid haham.*

I have used a plethora of sources in gathering the material for the biography. Additionally, I have interviewed many people who have received stories from their parents regarding the Rogatchover Gaon. Most prominently, Rabbi Mendel Morozov,one of the few (only?) people who remembers the Rogatchover personally, and Rabbi Yoel Khan who heard stories first-hand from people who knew the Rogatchover well.

Some of the sources utilized in the biography are the following:

Alei Tamar 2:241; Amudei Eish 72; Betzel Hachakhma 66; Hamodia, Tetzave, 12th of Adar 2003; HaOhr Sameach 73-79,80-86; Kovetz Ohalei Shem Gilyon 3 28; Kisvei Reb Yechiel 1:19 and on; Migdal Oz page 58; Marbitzei Torah Be'Olam HaChassidus 92; Pri Tamarim 19; Yemei Melekh 1:168; Yemei Melekh 1:179; Siach Zkeinim 4:377.

The most extensive sources are:

Kovetz Turei Yeshurun Choveret 44 Shvat-Adar 1975; Ishim Veshitot page 96 and on.

Additionally many sources from the Lubavitcher Rebbe's talks were drawn on.

The following are the sources from *Sihot Kodesh*, with the year the talk was delivered, followed by section or *seif.*

1951, *Vaera* 2; 1952, *Yud Gimel* Tamuz 28; 1953, Simchat Torah 6; 1954, second day of Sukkot 10 (*Laha"k*), footnote 40; 1964, *Motzaei* Shabbat, *Yud Aleph* Shevat 3; 1966, *Seudah* of the second night of Shavuot; 1968, *Balak* 3; 1968,*Reeh* 7; 1972, 19th of Kislev 3; 1974, *Yud Aleph* Nisan 3; 1975, *Mikets* 4; 1975, last day of Pesach 9; 1975, *Yud Gimel* Tamuz 5; 1976, Simchat Torah day, 6; 1976, *Mikets*, 13; 1976, *Zayin* Adar 4; 1976, last day of Pesach 6; 1976,*Kedoshim* 1; 1976, second day of Shavuot 2; 1976, *Naso* 1; 1957, *Bereshit* 9; 1959, 13th of Tamuz 7; 1961, Simchat

Beit Ha-Shoevah[?] 10; 1961, *Khaf* Av 1; 1964, *Bereshit* 37; 1977, second day of Shavuot 42; 1977, *Hukat* 22 and*Pinhas* 12; 1979, *Tsav* 41; 1979, *Gimel* Sivan 14; 1980, *Bereshit* 1980, *Devarim* 89, *klalim*.

Sources from *Likutei Sihot* are the following: vol.15, p. 36; vol.16, p. 454; vol.1, p. 117; vol. 16, p. 374.

Most stories have been passed down orally. Some are more credible then others, but usually any one story is corroborated by others that describe similar traits. Ultimately, we are dealing with a scant number of sources, some of them secondhand, based upon which we try to comprehend the image and identity of this great man. This would be difficult even if we were dealing with a plain and simple person. With that caveat, I will begin this attempt to depict the persona of the Rogatchover.

One of the most striking features of his personality is his impatience and sharp, often caustic attitude towards others. Coming from an integrated and consistent person, this manifests itself in two ways, as most of his behavior does: in his personal interactions and his scholarly style and writing. In his interpersonal behavior, it expresses itself as a stern, dismissive, and impatient manner. In his scholarship, it is exhibited by his rejection and sometimes disdain for *Aharonim*, and lack of wholehearted submission to the *Rishonim*.

This is not to say that he does not embrace and love other people. For every story we have of him being dismissive, there is another story of him being kind and humble. It simply means that he has no patience with things or people that waste his time. One of the episodes that bring out this facet of his character is the following:

At a certain point in his life, the Rogatchover was very close to the Kapuster Rebbe, Rabbi Shlomo Zalman Schneersohn, the author of the *Magen Avot*. In one of his letters to the Rogatchover he wrote, "The time has come for you to behave as your teacher did."

What was the meaning behind this mysterious message? The Rogatchover's teacher, Rabbi Yosef Dov Soloveitchik, had a tobacco jar with six letters engraved onto the cover: *shin, peh, vav, shin, mem, nun.* No one knew what these letters meant, and the Rogatchover was intensely curious about the matter. One day, they were learning a *Tosafot* on which Rav Soloveitchik had a question that he could not resolve. The students saw that the question was eating away at him, frustrating his every attempt to answer it. The Rogatchover saw his chance, approached his teacher, and said: "Let's make a deal. I'll explain this *Tosafot* to you in exchange for your explaining to me the meaning behind these mysterious letters." Rav Soloveitchik looked up, in the midst of a complex train of thought. "OK, I accept," he said. The Rogatchover proceeded to deliver a brilliant clarification on *Tosafot*, and his teacher kept his side of the bargain. "You see, when I was younger, I would speak sharply to other people, and not always with respect and sensitivity. In order to uproot that negative character trait, I engraved this mnemonic onto my tobacco jar, to constantly remind me of the need to speak nicely and patiently to people. The letters stand for *"shomer piv u-leshono shomer mi-tzarot nafsho"* ("one who guards his mouth and tongue guards himself from much trouble"). This was what the Kapuster Rebbe meant by telling the Rogatchover to adopt the behavior of his teacher; it was a message to him to be more careful to speak patiently to others.

✳ ✳ ✳

So sharp was the Rogatchover that many of the people who came to his home were afraid to go in, and so asked to be escorted and introduced. Zevuluni relates: "One Shabbos, I accompanied Rabbi Gronem Landau, one of the outstanding students of Kamenetz in Lithuania, who is today the head of Yeshivat ha-Darom in Rehovot. I introduced him to the Rogatchover, and after a polite exchange, I left for yeshivah, while Rabbi Landau remained behind. On *Motzaei* Shabbos I met Rabbi Landau, who said that the Rogatchover was looking for me. I was a bit nervous because the Rogatchover was suspicious of people illicitly taking *sefarim* from him—he did not have anything else to take—so I went to him right away. When he saw me, he took off his warm coat, put it on my shoulders, and said, 'Koidonover, the winter is in full force, and you go about without a coat. Take my coat. I do not have money to buy you a new coat, but if there is no choice, this will do fine.' I could not refuse, because one may not refuse a great man, and I had to take it. Till today, I still have it as a keepsake."

* * *

The hasid Eliyahu Althouse asked the Rogatchover about wearing two pairs of *tefillin*, Rashi and Rabbenu Tam.[4] "Generally we wear both pairs out of doubt which opinion is correct," he said, "but surely the Rav knows [which is correct]—so tell me, which pair do you put on?" The Rogatchover responded, "When someone asks me a halakhic question I feel duty-bound to answer, but insofar as my personal conduct is concerned, I feel no obligation to respond to you."

* * *

A Rav once came to Dvinsk, but was afraid of meeting the Rogatchover, who was famous for his dismissive behavior towards scholars. After debating with himself, he finally decided to go and see him. Much to his surprise, the Rogatchover treated him kindly, speaking to him pleasantly for thirty minutes as they discussed various *halakhot*. As he was about to leave, the Rav gathered his courage and said, "I thought you are known for being sharp with scholars, yet to me you were so nice!"

"Ah, that is precisely the point—I am only sharp with *scholars*. But to simple people I am nice and pleasant."

This was an interesting dynamic; the Rogatchover was extremely patient and unassuming with simple people, yet often dismissive of scholars. The hasidim in Petersburg who were with him during the war years told many stories to this effect. When asked why he does not respect rabbis and scholars, he replied, "It's not that I have any vendetta against scholars. I'll speak to anyone—I do not care about his lineage or background. I simply relate to people as they relate to me and as I see them. When a scholar relates to me with scholarship, I see the glaring deficiencies [in it] and thus do not think of him highly. A simple and innocent Jew, though—why would I respond to him with criticism?"

---

4   As told by the Lubavitcher Rebbe.

The greatest praise one could receive from the Rogatchover was the unassuming but profound, "I see you know how to learn a bit." Conversely, the Rogatchover would say about many of the leading scholars of the day, and of generations before him, that they "did not know how to learn."

A Rav once came to him complaining that the people of his town do not treat him with enough respect. "Why do you think you deserve to be respected?" the Gaon asked. "Because I am a *talmid haham* [scholar]," he replied.

"I know more then you by far and I still would not consider myself a *talmid haham*," said the Rogatchover.

A wealthy man once brought a prospective son-in-law to the Rogatchover to see if he was indeed the scholar that everyone claimed him to be. From the next room he heard the Rogatchover call the young man "*boch*," the Yiddish for goat. This occurred several times, and after they left, the wealthy man cancelled the wedding. A while later the Rogatchover saw this man and inquired when the wedding would take place. The man told him that after hearing the Rogatchover call the yeshivah student a goat, he had naturally cancelled the wedding.

"Fool! My goats know how to learn!"[5]

* * *

This facet of the Rogatchover's personality can also be seen from his responsa. Many of his letters are biting and critical in tone and style, sometimes indirectly and subtly, other times quite explicitly. To see this in action, one need go no further than Rabbi Shlomo Sabel's *Shalme Yosef*, his correspondence with the Rogatchover. Yet the Rogatchover never ignores a letter from Sabel or refuses to reply, and takes his responsibility as a public figure and halakhic decisor very seriously.

In his very first letter to Sabel, dated the 14th of Av 1929, he begins as follows:

---

5   *Teitz*, page 41.

"*Kibalti michtavo u-mah rotseh marbeh be-sheelot?*" ("I have received your letter, and do not know what you want. You are superfluous and excessive with your questions.")

In the third letter, as well as the sixth, eighth, eleventh, twelfth, thirteenth ("what do you want already? I wrote you concerning this!"), fourteenth ("I am astounded at you. I already wrote to you about this in the summer!"), nineteenth, twentieth, twenty-fourth, twenty-fifth, twenty-sixth, twenty-seventh ("I received your letter. G-d forbid that you write such a thing… the entire canon of Talmud is explicitly against this notion… please stop speaking concerning this since you will introduce a corruption in Israel and increase *mamzerim*"), and the twenty-ninth, he begins his response with "*mah rotseh?*" ("what do you want?"). This is a dismissive and biting opening to what is always a cryptic and extremely short letter, which is often signed "Yosef—*Akatzer*" ("I am being concise").

To add to this, in the third letter, in middle of a discussion, he writes, "*u-mah kotev shtusim…al yedaber hevalim*" ("why are you writing foolishness? Do not speak of vanities!").

Interestingly, in the sixth letter he writes, "I beg of you, tell me something. There is an old man in Yerushalayim whose name is Zalman Levin. He is one of my close friends for a long time, since my days in the city of blood, Petersburg. He is a Chabad Hasid, therefore find out for me how he is doing, and how he is situated there."

In the eighth letter, he again writes: "Why have you not responded to me to tell me how the old man Reb Zalman Levin is doing? He is amongst the elders in Yerushalayim."

In the twentieth letter he again signs himself: "Yosef—please tell me how Reb Zalman Levin is doing!"

In the seventeenth letter he signs off with an ambiguous statement: "Apparently you learnt in Radin."

In the thirty-first letter he writes: "Regarding printing my letters, if you want, you can do so."

In the twenty-sixth letter he writes: "I received your letter, and I had to pay a huge fine because you wrote on the letter in a place where it is illegal to write. Therefore I request that if you are writing to me, do not write so many questions in one letter."

✳ ✳ ✳

At the age of seventeen, the Rogatchover went on a tour of the major centers of Torah learning to, as he put it, "see if anyone out there knows how to learn a bit." His first stop was in Warsaw. From there he travelled to Lublin, where he spent some time. In Lublin he became close to Rabbi Schneur Zalman Fradkin, known as the *Torat Hesed* after his most famous work, who was a prominent Lubavitch hasid. Upon entering his study, the *Torat Hesed* looked up and said "Sit, my son." Right away, the Rogatchover fired back at him every source in the entire canon of Jewish literature where the phrase "sit, my son" is used. After hearing him out, the *Torat Hesed* replied, "Very nice, but you forgot one place where the *Rashba* has an alternate version of a *gemara*..." After this salvo of scholarship was exchanged, a discussion of Torah learning began which lasted several hours. After the discussion ended, the Rogatchover asked whether there are any other people in the city with whom he can discuss Torah. The *Torat Hesed* gave him the address of Reb Tsadok ha-Kohen and sent him on his way. "The old man knows how to learn! The old man knows how to learn!" he exclaimed, while walking down the street.

The next stop was the home of Reb Tsadok. The Rogatchover entered his study and immediately began shooting scholarly ideas at the saintly man in rapid-fire style. Reb Tsadok looked up from the *sefer* he was learning and asked, "Do you have a question that you need help with?" "No, I simply would like to test my scholarship against yours." The saintly man closed his eyes and sharply stated, "Listen here, young man. I, too, was once like you. I tried testing my prowess in learning against all the sages of the time. None were able to best me. But, after meeting my master [the Ishbitzer Rebbe] and learning from him, I realized— none of this, ultimately, is important. What matters is your fear of heaven and degree of sincerity. And besides, what will G-d gain if I best you or you vanquish me? Listen to me—you need to find yourself a teacher, a rebbe who will induct you into the proper path of serving G-d." The Rogatchover left the house and slowly, reflectively walked down the street, whispering: "Wow. His sharp and true words penetrate to the core..."[6]

At the age of eighteen, he married the daughter of Rabbi Moshe Gorfinkel, who agreed to support him for eight years. A couple of years later his wife died and it was decided that he would marry her younger sister. When it came time for the chuppah, the esteemed groom was nowhere to be found. After much searching, someone thought to go look in the local study hall, where they found the Gaon hunched over his precious Rambam, in the midst of unraveling a complex theory on *hilkhot maaseh korbanot*. People informed him that it was time for the wedding and he had to go. He gazed at the Rambam and closed it softly, saying, "Forgive me master, I must go to the chuppah..."

* * *

Rabbi Zevin described the Rogatchover's character as follows:

"The Rogatchover well knew his own worth. He did not hide himself from his own perception. He did not value the great *Aharonim*, even the early ones. He does not mention them or bring them at all in his writings. Even the *Rishonim* (Rashi, *Tosafot*, the *Rosh*, and others) that he expounded upon, showing us wondrous pearls hidden in their words, even with them, he did not accept their superiority in an absolute way. Often he would explain a *mishnah* or *gemara* in a creative and original way, diametrically opposed to the explanations of the *Rishonim*. And every time he would do this he would bring copious amounts of sources to buttress, support, and adorn his unique theory.

If this is so with the Mishnah and Gemara, into which the *Rishonim* delved, bequeathing to us large amounts of commentary, all the more so is it true with the Tosefta and the Talmud Yerushalmi, on which the *Rishonim* did not write much material.

---

6   Ishim Ve'shitot

On the pages of his books are spread thousands of entirely original explanations, perhaps tens of thousands, on the Tosefta and the Yerushalmi. It would be very worthwhile for someone to publish all his explanations and commentary on the Yerushalmi as an independent work. It is unfortunate that his style of writing was so cryptic, brief, and difficult to decipher. Much struggle and exertion is required in order to understand what he is saying.

The Rogatchover's written Torah and oral Torah could not have been more different. He was a great orator and speaker with a clear and crisp articulation that none matched. When he would hold forth on his deep theories in the Talmud, his words would shine and smile, fitting beautifully and seamlessly into the text. It seemed as if it would be impossible to hold a different opinion. Even simple people who did not know much Talmud would feel and appreciate the sweetness and brilliance of his theories when they heard his words. People would come and sit for hours just to hear him, taking great pleasure from his speeches and not feeling impatient or fidgeting. But in writing, to our great misfortune, he is as one impaired. His style and narrative voice are incredibly difficult. So much deep light is hidden in his books, radiance with which he gazes from one end of the Talmudic world to the other. But much effort is required to decipher his secrets.

Yet, as much as he is cryptic in his writings, so too is he prolific. He writes and writes and writes. Books, published and unpublished, and tens of thousands of letters. From all corners of the globe people turn to him every day with different questions. Questions of theoretical halakhah and practical queries. Questions of depth and questions of breadth. All of them, without differentiation, he answers right away, on the spot, without thinking or glancing in a *sefer*. His responsa are also staggering in the number of sources cited and the innovative approach he brings to these sources.

Here is one small example of his originality. Someone asks him if they need to say the prayer for traveling on an airplane. He responds on the spot in the negative, giving the following source as a proof:

The Talmud in *Hulin* (139b) brings the verse, "when you chance upon a *kan tsipur* before you on the path."

Commenting on this, the Talmud states "if one found a nest at sea [on a small islet or rock in the ocean], he is obligated to send away the mother bird and perform the mitzvah. As it says, 'He who gives a path [*derekh*] at sea.'" In other words, since the Torah states that the obligation is when the nest is "before you on the path," this means that the obligation is only active when one is on a halakhic path. The Gemara then tries to deduce that by this logic, one who finds a nest in the heavens should be obligated in the mitzvah, since it says "the path of the eagle is in the sky," implying that there is a path in the heavens. To this the Gemara responds, "No, this is different. It is indeed called the path of the eagle. But in general, there are no paths in the sky."

Therefore, concluded the Rogatchover, halakhically the sky is not considered to be a path, and thus the prayer said on the path of traveling, *tefilat ha-derekh*, is not said on an airplane.

This is merely an example of his method. I am not entering now in to the actual question of the halakhah. One can argue with his reasoning, since there is, in fact, danger in the sky. Indeed, the danger when traveling by plane may even be greater than otherwise, and thus we would reason that a traveler is in even greater need of G-d's assistance. However, the Gaon is answering simply. The prayer for safe travel was not instituted for every danger. It was instituted for danger when traveling on a path, and therefore anything which is not halakhically a path does not mandate the prayer. What I am interested in right now is in the incredibly adaptive and original understanding and application of that *gemara* in *Hulin*.

This is his approach not only in questions concerning man's relationship to G-d, but also in questions dealing with interpersonal relationships. Again, the same rapidity of response and simplicity of approach is evident. One example is of a wealthy man who died, leaving an inheritance for his son. But there was a unique condition in the will. The whole estate was left to the older son, except for the army expiation receipt.

There was a period in Russia where everyone who paid a large sum of money to the government was exempt from being drafted into the army. The government would give the person a receipt, but the person could sell the receipt to whomever he wished. When they abolished this system of paid exemptions, it was only abolished going forward; whoever had a receipt still qualified for an exemption from the draft. Obviously, the price of these receipts greatly increased. People were paying vast sums of money for them.

The younger son of this wealthy man who died decided to show up for the military physical examination as usual, and wait and see. If they were to exempt him, he decided, he would sell the receipt for a large sum, and if they were to clear him for the army, he would present the receipt and get his exemption. As it happened, his medical doctor exempted him, and he therefore wanted to sell his inherited exemption receipt. The older son, however, claimed that their father had only bequeathed the receipt to the younger son in order for him to be freed from the army. Since he was freed by other means, the receipt should revert to being part of the estate. The older brother inherited the estate, which means he should then take ownership of the receipt as well. The younger brother rejected this, claiming that when their father gave the receipt to him, he did so without qualification, and that it was not the older brother's concern how the younger gets out of serving in the army.

These disputing brothers came before the Rogatchover and asked him to adjudicate the argument. They both presented their claims to him. After hearing them, the

Rogatchover turned to the younger brother, saying, "Come here, young man, and let me learn with you a little piece of Gemara." He opened to Tractate *Nazir* (24a) and read: "A woman made a vow to become a *nazir* and set apart her cattle for the sacrifice [*korban*]. Her husband then revoked her vow. The law is as follows: if the cattle were his, then… if they were hers, then…"

He then showed him that the Gemara asks on this *mishnah*, "What difference does it make if the cattle had originally been hers or not? Even if they were her husband's and he gave them to her, in the end, they belonged to her." The Gemara answers, "He only gave her the cattle for something she would need, and since he revoked her vow, she does not need the cattle. It is as if they were never hers."

"And so it is with you, my friend," the Rogatchover continued. "Clearly, your father only designated the waiver for you because he feared for you should you be drafted. Now that you are free without the waiver, the halakhah views it as if it never belonged to you." The younger brother accepted this ruling and they left.

The Rogatchover treasures his authored works and does not hide from himself. He writes: "G-d willing, this winter I will publish my compilation, which is called *Tsafnat Paneah*. There one can find wonders from G-d's Torah, and all doubts will be resolved."

Aharonim and *Rishonim*

His sharp manner manifests itself in his relationship to the *Aharonim*, to a lesser extent the *Rishonim*, and in general, throughout his responsa. The scarcity of Aharonic literature cited in his writings is astonishing. He rarely cites the *Shulhan Arukh* or any other major *Aharonim*. Even finding a *Rishon* can be difficult. Besides not quoting them, he is often critical of *Aharonim*, and while he is usually respectful of the *Rishonim*, he does not accept their superiority unequivocally. Instead, he on occasion draws conclusions straight from the Talmud itself, something that had not been done for hundreds of years. Does the Rogatchover not quote *Aharonim* because he does not accept their scholarship, or because he has such a different method-ological framework that it is simply incompatible? It is difficult to say, and the answer almost assuredly is a bit of both. Certainly he knows the Aharonic literature. Although there were claims that he never learnt the works of major *Aharonim*, it appears that in fact he is extremely well versed and proficient in them.

Rabbi Eliezer Nannes, a Lubavitcher hasid who lived with the Rogatchover for a period (and who was also in the *Gulag* for nineteen years without ever once breaking Shabbat), related the following. "One day the Gaon told me I could ask him whatever I wanted and he would resolve it for me. I asked, 'They say the Rav does not learn *Aharonim* …is it true?'

'G-d forbid,' he replied. 'It is a complete falsehood. You can test me if you wish on any *Aharon* who is a commentator on the *Shulhan Arukh*, and I will repeat their work word for word!' I took out a *Ketzot ha-Hoshen* and opened it to one of the chapters. The Rogatchover started reciting it word for word!"

Once a scholar was debating with him in his study and started looking for a *Taz* to quote to the Rogatchover. "Here, this is the only *Shulhan Arukh* I have here," the Rogatchover said, offering him a small book containing only the words of the actual *Shul-han Arukh*.

* * *

It is important to keep things in context. Not quoting an *Aharon* is not the same thing as being disrespectful. Once a yeshivah student was learning Torah with him, and thought that since the Rogatchover was supposedly not very respectful of Aharonim, he could say something derogatory about Reb Akiva Eiger. "Get out of here! You disgrace *talmidei hahamim*? Out!" said the Rogatchover.

In a similar vein, there is a letter from the Rav of a town who wants to abolish a practice upon which the *Rama* insists. This Rav thinks that he can enlist the Rogatchover in this project. The Rogatchover writes back, "I received your letter, and I'll tell you the truth—I did not even want to respond. What kind of ques-tion is this, trying to uproot practices and halakhot from the

Rishonim without any substantive reason? G-d forbid that we rule against the *Rama*...do not move one inch from the ruling of the *Rama* in this."

* * *

We do, however, find some conflicting messages regarding how much allegiance the Rogatchover displays towards the *Rishonim*. In one letter (*Sheelot u-Teshuvot*, Dvinsk, no. 3) he writes: "I have no power to argue with the *Ri*, even though the truth is as I see it." In another letter (*Sheelot u-Teshuvot* no. 267) he writes, "If not for the *Rishonim*, I would have said..." He is extremely hesitant to deviate from their opinions. A striking quote on this theme is in another letter (*Sheelot u-Teshuvot*, Dvinsk, volume 2, no. 1), where he writes: "But what can we do, since our teacher the Rambam wrote otherwise? [...] Where did he know this from? But against our will, we must bow our head to our great master the Rambam, since the halakhah is in accordance with him in every place."

Rabbi Kasher maintains that even among the *Rishonim*, the Rogatchover's style is to utilize only a select few, such as Rashi, *Tosafot*, the *Ramban* and Rambam, *Sefer ha-Yashar*, *Sefer Yereim*, *Raavad*, and a couple of others. Therefore the Rogatchover writes (no. 257): "Regarding the explanation of Rabbenu Hananel on *Sukkah*—I have not seen it."

* * *

Although the Rogatchover displayed impatience with *Aharonim*, he is extremely reverential towards the *Alter* Rebbe, Rabbi Schneur Zalman Schneersohn, the author of the *Tanya* and *Shulhan Arukh ha-Rav*, and the first Lubavitcher Rebbe.[7] This is all the more impressive when seen against the backdrop of his neglect for almost all other *Aharonim*. When the Rogatchover would study the *Kuntres Aharon*, a later commentary of the *Alter* Rebbe on his own *Shulhan Arukh*, he would run about in bewilderment and shock, muttering all the while, "[He is] as one of the *Rishonim*!" He often calls the *Alter* Rebbe "the true genius,"

---

7   Shu"t Tsafnat Paneah haHadashot, 1:104

ha-gaon ha-amiti.[8] "The rule is—in almost every instance that the true Gaon of Liadi rules it is truth."[9]

It seems that he holds the *Alter* Rebbe's son, the *Mittler* Rebbe, in even greater esteem. Once, in the middle of the study hall in Leningrad, he shouted, "The *Mittler* Rebbe was a *gaon ha-geonim* (genius among geniuses)!" One of the students asked him, "But we have almost no writings of his on the Gemara." The Rogatchover replied, "From his hasidic writings one can tell how profound his mind was!"

Further proof of the respect he has for the *Alter* Rebbe is offered by Rabbi Zalman Shimon Dvorkin and Rabbi Avraham Drizin, who visited the Rogatchover in Petersburg on the 4th of Tishrei, 1925. They sat with him for several hours discussing various concepts in the Gemara and *hasidut*. During the conversation, they described to the Rogatchover what the night of Rosh Hashanah had been like, specifically concerning the Rebbe *Rayatz*. One of the things they told him was that the Rebbe prayed at great length by night.

"This is hard to believe. The night of Rosh Hashanah is classified in Kabbalah and *hasidut* as a time of dormancy when the world is asleep. [This is based on the doctrine that we need to renew G-d's desire to rule the world every Rosh Hashanah; the world is thus said to be in a state of transitional "slumber."] How then can he pray for so long?"

Immediately he answered his own question. "The truth is that the Alter Rebbe also prayed at length Rosh Hashanah night—and he was a *gaon* and a philosopher!" The Rogatchover then launched into a complex halakhic discussion. But after finishing his monologue, he again exclaimed, "The *Alter* Rebbe was a *gaon*! A philosopher!"[10]

* * *

Someone once asked the Rogatchover how many times in the Talmud it records Resh Lakish questioning a statement of Reb

8   Ishim and interview with Morozov April 7, 2013
9   Shu"t Tsafnat Paneah haHadashot, 1:104
10   Buruchav

Yohanan.[11] He answered that it was seven times. The man then said that the *Alter* Rebbe wrote seven or eight. The Rogatchover thought for a while and jumped up exclaiming, "Indeed! There is another place where, depending on how you understand the dispute of the variant texts, it states that Resh Lakish challenged Reb Yohanan. What an incredible scholar. To hint at such a deep understanding with one extra word!"

The Rogatchover also displayed a personal appreciation for the *Alter* Rebbe. The 19th of Kislev, *Yud Tet* Kislev, is a holiday among Lubavitcher hasidim because the Alter Rebbe was released from Czarist prison on that day. One year, the Rogatchover walked into shul just as a hasidic gathering was getting under way. Immediately the hasidim begged him to come sit with them and expound upon the auspiciousness of the day. The Rogatchover obliged them and sat for an hour lecturing. After getting up he said, "Without the *Alter* Rebbe, there would not be Judaism in Russia today," and walked out.[12]

* * *

In stark contrast to all the other leading rabbis of his day, the Rogatchover had a small bookshelf and very few *sefarim* that he would use on a consistent basis. The *sefarim* he did have included a Talmud Bavli and Yerushalmi, a *Tur*, and some *Rishonim*. The crown jewel of his small study was his Rambam, whom he considered to be his teacher. He would even refer to the *Rambam* as "my master" and reportedly would talk to the Rambam, bidding him good morning or expressing his delight when unraveling a complex concept from his works.

He answers very concisely and summarily to those who came to him with questions. Many of his responses are extraordinarily biting and dismissive, or, at the very least, incredibly short, with *ayin* after *ayin* and nothing more. (*Ayin* is the Hebrew shorthand to look up the source referenced.) For example, he writes "*ayin Makot* page 17." Aside from being indirect and forcing the questioner to look up numerous sources, it is usually extremely ambiguous to what part or concept on the page he was referring. It is as if he did not have the time or inclination to craft a nor-

---

11   As told by the Lubavitcher Rebbe.
12   Interview with Kahn April 22, 2013

mal response to the questioner. He has more pressing matters to attend to—his learning. This is not to say that he takes his obligation to respond lightly. As we will see, he considers it his grave responsibility to answer all those who request his advice and scholarship.

* * *

His *sefer, Tsafnat Paneah,*[13] was and generally remains, a closed book, even for scholars. It is written with extreme conciseness and is riddled with ambiguous hints as to his intent. Adding to the difficulty is that often the sources cited are so numerous and dense as to make the smooth rendering of his text a near-impossible feat.

Another obstacle is that, usually, his theory on a given subject does not lend itself to compartmentalization or incrementally increasing building blocks. If that were the case, it would be easier to digest a piece of his writing, by breaking down and understanding just one line before advancing to the next. The problem is that often what he is trying to convey can only be understood in conjunction with all the other parts of the theory. Standing on its own, one part may not be comprehensible in the slightest. This creates a situation where the reader is forced to jump into the nucleus of the idea without the aid of independent pieces of information to indicate where his argument is headed.

This, however, is his "Written Torah." His "Oral Torah" is entirely different. He has a unique ability to communicate even dense and technical ideas in a clear and lucid manner. Most of the content in his books is taken from what he wrote in the tiny margins of his *sefarim*. Yet when asked what he means in a particular place of his writing, he often explains it at length and unambiguously. In this he was the polar opposite of the Lithuanian Rav of the town, Rabbi Meir Simhah Ha-Kohen, who reportedly was

---

13   Literally "Decipherer of Secrets" meaning that the book deciphers the secrets of the Torah. However there are those who, in a play of words, interpret the title of his book to mean that one must decipher the secrets of the book itself.

extremely brief in his verbal responses to people, yet very clear and explanatory in his writing.

* * *

Shmuel Yosef Agnon, a Nobel laureate and one of the central figures of modern Hebrew literature, writes about a visit to the Rogatchover:[14]

"I went into his room and found him suffering immensely from his sickness. When he noticed me, he started to pour out his heart to me. 'I am afraid,' he said, 'that all my suffering is a result of my not being respectful enough of the *Rishonim*. All my days I immersed myself in the Rambam's *Mishneh Torah*—it was my central focus and toil. Even when I learnt other *Rishonim*, I only studied them to gain more understanding of and perspective on the Rambam's approach.'

He then started to cry, continued Agnon, and yelled out, 'Where are the other masters of the Torah? Where are Rashi and *Tosafot*? Where are the *Raavan* and the *Ri*? What have I done? Why did I not put effort into understanding and expounding upon their words? It is because of this I am being punished.'

He was silent for a bit, and then a spirit of calm settled over him. 'It is all worth it,' he declared suddenly. 'If I am suffering because of my connection and bond to the Rambam, I accept the pain joyously!'"

Yitshak Horenstein relates: "I myself saw, with my own two eyes, how the Rogatchover used to learn the Yerushalmi with both of his forearms covering the commentaries on either side of the page. And whenever his forearm did not cover the commentary completely and he saw snippets of commentary, he would sharply deride the commentator's explanation."

Shmuel Katz was the av beit din in Los Angeles. He told my father the following:

"As a young boy I was known as the ilui of Brezhnitz and was chosen to be the bochur hameshamesh, the attendant, of the Roga-

---

14   In *Sefer Sofer Vesipur*.

tchover. I remember the long lines of people coming to meet with the Rogatchover. Ah! He was so sharp. A big Litvish Rav once came with a sefer to get a haskama from him. After perusing the book for several minutes the Rogatchover looked up and exclaimed—benheima betzuras ox ferd!—animal in the form of a cow and horse! After the Rav made a hasty exit, the Rogatchover turned to me and gently with a sweet smile said, 'Shmulekel, would you be so kind as to get me that sefer on the top of the bookcase?' I waited until he was in a great mood before asking him, 'How could it be that to this big Rav you are so dismissive but to me, a little bochurerl you are so kind and patient?'. He replied, 'That Rav is already entrenched in his ways and there is no hope for him. You however, are young and therefore with Gods help you can correct your ways. Therefore I am patient with you."

In a similar vein, Louis Jacobs reported that his teacher Rabbi Rivkin, used to brag that the Rogatchover deigned to call him a 'beheima'.[15]

Jacobs also reported that Chaim Chernovitz once asked the Rogatchover a question on a perplexing Tosafot. The Rogatchover responded, "This is one of 120 Tosafot's that contain an inaccuracy."

Absorption in Torah

The Rogatchover was intensely, even ferociously, immersed in his cognitive system of Talmudic analysis. This immersion was so utterly and absolutely powerful that he ceased to behave in a normal manner and experienced reality solely through his intellectual *Weltanschauung*. There are several stories that have trickled down to us which exhibit this.

When Agudath Israel was forming, its rabbis sent letters to all the leaders of the generation, asking them to sign an approbation of the Agudah. Much to their surprise, the letter they received from the Rogatchover was simply a long list of sources, and each source seemingly had nothing to do with their request for approval. They saw no commonality between all the sources cited, so they decided to send a representative to the Rogatchover to find out the meaning behind the letter. When they

---

15   http://louisjacobs.org/news/videos.php

confronted him, the Rogatchover replied, "As soon as I saw you were forming an *agudah*, I right away began thinking about the concept of *agudah* (organizational entity) in the Gemara. So I wrote to you all the sources where the concept of an *agudah* is discussed in the laws of the four species of Sukkot, as well as in reference to *agudat eizov* in the Torah."

Consider that even the greatest scholars, who immerse themselves entirely in Torah study, would reply to a letter from the Agudah with an answer to the matter at hand. Yet the Rogatchover was so wrapped up in his world of Talmudic analysis that he was eccentrically removed from practicalities. When asked about an organization, his mind immediately began contemplating the concept of groups and organizational entities. Even then, a normal scholar would stop thinking about this tangential line of inquiry and write an actual response. Not the Rogatchover. Instead he wrote down his tangential analysis and sent that as a reply! Unique and exceptional character went hand in hand with unique and exceptional scholarship. In this sense, one might say that the Rogatchover was a wholesomely and fully integrated man, from top to bottom.

* * *

Another angle on this can be gleaned from the following story. When the Rogatchover was asked about something that had to do with Moshiach, he replied "It is a Gemara in *Sanhedrin*." It was pointed out to him that it is in fact a verse in Tanakh. He replied, "I learn Gemara, and thus my reference point is the Gemara in *Sanhedrin*."

A similar story is that once the Rogatchover quoted a Bible verse during a conversation. His colleague pointed out to him that the verse is in fact slightly different in the text. "I am quoting the verse as the Gemara brings it. If you have a question, it is on the Gemara, not on me," replied the Rogatchover.

The Rogatchover lived fully and unapologetically in the world of Talmud. Even Biblical verses were understood via the prism of Talmud and halakhah. Everything went through that framework and came out the other end clear and concise. This is intensely typified in his Biblical interpretive style.

Another story demonstrating the Rogatchover's abstract view-point is as follows. In 1929, Rabbi Yitshak Hutner travelled from Hebron to Europe and met the Rogatchover there. He entered the room and said "I come from Hebron to..." The Rogatchover cut him off and began discussing the status of Hebron, its level of holiness, and whether it was one of the *arei miklat* (cities of refuge). For forty-five minutes straight, Rabbi Hutner could not get a word in edgewise. Finally, after finishing his complex lecture, the Rogatchover asked, "So how are the Jews of Hebron?"

Yet another episode indicative of this holistic approach was when the Rogatchover was informed that he had kidney stones. He right away responded, "I wonder if *tumat rekev* [ritual impurity from the grave] applies here." The Talmud explains that a dead limb only has *tumat rekev* if there are no external items in it. The Rogatchover was therefore wondering about the halakhic status of kidney stones. Are they considered an organic natural part of the body, to which *tumat rekev* applies? Or perhaps they are considered a foreign agent, and thus do not have *tumat rekev*.

An even more extreme example can be seen in the following story. During World War I, a Jew was caught outside in the streets while a bombing raid was taking place. He started running down the street and saw a man standing by the door. As he got closer, the man (who was in fact the Rogatchover) started excitedly yelling to him, "Come in, come in! Just now I uncovered a deep insight into the Yerushalmi which is implied by the Tosefta! Perhaps with this we can also explain an ambiguity in the Rambam. Come in!

The Lubavitcher Rebbe related a story which is further suggestive of this eccentric and Talmud-centric worldview. One Shabbat afternoon, as dusk settled in, the Rogatchover was seen sitting at a table gazing at the clock. With every tick-tock of the clock, he swayed his head from side to side, keeping time with the clock while deep in thought. "It's gone!" he suddenly exclaimed. One of the people there could not contain himself and asked the Rogatchover the meaning behind this. "Amazing—until that last second, Shabbat was here in full strength, and one would receive the death penalty for breaking it. Yet one second later, it's completely gone!"

The Gaon would get so completely absorbed in Talmudic discussions that he would exhibit behavior totally at odds with social niceties. Once he was debating a scholar on the precise halakhic status of bright colors (*tsahuv*). "Here—this is halakhically bright!" He strode over to an old man with a long white beard who had just come in to shul. Grabbing the old man's beard, he walked back to the astonished scholar. "This is what I'm talking about—this is halakhically bright."

* * *

Rabbi Broyda relates: "When the Gaon was speaking to us …he would pace excitedly about the room. Whenever he needed a *sefer* …he would jump up and run to get it. He was not a young or healthy man at this point. But with almost childlike glee, he would exert himself in his learning. For the higher shelves in the room, there was a ladder that he would scale quickly to get the book he wanted. He knew precisely where each and every *sefer* was. A curious phenomenon occurred. Even when running about or climbing the ladder, he would never let go of the Gemara that started the original conversation. He would keep one hand inside it to not lose the place and would take it with him everywhere he went for the duration of the conversation. We asked him why this was, and he said, 'It says in *Mishlei* that "*hisif eneicha*"…blink your eyes and it is gone. How can I put down the Gemara for even one second, then?'" Rabbi Broyda explained that he was referring to the Gemara in *Berakhot* (5a) which compares the Torah to a bird, an *of,* since it says *hisif eneicha,* which Rashi explains to mean that if you close your eyes from Torah learning, you will forget it.

Rabbi Broyda continued: "During the course of the discussion, the Gaon admonished us that we are forgetting a clear *mishnah* in *Masekhet Kelim.* Now, I had just been studying *mishnayot* intensely for the anniversary of our *Rosh Yeshivah*, Rabbi Moshe Epstein, and had just reviewed that *mishnah.* I was able to tell him what *mishnah* he was referring to. His eyes lit up. He was immensely pleased and told us we must come back to visit him again. But when we returned he was gone. He had travelled somewhere due to his illness. They told us however, that he often asked about the yeshivah students from Israel and when they would return."

* * *

The Lubavitcher Rebbe related: Once the Rogatchover received a letter from the town council saying that he had to pay two different taxes. After reading the letter, he said, "One tax is legal according to halakhah, and I will therefore pay it. The other has no standing, so I refuse to pay it." A couple of days later, he received an official letter saying that there had been a mistake. He only had to pay one tax—the one he had agreed to pay. After telling the story, the Lubavitcher Rebbe exclaimed: "See the power of the Rogatchover. He was truly an officer of the Torah (*sar ha-Torah*). He was able to affect reality through the energy of Torah!

* * *

Another perspective on his immersion in Torah can be seen from the following two letters. One letter[16] is dated the 11th of Tishrei. For other letter-writers of the past generations, the date, as a simple recordkeeping matter, would be sufficient. Not so for the Rogatchover. This date immediately conjures up for him the Mishnah in *Keritot* (25a): "It is said that Bava ben Buta would offer an *asham talui* (a conditional sacrifice for a possible transgression) every day, except the day after Yom Kippur, the 11th of Tishrei." The Rogatchover then explains the unique status of this day based on a statement in *Meilah* (14b) that one need not worry about an unwitting transgression if only one day is involved. The 11th of Tishrei is only one day after the atonement of Yom Kippur, so no such sacrifice could be brought.

His every letter between Rosh Hashanah and Yom Kippur reflects the awe of the season. A letter[17] dated during this period in 1927 responds to the query whether one may wear glasses on Shabbat when one is not totally dependent on them. The letter begins with a short aside, "Tuesday, the 8th of Tishrei, 5688—may we, G-d willing, merit receiving the Second Tablets this coming Yom Kippur," which is not a unique expression in responsa literature. But then he launches into a deep exploration of the dif-

---

16   Shu"t #124
17   Shu"t #33

ferences between the first and second *luhot* (tablets of the Law given to Moses) and other aspects of the giving of the Torah. In a letter of thirty-eight lines, only three are devoted to an answer to the question (if they help the wearer in walking, wearing them is permissible), and thirty-five to an exposition on the date.

This trait, of instantly exploring the halakhic nuances of anything that came before him, even the date of a letter, was further typified by the fact that according to the Lubavitcher Rebbe[18], Shabbat was a difficult time for the Rogatchover. This was because he could not write down and categorize the torrents of thought coursing wildly through his head.

Rambam

The Rogatchover's fascination and loyalty to the Rambam began at an early age, during his partnership with Rabbi Chaim Soloveitchik, and endured, indeed grew, throughout his lifetime.

Rabbi Yehiel ha-Kohen, in one of his letters, posits that the Rambam deviates from the Gemara in a certain ruling. The Rogatchover responds sharply, vetoing any such notion. "The Rambam is founded on Gemara—how could he himself argue on his own basis?"

The Rogatchover, when speaking about Islam, makes the following intriguing observation. The Rambam, in *Hilkhot Yayin Nesech* (laws of wine in worshipping idols), states that Christians are considered idol worshippers, while Muslims are not, because Muslims also believe in one G-d. The Rogatchover asserts that, in fact, Muslims are also halakhically considered to be idol worshippers. He bases this on the assertion that Muslims serve the moon, which is why the flag of the Ottoman Empire is the half-moon crescent. He even offers an explanation why they serve the moon. It is because they live in arid deserts and the moon is what influences precipitation and waves. Why, then, does the Rambam not write this? "The Rambam lived amongst Muslims! Do you think he would write that they are idol worshippers? Such a thing would have been foolhardy and dangerous, and halakhah forbids such actions."

---

18   Sihat Parashat Vaera, 1951.

Once the Rogatchover was baffled by a passage in the Rambam. After much exertion and confusion, he resolved the issue, shouting, "Ah, Master! You should live to 120!"

Scholarship

The Rogatchover's mastery of Torah was renowned and admired from several different angles. But certainly the most immediately appreciable trait was his absolute command of the entire canon of rabbinic literature. Indeed, some have stated that only with the advent of computers can one comprehend what the Rogatchover's command was like.[19]

Rabbi Chaim Zev Cheresh was close to both the Rogatchover and the *Or Sameah* and received *semihah* from both. He was once asked what was the difference between the two in terms of scholarship.

"When you ask the Rogatchover a question, he instantly fires back an answer buttressed by numerous sources in Gemara. When you ask the *Or Sameah*, he contemplates for a little bit before answering. That minute, that tiny bit of thought before answering—that is the whole difference between them."

Rabbi Cheresh also once was asked if he saw any changes in the Rogatchover over the years. He replied, "In terms of mastery of the breadth and scope of Gemara, there was no difference. But I did notice changes in his depth of understanding. In fact, I once asked him a difficult question that he masterfully resolved. A couple of years later, I asked him the same question, and he gave me an entirely different answer. I said, 'I once heard a scholar give a different answer,' and I proceeded to tell him the very answer that he himself had told me many years prior. 'Who told you this answer?' he demanded. I told him that I had heard it from him himself. He looked down and reflected for a bit. Finally he looked at me and said, 'That previous answer was wrong.' He explained to me at length where his mistake had been."

This story is contrasted by the following. Rabbi Chaim Ozer Grodensky was once sitting with Rabbi Yisrael Soloveitchik on Shabbat, and they were discussing the Rogatchover. "What an

---

19   *Teitz*, page 37.

incredible man he was!" exclaimed Rabbi Grodensky. "Rabbi Meir Simhah, the *Or Sameah*, used to be a hard man to interact with in his first city, Bialystok. Yet later he was revered and loved by all in Dvinsk. The Rogatchover, however, was loved in his first city and in Dvinsk. What was the difference? Perhaps it was an outgrowth of their different scholastic styles. The *Or Sameah* was exceptional in his depth. And it is in the nature of depth to change. The Rogatchover, however, never innovated anything, and therefore there was no change in his behavior or philosophy from before to later."

The *Or Sameah* would often praise the Rogatchover's skill in depth, saying that it far eclipsed his command of scope and breadth.

* * *

It once happened[20] that while talking in learning, the Rogatchover momentarily forgot what Rashi says in a certain place. He immediately stamped his foot and said: "One who forgets something from his learning is considered as liable for his life" (*Avot* 3:10). But then he immediately remembered it and continued.

This story casts aspersions on the famous depiction of him as someone who simply was not able to forget something. The *Or Sameah* once said that the Gaon does not have a great memory, because he sees the text in front of him and is constantly learning it. However, this episode would suggest otherwise.

Rabbi Pinchas Teitz also remarked, "It is not that the Rogatchover has a phenomenal memory; he simply has an inability to forget anything." He also said that the Rogatchover once told him, "I remember every moment of my life from the age of three."[21]

Once Rabbi Naftali Bainish Wasserman came into his study and began quoting a Yerushalmi. "It does not say that," the Rogatchover said, cutting him off. "What do you mean—I just now saw it!" responded Rabbi Wasserman. "I am telling you again, there is no such line in the Talmud Yerushalmi." They looked at

---

20   Zevuluni.
21   *Teitz*, page 40.

the source, and indeed Rabbi Wasserman had added a couple of words that were not there.

The Gaon visited the *Sefat Emet*, who later remarked, "I can tell from his capacity of memory that he is entirely absorbed in holiness."

* * *

"I can only learn as I see it," the Rogatchover would explain to people who were astonished at his original and non-traditional explanations of various *gemarot*. "As a *posek*, one must take into account precedent, but as a simple person learning, just trying to understand the right *peshat*? Not at all!"

* * *

One familiar with the Rogatchover's style of analysis knows that he does not actively seek a *hidush* (novel interpretation). He simply sees a different world. A person who sees the atoms that comprise physical matter will describe a chair in non-normative terms unused in common parlance, but not because he is trying to sound poetic or flowery or different. He simply is unable to describe the world otherwise, for he sees the particulars, not the general image of the chair as most humans do. This story further brings out this point *vis-a-vis* the Rogatchover's penchant for novel interpretations. There is no agenda or concerted effort in his originality. As the Lubavitcher Rebbe remarks, "The Rogatchover was *unable* to analyze or indeed write his analysis in a different style. It was part and parcel of him."

Rabbi Zevin writes:

> "His perspective was not bound to the natural parameters of the subject at hand. Instead he flew like an eagle, carrying the concept to strange shores and expansive proportions. It did not interest him if others had an alternate explanation. His building blocks were Rambam, Rashi, *Tosafot*, and a few select commentators. This was his material from which he constructed structures of multiple and varied layers of depth."

Hasidut

The Rogatchover had an intimate and strong connection with the *Rashab*, Rabbi Shalom Dov Ber Schneersohn, the fifth Lubavitcher Rebbe. It is unclear if they ever met, though some reports indicate that they met at the rabbinic conference in Petersburg. Indeed, it would appear that the *Rashab* was instrumental in having the Rogatchover appointed as the Rav in Dvinsk. In his book *Keshet Giborim*, Rabbi Aharon Ben-Tsiyon Shurin writes: "In 1889, the hasidic Rav of Dvinsk died and they needed to appoint a new Rav. The Rebbe *Rashab* instructed his hasidim to travel to Warsaw and convince the Rogatchover to leave Warsaw and become the Rav in Dvinsk."

There are four letters that we have from the Rogatchover to the *Rashab*. In the first one, dated the 23rd of Nisan, 1917, he bemoans the secular forces trying to contaminate the pure learning of Torah. "They want to make decrees concerning the learning of Torah, especially among young schoolchildren, about whom it states, 'do not touch my anointed ones.' Their main desire is to make an unholy marriage between Torah and secular knowledge. Since you are involved in these matters, I am writing to you to awaken you to fight this encroachment."

In the second letter, dated the 7th of Iyar, 1917, he warns of a gathering of false and crooked rabbis who were conspiring to do harm.

In the third letter, dated the 21st of Tamuz, 1917, he writes that he is trying to gather together the different Orthodox camps to unite into one force. "How long will the Torah be like bald spots, without cohesion? We must band together, and only afterwards can we split up into differentiated separate forces. For first there must be a collective, and only then can there be individuation."

In the fourth latter, dated the 28th of Av, 1917, he writes again concerning different gatherings that were taking place. "Since the voice of confusion is heard in our lands, therefore our brothers have started to make various organizations and groups. Thus we must make a great disclaimer and condemnation if any group tries to make changes, or create a breach in anything concerning the holy Torah, as was done by our masters, the Talmudists. As the Rishonim did also, and at their forefront the Rambam. For we are as slaves who have been pierced and will not go free..."

Whenever the *Rashab* would receive a letter from the Rogatchover, his face would light up and he would express great joy, exclaiming, "the whole house is filled with light."

* * *

Shmuel Levitin was present when the *Rayatz*, Rabbi Yosef Yitshak Schneersohn, the sixth Lubavitcher Rebbe, visited the Rogatchover when he moved to Petersburg in 1924. He reports that the only other person present was the Rogatchover's son-in-law, the Rav of Moscow, Rabbi David Abba Goldfine. They spoke about how the coming of Moshiach will take place, and the Rogatchover walked him out to the stairwell.

Rabbi Shaul Brook wrote the following to Rabbi Yisrael Jacobson:

"I will now tell you what I heard from Zalman Chanin, who was in Leningrad at the time of this story. The Rogatchover came to visit the Rebbe [*Rayatz*] after the Rebbe had visited him first. The hasidim asked him what he was going to speak to the Rebbe about, and he said, 'I am coming to give your Rebbe *semihah*.' They were together for a long time, and when he came out, the hasidim asked him, '*Nu*, what do you say about our Rebbe?' He replied, 'Jews need to have a *nasi* [leader]. His father was worthy to be a leader. In general, a son-in-law comes before others, and a son before a son-in-law. Now that he is his father's son and worthy in his own right, he certainly has to be a *nasi*."

* * *

Yisrael Devoritz decided he wanted to learn at Tomche Temimim, a Lubavitch yeshivah. His family, however, being staunch *mitnagdim*, fiercely opposed this decision. The family turned to the Rogatchover to resolve this familial dispute that threatened to rip the fabric of the family apart. "Do not bother the boy. Wherever he wants to go, let him. It is his decision," was the reply.

A couple months went by and the family did not hear from their son Yisrael. They began to worry and wrote to the management of the yeshivah to inquire about their son, but received no reply. In fact, their son had become sick and was too weak to write a letter. Fearing the worst, they turned to the Rogatchover and asked him to help. The Rogatchover immediately sat down to write a letter to the Rebbe *Rashab* inquiring about this boy. This time, the management took notice and sent back a detailed letter informing the family about the boy's spiritual and physical well-being.

* * *

The Rogatchover's correspondence and connection to the seventh Lubavitcher Rebbe, Rabbi Menahem Mendel Schneersohn, was quite interesting. The Rebbe's mother reports that the Rebbe began corresponding with the Rogatchover at the age of 16 or 17. The Rebbe signed with a pseudonym, Mordechai Gourary, to avoid using the family name of Schneersohn, which was a red flag to the Soviets.

The Rebbe describes the Rogatchover in astonishing terms. In his correspondence he calls him "the minister of Torah" (*sar ha-Torah*), "the teacher who glides through the sea of Talmud" (*rav ha-hovel be-yam ha-Talmud*), "a wondrous man" (*ish pele*), and the like.

"His thought is beyond the normative understanding of what constitutes a novelty," "his teachings are pearls," "no one imagined such a level of learning in earlier generations," and "incredible concepts." The Rebbe cites the Rogatchover hundreds of times in *Likute Sihot* and expands the narrative the Rogatchover began. He often develops ideas the Rogatchover only began and builds them into a discussion of broader or deeper scope.

The Rogatchover gave semikha to the Lubavitcher Rebbe as well. Naftali Nimotin, in 1978 Leningrad, told Ilya Meschaninov that he went in to the Rogatchover along with the Lubavitcher Rebbe to get semikha.[22]

Two of the letters between them are the following:

---

22   Interview April 6, 2013.

1. [To] his honor, *ha-Rav ha-Gaon*, who is famous for his name and praise, a master in the secrets of Torah. The prince of Torah, a ruler and instructor, the Rav who sails the sea of Talmud, and who lights the path in its commentaries…our master, Rabbi Yosef Rosen:

Your letter reached me regarding the wisdom of astrology. We find in the *Yad ha-Hazakah* of the Rambam much material that is relevant to this. It appears that the Rambam leaned on the works of the nations for this, as he wrote concerning the calculations in *Hilkhot Kidush ha-Hodesh*, chapter 17, halakhah 25. Also, what he wrote in *Hilkhot Yesode ha-Torah*, chapter 3, is found in the books of Greek philosophy, especially the books of Aristotle and his students and commentators. And I have turned to his honor to explain the thinking of *Hazal* in this discipline, especially to reconcile the many apparently conflicting passages.

For example, in *Berakhot*, page 58, and in *Pesahim*, page 94 and even there, there is an argument between the Sages of the Jews and the Sages of the nations, and their words appear to [be correct], and see *Hagigah*, page 12, and *Yoma* 20a, and *Bava Batra*, pages 25 and 74.

My primary question and request [to you] is to explain, as much as can be done on paper, the opinion of *Hazal* regarding astrology as it is sourced in *Sha"s*, the Tosefta, etc., specifically concerning the heavenly spheres [*galgalim*], the movement of the sun and moon, the four elements, and the fifth element, from which stems the *galgalim*, stars, etc..

[signed] Menachem Schneerson

2. The 7th of Av, 1932

[To] his honor, *ha-Rav ha-Gaon*, who is famous for his name and praise, a master in the secrets of Torah, a master of flour, a *sadran* and *palpelan*, our master, Rabbi Yosef:

Peace and blessing!

Our teacher should explain to us the law of *hefker* in *yovel*, if it goes from the possession of the the *zocheh* to *hefker* and returns to the possession of the *mafkir*, etc..

Also [please explain] the reason of the Rambam in *Perush ha-Mishnayot, Nidah* 45b, that he interprets the years of a female for vows to be two years less than the years of a male, since their years are short, etc., and not like the rationale in *Sha"s ad loc.*. Also, what is the reason that their lives are short, etc.?

One who honors you as befits your exalted and great stature, [signed] M. Schneerson[23]

The Rogatchover on occasion references the Kabbalistic and hasidic dimensions of Torah. Thus, for example, he writes, "concerning this dispute between the Bavli and Yerushalmi, it is taught that wisdom is the essence of speech, while understanding is the differentiation of detailed analysis..."

On another occasion, the Rogatchover writes: "But what already can I write about this to a *mitnaged* like you? If you were a hasid, I would reveal to you secrets about this topic, but for a *mitnaged* like you, this is sufficient."

Interestingly enough, in the line after this, he writes, "Please pray for me—I have a cough. The angel of cold has touched me."

Once one of the younger Chabad hasidim told the Rogatchover that he should learn more *Hasidut*. The reply he got was, "Do you think it's such a simple thing to learn *Hasidut*? Why, just to comprehend the concept of *tsimtsum* would take a year and a half." (*Tsimtsum* is the Kabbalistic doctrine of divine concealment to bring about creation.)

* * *

Refael Nimotin used to walk the Rogatchover from his house to shul every day, and said that the Rogatchover would invite him to ask any question of him. Whenever Nimotin did ask some-

<hr>

23   See the Reshimot for more correspence between the two —Reshimot no. 33, pages 4-16; no. 159, pages 8-15; no. 104, pages 3-8 and 10-11.

thing, the Rogatchover explained it clearly and slowly, so that even a child would be able to understand.

Once, a woman entered his study when a close friend of his and a famous rabbi were present. The woman asked the Rogatchover to bless her. As was his wont, he refused, saying, "I am only a simple man; I only bless after eating."

The visiting rabbi then asked, "Why not bless her? The Mishnah states that 'Even the blessing of a simple man should not be light in one's eyes,' and all the more so (*kal va-homer*) does this apply to your blessing."

The Rogatchover responded, "Why wait for me to deliver the blessing with the aid of an *a fortiori* argument? You can do it even without a *kal va-homer*."

This story is sharply contrasted by the fact that the Rogatchover well knew his own worth and did not fear to display a self-confident and almost aggressive manner at times.

But the resolution is simple. He did not think he had saintly powers. He simply knew that he was concious of his exceptional scholarship.

1.2 Rav of Dvinsk

Zevuluni relates: "A virtually unknown, fascinating first-hand story about the Rogatchover Gaon was written in Yiddish by Rabbi Ephraim Oshri in his *sefer Hurban Lita*.

Rav Oshri authored *Sheelot u-Teshuvot Mi-Maamakim*, which dealt with halakhic questions during the Holocaust. There is a chapter in the book *Hurban Lita* in which he discusses the *gedolim* (great Torah scholars) of Lita (Lithuania).

He told me the following story, which he witnessed himself, about the Rogatchover Gaon.

Rav Oshri writes (p. 214): "I personally witnessed an episode with the Rogatchover when I was a guest in his house. He invited me for Shabbat. *Motzaei* Shabbat, after *havdalah*, the servant brought in the mail that had arrived on Shabbat. It consisted of twenty-two letters and ten post cards which had arrived from all over the world. The Rogatchover opened every letter himself, and on each one he made a notation. Some he put into his jacket pocket and some in his table drawer. Then he sat down immediately to write, from memory, answers to the letters. He never referred back to the letters, nor did he refer to any *sefer*. When his responses were ready, he wrote the addresses on the response envelopes. He remembered the addresses, the numbers of the houses, and the names of the streets.[24] Reading all of the letters, including writing responses, took him only two hours and eleven minutes."

Twenty-two letters plus ten post cards is thirty-two pieces of correspondence. The whole endeavor took him two hours and eleven minutes, or one hundred thirty-one minutes. This yields an average time spent per item of four minutes, six seconds ($131/32 = 4.09$). This includes reading, writing responses, and writing the address.

A similar recollection was offered by Rabbi Teitz, who said that he once brought a heavy bundle of mail to the Rogatchover. Yet a mere ninety minutes later, all the mail was answered and ready for the post office—all this without referencing a single *sefer*.[25]

* * *

The Rogatchover feels a tremendous responsibility to respond with halakhic answers to all those who write to him. In one of his responses, dated the 5th of Kislev, 1936, right before he died, he writes:

"I received your letter. Why are you harassing me? I am sick, literally bedridden. Do not continue bothering me because I am very sick right now." Yet he goes on to respond to the questioner!

---

24   His wife, who was learned and knew several languages, was usually the one who addressed the postcards.
25   *Teitz*, page 45.

More proof that the Rogatchover takes his obligation as a *posek* very seriously is that as soon as he finishes each letter, he requests that it be sent to the post office.

✳ ✳ ✳

In another letter (*Sheelot u-Teshuvot* no. 3) he writes: "Believe me, I answer each day many letters, and it is impossible for me to respond at any length because of the time constraints, not to mention the cost of mail." In another letter (no. 86) he writes: "I wrote chaotically because time runs away from me because of an overload of responsa I must write…" In yet another letter, he writes: "You write that I did not answer you. G-d forbid! I answer to all who ask—just concisely." Another time he writes (*Sheelot u-Teshuvot* Dvinsk no. 126): "I am being concise because I am weighed down right now by many letters." Finally he writes (Dvinsk no. 77): "This is enough. I want to go to sleep. There will be other times." Yet he generally does not want people to stop writing to him. In a different letter (*Sheelot u-Teshuvot* no. 106) he states: "Do not hold back from writing and making demands of me, because this is the gist of learning Torah. On the contrary, I am very pleased by this."

He often begins a letter with "I just now received your letter" or "your letter came just now," indicating the sense of immediacy and urgency with which he responds to people. By many accounts, it was one of the first things he did every morning.

✳ ✳ ✳

Some people knew of the Rogatchover's dire poverty and sent money for return stamps. Sometimes people would write that they are attaching money. Yet it happened more than once that the money was stolen somewhere along the way. When this occurred, the Rogatchover writes back to them, admonishing them for lying. He forewarns them against claiming that someone took the money by citing a Talmudic source from *Hulin* (105a) *"Midi de-tsayir ve-tachim leit lehu reshu."*

כל מילי דצייר וחתים וכייל ומני - לית לן רשותא למשקל מיניה, עד דמשכחינן מידי
דהפקרא

This *gemara* means, "all things that are tied up, sealed, measured, [or] counted—we do not have permission to take from [them]. Only when we find things that are ownerless [may we take from them]."

The context is, a *mazik* is accused of breaking a barrel, which is a measurable thing. But he claims that it was *hefker*, since it was abandoned. The *mazik* says that we (i.e., *mazikim*) are not allowed to take measurable or countable things. But we can take *hefker* things. Presumably, the Rogatchover was saying do not blame the missing money on a *mazik*, because *mazikim* cannot take countable things like coins.

* * *

Occasionally, one of the Rogatchover's letters gets lost in the mail. He takes this very seriously as a sign from heaven that something is wrong with his response. He writes, "It appears to me that you did not receive my first letter. I am very disturbed by this. Apparently they [i.e., those in heaven] did not agree with what I wrote. Therefore I beg you to let me know if you received my letter or not."

The Rogatchover is very relaxed about people publishing his letters. In many letters, he gives permission to print the letter, as long as it is published "without additions, deletions, or abbreviations, just as I wrote it." In fact, he states that people who do not allow these works to be published are considered thieves, since they are stealing from the many.

* * *

There are people who write constantly to the Rogatchover, or who simply ask questions that do not require his world-class expertise, and this infuriates him. He has a special boilerplate response that he reserves for such people.[26] It is a long list of sources that apparently have no common thread uniting them. The questioner would invariably organize his yeshivah, circle of friends, and local scholars to help him unravel the message from the prestigious Rogatchover. Finally someone would notice that

---

26   My father heard from Rav Shmuel Katz who was a live-in assistant for the Rogatchover that he saw this template letter often.

the only common denominator is that every source cited has the word *am ha-aretz* (ignoramus) somewhere on the page!

* * *

Once a Jewish woman came before the Rogatchover with her disputant, a gentile woman. The gentile claimed that the Jewish woman owed her money. The Rogatchover was stymied by the case and started pacing back and forth. Finally he went over to the Jewish lady and whispered to her, "Do not give her the money you owe her." The lady responded, "Of course I would not! Do you think I would give her back her money if I don't have to?"

Right away, the Rogatchover said "Aha! So you were lying. Pay her immediately!"

* * *

According to some accounts, it was extremely hard, nigh impossible, to receive *semihah* (rabbinical ordination) from the Rogatchover. Yet by other accounts, he gave *semihah* to people regularly. One story that fits the latter account is related by Rabbi Yisrael Devoritz: "In my youth, I studied *shehitah* and *bedikah* (the laws of ritual slaughter and checking an animal to certify its kosher status) in Rogatchov, and upon completion of my studies, I went in to the Rogatchover's study to get tested. 'I am sure you know all the laws of *shehitah* and its accompanying fields of law,' he said. He then asked me a few questions concerning complications with an animal's liver and gave me *semihah*."

In fact, there were students who came before him that he barely tested, and then there were students that he tested to the utmost extreme, making sure that they knew each and every halakhah in *Shulhan Arukh*. When asked about the inconsistency of his approach, the Gaon responded, "When I see a student that fears heaven and is humble, I do not really need to test him. Because when he is asked a halakhic question, he will either give an answer, or if he is unsure, he will tell the person to come back to him, since he needs to review the question and look up the answer. If he still cannot answer, he will send the halakhic query to a greater Rav, and no harm will come from his lack of expertise. However, when I see that a student is lacking this sensitivity, then I must test him in every law to make sure he knows it perfectly. For I know that if someone asks him a question that he does not know, he will not have their requisite humility to tell the person that he must review the material, or that he must ask someone more knowledgeable then himself."

A similar story is that the Gaon was conversing with someone to whom he had given *semihah* a while back. During the discussion, the Gaon brought a *mishnah* to support his statement, to which the student nodded and agreed. Immediately, the Gaon asked for the certificate of *semihah* he had given him, and tore it up right there on the spot! "I was testing you. There is no such *mishnah*. it is in fact a *baraita* (a non-authoritative Tannaitic teaching). I do not mind if you do not know something, but to pretend to know means you are not fit to have *semihah*."

Another story along these lines is that a young man came before him to be tested for his *semihah*. The Gaon looked at him with his piercing eyes and began asking him questions in *hilkhot kriyat ha-Torah* (laws concerning communal Torah readings in shul). The student was caught unawares, because the test for ordination is traditionally on an entirely different section in *Shulhan Arukh*. Not having prepared this section, the young student did not respond.

"Do you understand why I am testing you on these laws? I see that you are a G-d-fearing person, and I am confident that when you are a Rav and you do not know something, you will research the answer properly. But what about when something occurs in shul during services? There will be no time to research or ask another Rav. These laws are the most important for you to know!"

* * *

Rabbi Pinchas Teitz writes: "The amount of letters the Rogatchover wrote was vast. I think it was about forty thousand letters. He remembered every letter he wrote—the content, the addressee, the time and date—everything!"

* * *

When people would come to the Rogatchover for a blessing, he would usually say, "Go to the *kohen!*" By this he meant the *Or Sameah*, who would give people blessings.

Once two Jews involved in a dispute came to the Rogatchover's house. The Rogatchover was in the middle of a complex and involved discussion on the Yerushalmi at the time, so he sent them away to the *Or Sameah*. They came before the *Or Sameah* and told him that the Rogatchover had been learning the Yerushalmi and had sent them away.

"It is an explicit Gemara. The Gemara in *Bava Kama* (6b) asks why the Mishnah uses the word *hov ha-mazik* and not the more generic term *hayiv ha-mazik*. The answer given is that the author of the Mishnah was from Israel, and people there use a very concise terminology. Thus the Tanna wrote *hov*, thereby taking out two *yuds* from the word [*hayiv*]. Is it any wonder then that the Gaon also sent two *yudden* away?" (*Yudden* can mean two of the letter *yud*, or can mean two Jews.)

* * *

Chana Elka Eisner came to the Rogatchover and asked him whether she should fast on Yom Kippur, since her bat mitzvah fell right afterwards, on Simchat Torah. Without looking up, the Rogatchover said, "Do not fast." She walked out and decided that she was still going to fast and be stringent with herself. She was already down the street when she heard a man calling her. Lo and behold, it was the Rogatchover himself. "Listen to me, *maideleh* [little girl]—do not fast!"

* * *

The Rogatchover was offered the position of *Rosh Yeshivah* in the yeshivah of Chachmei Lublin. Rabbi Meir Shapiro sent him three letters begging him to come, but the Rogatchover did not take the position. Rabbi Shapiro even offered him a substantial sum of money (at a time of dire need in the Rogatchover's life). Still he did not accept. Perhaps he felt a responsibility to remain in Dvinsk for his community there, or possibly he refused for other reasons. Either way, this offer was rejected, and a year or so later, he returned to Dvinsk.[27]

* * *

There once was a famous *din Torah* (halakhic dispute) about an astronomical sum of money. It dragged on for a long time and ended in a compromise. The *bet din* was comprised of three rabbis, including the Rogatchover, the Rav of Shavli, Meir Atlas, and either the famous Rav Chaim Brisker, or Rav Chaim Ozer Grodensky of Vilna. It is not clear which one, because the Rogatchover said only that he sat with Chaim and Meir at the *din Torah*. He called all scholars, even those of previous generations, by their first names.

After the two sides agreed to compromise, they took out money with which to pay the members of the *bet din*, but Rav Meir and Rav Chaim refused to accept it. The Rogatchover, on the other hand, swept the money off the table and put it in his pocket, saying:

"Regarding the mentally deficient, it says in *Hagigah* (4a), 'Who is a mentally retarded person (*shoteh*)? One who destroys what he is given.' The question is asked—we would expect it to say that he destroys what he already has, not what he is given. From here we see that if one is given something and he refuses to take it, he is called a *shoteh,* and I do not want to be included in that category."

* * *

Zevuluni relates: The Rogatchover feared no one, not even his supporters. He was a fiercely independent man. With my own eyes, I saw the head of the community bring him a letter about an important communal matter that needed the Rogatchover's signature. The Rogatchover took the pen and the stamp and stamped in the middle of the letter, saying: "Up till here, I am an agreement with what it says in the letter, and I have signed. From this point on, I disagree, and I will not sign." The head of the community's pleading was to no avail.

---

27   Teitz's intro to Makkot

There was a *mohel* (a ritual circumcisor) in Rogatchov, Avraham Leib Devoritz, who refused to accept payment for his services. After some time, his family came to the Rogatchover, begging him to convince their father to accept payment, since they desperately needed money. The Gaon called in the *mohel* and stared at him, contemplating for a while. Finally he said, "You must accept payment. It is a halakhic requirement. In fact, if you do not, it is possible that the father of the circumcised child has not fulfilled his obligation!" After hearing this, Avraham Leib agreed to accept payment from those families that could afford it.

* * *

Yisrael Devoritz relates: "During World War I, I was afraid of being drafted, so I asked the Rogatchover for a blessing. He paced back and forth, torn about what to say. Finally he turned to me and said, 'The salvation of G-d can come in a second.' After receiving a blessing from the Rebbe *Rashab* as well, I was bizarrely and inexplicably released from the draft. Although the Rogatchover did not like to give blessings, he apparently made an exception here, though he did not phrase his statement as a blessing, but rather as an assertion of hope."

By many accounts, the Rogatchover was revered by the gentiles in the city as well, who would occasionally come to him to resolve their disputes.

One year, the townspeople asked the Rogatchover to deliver a sermon before blowing the *shofar* on Rosh Hashanah. "Why are you asking me? This is not my style. There are many rabbis steeped in the *Mussar* tradition who are more fitting to speak to you," he said. But the townspeople would not take no for an answer, and finally he relented. When the time came for him to speak, the Rogatchover slowly walked to the head of the congregation, and, with a quavering voice, spoke. "A couple of days ago, a very difficult question came before me. Difficult from a halakhic perspective, but also difficult on a personal level. A woman had gone into premature labor and the fetus was endangering the life of the mother. The doctors said that if we do not abort the fetus immediately, the mother's life was forfeit. Without a choice, I ruled that they, G-d protect us, should dismember the fetus to save the life of the mother." The Gaon began to weep in front of the deathly silent congregation. "Our Sages elaborate at length about the value of a single life. Indeed, one who saves a life has saved a whole world. ...but I had to rule to kill this precious soul that was pure and innocent..." The Rogatchover just stood there sobbing. The congregation began to cry with him, and in this grave, serious moment began the *tekiyot* (*shofar* blasts).

* * *

Once the Rogatchover had to travel, and left his son-in-law, Rabbi Abba David Goldfine, in charge. Upon returning, he asked him if there were any halakhic questions that had been asked in his absence. "Yes, a woman came with a chicken, but the whole thing was nothing. There was no problem, no halakhic complication; it was kosher." Right away, the Gaon called for that woman, looked at the chicken, and declared it not kosher. It turned out that the woman had brought the wrong chicken before. "How did you know?" his son in law asked him. "There is no such thing as a woman bringing a chicken that has no halakhic complication. Sometimes it's kosher and sometimes not, but for there to be no problem at all? Does not happen."

* * *

Rabbi Zevin writes:

> "The Rogatchover's skill in sharp criticism was very interesting. A Rav sent him the Yerushalmi on *Kedoshim* which had recently been 'discovered' (in our days it has already been clearly shown to be a forgery), and he responded:[28]

> 'Last night I took some time to peruse the book you sent me. And behold, I am perplexed, because in my opinion, it is replete with gross and shameful mistakes. On almost every single page, the eye can clearly see that false men had to do with it. When I will have some time, I will send it back to you in the mail, since I fear to infringe the Torah's prohibition on possessing deceitful items.'

In the very next letter, he wrote:

---

28   Siman 114

'Today I returned the volume and it is merely a compilation of pieces from the Yerushalmi and *Rishonim*. There are things in there that should not have been written. Certainly we should publish a pamphlet against it so that none will stray after it.'

He cited several examples of forgery. I shall bring just one. The false Yerushalmi brings a Tosefta that according to Rabbi Akiva, we can tithe from one animal onto another. The Gaon wrote that this is a corrupted version of the Tosefta. Instead it should say that Rabbi Akiva stated we cannot do this. He then proceeds to prove this point thoroughly. He then ends off by saying that if the Yerushalmi was not a fake, then it would not have quoted this Tosefta in the version that had become corrupted in exile!"

The *poskim* in the latter half of the century after the Rogatchover's demise did not quote him too often. Perhaps this was in line with the Talmud's statement concerning Rabbi Meir:

אמר רבי אחא בר חנינא: גלוי וידוע לפני מי שאמר והיה העולם שאין בדורו של רבי מאיר כמותו, ומפני מה לא קבעו הלכה כמותו - שלא יכלו חביריו לעמוד על סוף דעתו

"Rabbi Aha, the son of Hanina, said: it is revealed and known before the One who spoke the world into being that there are no Sages comparable to Rabbi Meir in his generation. If so, why is the halakhah not in accordance with him? Because his colleagues could not fully comprehend the depths of his thought."

However, some of the *poskim* who did cite the Rogatchover are the following:

1. Rabbi Yaakov Yitshak Weiss, *Sheelot u-Teshuvot Minhat Yitshak*, 1:29, 2:5, 3:101, 9:130, 10:97.

2. Rabbi Yaakov Mordekhai Baryesh, *Sheelot u-Teshuvot Helkat Yaakov, Even Ha-Ezer, simanim* 3, 36, 59, 64, 74.

3. Rav Yehiel Yaakov Weinberg, *Seride Esh, helek* 1, *simanim* 114, 131, 162, 173, 181.

4. Shlomo Zalman Oyerbakh, *Minhat Shelomoh, helek* 1, *simanim* 7, 37, 56, 58, 60, 69, 71, 89.

5. Eliezer Yehudah Waldenburg, *Tsits Eliezer*, 8:22, 9:51, 10:40, 11:29.

6. Shemuel ha-Levi Vosner, *Shevet ha-Levi, helek* 1, *siman* 50, *helek* 2, *simanim* 118, 187, 196.

7. Rav Menashe Klein, *Sheelot u-Teshuvot Mishneh Halakhot, helek* 4, *simanim* 52, 114, 151, 162, 165, 208.

8. Rav Yekutiel Yehudah Halberstam, *Sheelot u-Teshuvot Divre Yetziv, Hoshen Mishpat*, 87.

9. Ovadyah Yosef, *Yabia Omer* and *Yechave Daat*.[29]

Zionism

What are the Rogatchover's opinions on Zionism? We must look to his letters in order to glean some approximation of his attitude.

In a letter of reply to Rabbi Yitshak Sternhell of Sanz, editor of the monthly Torah journal *Ha-Kokhav*, he writes:

"Regarding what you asked about settling the Holy Land, this is only for individuals, and we must not do it as a group. As it states at the end of *Ketubot*, we must not go up as a wall (*she-lo yaaleh ke-homa*). In other words, we cannot go to Israel en masse, as a distinct group. See Yoma 9b [where it is clear that group immigration, even when peaceful, is considered 'as a wall']. The Rambam also holds that only settling Israel is a mitzvah, not buying land there. For in this matter there is a contradiction between *Gitin* 8b [where it states that there is a mitzvah to buy fields in *Erets Yisrael*] and *Bava Kama* 80b [where only houses are mentioned]. The Rambam [*Hilkhot Shabbat* 6:11] rules in accordance with *Bava Kama*."

We see an interesting approach here. Certainly it is a good thing to go to Israel, but only as individuals. It is not, however, clear whether he means that Jews cannot set themselves up

---

29   This list is taken from

פילוסופיה בשירות ההלכה: עיון בבעיית האישיות המשפטית

by Yitzchak Brand.

as a self-governing entity, or whether he means that the movement cannot possess a national flavor. Perhaps a couple million individuals could and should go to Israel, just not as a distinct nation. (See Chapter Five for more context on the conceptual difference between groups and individuals.)

An interesting story is told by Rabbi Moshe Blau. Rabbi Blau was sent from Yerushalayim to seek guidance on the Kookian controversy that was growing about who should be the Rav of Yerushalayim.

"I entered the room, even though [the Rogatchover] was sick and the doctor was in middle of treating him.

'Who are you?' he asked.

'Moshe Blau from Yerushalayim,' I replied. 'Perhaps I should come back later when the doctor is not here?'

He said, 'No, no, it's fine. It's nothing, foolishness—I just have a slight problem with my throat. Foolishness. The doctor will leave any moment. The Rebbetzin summoned him. She is extra zealous with the mitzvah of health. Sit, sit, we'll hear the doctor's directive, and then we'll talk a bit.' After the doctor left, we started talking. 'Why are you here?' he asked. I told him about seeking guidance on the Zonnenfeld succession and the controversy with Rabbi Kook. He was very interested in the whole matter. He started speaking about Zionism in general and told me:

'You know that I was one of its fiercest opponents. Everyone knows about the famous letter…Recently I have stopped writing against them, since my daughter lives in Petah Tikvah and wrote to me that they are threatening to fire her if I keep on battling them. She has no other source of livelihood, and so I stopped writing public letters against them. I believe that the Zionists are suspect in everything…even in bloodshed.'

I suggested, 'Maybe his honor would consider moving to *Erets Yisrael*?'

'Where would I get an income from?'

'Israel will take care of you.'

'I do not like this type of income. Besides, I worry about the Zionists, and one is not allowed to enter a dangerous situation.'

After some more conversation, I left, but this hour of pure pleasure remains etched onto my mind and heart."

The famous letter the Gaon referred to was printed in a journal called *Peles* in Berlin in 1901. The title of the letter was "Zionism—What For?" The letter was written under the pseudonym of Rabbi Banaah. The letter begins, "Regarding this crooked cult that calls itself 'Zionists' ...indeed this is an apt name, since Zion is outside Jerusalem proper..."

* * *

Once a group of scholars, among them Rabbi Schneur Zalman Broyda, arrived from Israel and entered the Rogatchover's study. "Ah! Thank G-d for the *Ramban*," he said to them. "He saved the holiness of *Erets Yisrael*!"

Rabbi Broyda explains the meaning behind this strange statement. The Talmud, expounding a Biblical verse, states that the sanctity of Israel departs if bad and unworthy people, *pritsim*, settle there. The *Ramban* comments that this only applies if non-Jews settle there. Thus the Rogatchover was stating that if not for the *Ramban*, the holiness of Israel would depart, since the Zionists, whom he regards as *pritsim*, settled there.

* * *

In *Tsafnat Paneah* on *Parashat Mikets*, he writes that when Yaakov faces danger from the ruler of Egypt, who is actually his own son, Yosef, he employs two of the same strategies he used when meeting Esav. Just as he met Esav's challenge with a gift and a prayer, so too here he uses a gift of the best fruits of the Holy Land with a prayer: "May G-d Almighty give you mercy before the man..." But he does not use war, because he wishes to teach a lesson to his descendants not to fight wars during the exile, as it states in *Ketubot* 111a: "He made them swear not to rebel against the nations."

It seems that the Rogatchover understands that Yaakov's exile in Egypt really begins at this point. Previously, when meeting Esav, he was not considered to be in exile, and thus was permitted to fight if necessary. (This notwithstanding the fact that Yaakov indeed fought Esav in Israel!)

* * *

As an aside, Rav Shila Refael, the Rav of Kiryat Moshe in Yerushalayim and the grandson of Rav Yehudah Leib Fishman, relates an interesting story which shows the Rogatchover's greatness and his quick grasp of difficult situations. It was when the Turks ruled Palestine, when every Jew who was not born in *Erets Yisrael* expected to be expelled. Many of those who were born abroad swore they were born in *Erets Yisrael*, and that satisfied the Turks.

The *rabbanim* in Israel discussed whether it was halakhically permitted to make this false oath. Rav Fishman and Rav Abba Citron, rav of Petah Tikvah and the Rogatchover's son-in-law, turned to the Gaon for an answer. The answer he wrote them said merely, "It is surely permissible; see *Ketubot* 75a."

The Gemara there comments on the verse, "And of Zion it shall be said, this man and that man was born in her, for the Most High Himself will establish her."[30] Rav Maisha, the grandson of Rabbi Yehoshua ben Levi, said, "One who is born in it, and one who anticipates seeing it." Rashi there says, "One who anticipates seeing it is called one of its children."

With this the Rogatchover resolved simply this frustrating dilemma.

1.5 Personal Matters

The Rogatchover's material circumstances were severely austere. The Jewish community in Dvinsk was impoverished and did not receive government assistance. For this reason, he thought twice about every letter he answered. Those who included a stamp solved the financial problem, but most correspondents did not know of his impoverished state. He would calculate and affix a

---

30   Tehillim 87.

stamp that was half of what the postcard required, and the recipient, by law, had to pay the rest.

The Rogatchover, who lived a life of material deprivation, was very particular about not making long-distance calls from his home. In Dvinsk there was a flat monthly charge for unlimited phone usage, except for long-distance calls, each of which was marked down and required payment.

Zevuluni relates: I once was witness to the following. The *gabbai* of the Planover shul where the Rogatchover prayed, Mr. Vafsi,[31] came into the house and asked to use the phone. Permission was granted, but the Rogatchover motioned me to come over to him. He said to me, "Koidonover [he called me after the city I came from], please see to it that Vafsi does not call Riga."

1.6 Family

The Rogatchover's son-in-law, Rav Abba David Goldfine, was an outstanding prodigy. It is said that when he studied in Brisk, Reb Chaim himself made time to learn with him one-on-one. He met the Rogatchover while traveling through Dvinsk and heard a lecture from him. After the lecture, Rav Abba came over to the Rogatchover and began challenging many of his assertions. "I see you know how to learn. Stay with me a bit. I want to discuss some things with you," the Rogatchover said. Eventually he married the Rogatchover's daughter. Rav Abba was removed from the ways of this world and was a bit naïve and absentminded. One can see the Rogatchover's understanding of his son-in-law from the following story:

A town offered R. Abba a position as a rav in their town. He was not sure if he should accept, so he turned to his father-in-law for advice. "Do not accept. You are too outstanding a scholar to go to a small town. And a large town would not work for you, either, since you are too simpleminded and naïve."

During World War I, while fleeing, he ended up in Moscow and became the chief rabbi there until he died in 1936.

---

31   The father of Dr. Vafsi, one of the doctors accused in Stalin's Doctors' Plot),

His other daughter, Rochel, married Yisrael Abba Citron. Rabbi Citron was born in 1881. He was appointed to the *bet din* in Petah Tikvah in 1911. He studied in his youth in Telz and Volozhin and gained fame as an incredible genius. He died in 1927, leaving his wife a widow. She later returned to Europe and died there at the hands of the Nazis, may G-d avenge her blood.

In an incredibly revealing and intimate letter[32] that he wrote to his daughter in Israel in 1919, the Rogatchover wrote these passionate words. "To my son-in-law and my dear daughter, who are bound to the walls of my heart, and to my nephew, who is as precious to me as the pupil of my eye, may you all live long. Thank G-d, everything with us is peaceful. I received your letter and my spirit is awakened. I will describe to you things that I never wrote, things I have only spoken about. I will describe to you the situation as it was recently. I already wrote you that many of the refugees that came were killed, either as dissidents or for money. Many wealthy people are in dire straits right now. The Rav here has lost his source of livelihood. You cannot believe what is going on—a strong and crippling hunger. A loaf of bread is sixteen rubles and sometimes eighteen rubles, and this is not even for clean bread from the time of Yehezkel. Kosher meat is nonexistent. A scrawny and thin chicken is eighty rubles! Liquor is twenty-five rubles for a liter, kosher butter is fifty rubles for a liter, and sugar costs seventy-five rubles. As for me, I need a minimum of seven rubles for each month, and where will it come from? But I pray to G-d, who sends help from nowhere..."

The Rogatchover's sister's name was Musya Raizel Dimichuvski. She had a son, Ephraim Fishel, who was named after their father. When she died and left him an orphan, the Rogatchover took this child into his home and raised him. When he reached the age of eighteen, the Rogatchover sent him to Tomche Temimim, the Lubavitch yeshivah. In a letter to Rabbi Zevin (*Sheelot u-Teshuvot*, p. 144), who helped the boy get set up in Lubavitch, he writes: "I just now received your letter and you have brought me much joy. I will send ten rubles each month. I beg of you, please look after him in every matter. Please [help me] with this, for right now, watching him is like preparing the *matzo*..."

---

32   Published for the first time in Buruchav page 172

1.6 Illness

The Rebbe of Kopshnitz heard the following story from the Rebbe of Sadigora (the *Abir Yaakov*). "The Gaon of Rogatchov came to Vienna for treatment during his illness. When we heard this, we all came to visit him. I entered the room and, G-d protect us, saw him fidgeting from the torturous pain. But I'll never forget— when we started to speak about a Rambam he became still and the pain went away." Perhaps another possibility is that the pain was still there but the Rogatchover did not feel it, so intensely did he immerse himself in the Rambam's thought.

Although the Rogatchover was wracked by pain, he did not decrease his immersion in study and writing. Several letters attest to this. In one letter (*siman* 122 n.y.) he writes: "I was in Riga for three weeks and, praise G-d, there were many rabbis and people with whom to interact. We delved into all different fields of Torah, even though there was tremendous suffering, and we rejoiced on Purim *ad de-lo yada*."

In another letter, from the 22nd of Kislev, he writes: "I am incapacitated by my doctors' advice after having had an operation, may G-d protect us. May G-d send me healing…"

Rabbi Isser Zalman Meltzer relates that when he visited the Rogatchover, he was in pain and bedridden. The Rogatchover told him that he feels bad for always arguing against the Raavad, but what can he do? The Rambam's thought is so compelling that it is impossible to argue against it!

When the *Rayatz* heard that the Rogatchover was ill, he wrote a letter to the hasid Rabbi Eliyahu Chaim Althouse.

"*Motzaei* Shabbat *Vaera*, 1936. Peace and blessings. I received your letter and I am in great pain from the news about the Rogatchover. I am certain that all hasidim and all those who fear G-d are praying fervently for his recovery… please inform me what the situation is now. I eagerly await good news. Your close friend who seeks only good for you and who blesses you, Yosef Yitshak."

While travelling to Vienna for treatment, the Rogatchover stopped in Riga for Shabbat *Yitro*. He was called to the *haftarah*, read the blessings, but then stopped and took a deep breath. He motioned to the reader of the Torah, Rabbi Shalom Yaakovson, to take over. Interestingly, the *haftarah* contains the verse "In the year that King Uziyahu died."

The Rogatchover was sick at various times in his life. One report about his sickness comes from the famous Lubavitcher hasid Reb Yitshak Horowitz. He writes: "I do not think I will be able to raise money here. The whole town of Dvinsk is funding the medical bills of the Rogatchover Gaon. They just paid two thousand rubles to have a specialist come from Vienna."

From a letter of the *Rayatz*, we see that another name was given to the Rogatchover to help heal his illness, an ancient custom amongst Jewry. The letter is dated the week of *Vaera* 1936:

"Peace and blessings. I received your letter and am in great sorrow regarding the current state of the Gaon. Certainly all the hasidim are praying and begging G-d to have mercy…G-d should send a speedy recovery to the prince of Torah, our master *Chaim Yosef*…"

1.7 General Stories

Contrary to popular practice, the Rogatchover did not bake his own matzot, nor was he involved in the process at all. He once explained this behavior, saying, "If I go to the bakery, I'm bound to see problems that arise from variant and minority opinions of different *sugyot*. I will demand that the bakery be structured differently to forestall these problems, but I won't be listened to. I thus won't be able to eat matza. Therefore, better I stay away and be able to eat matza in peace."

* * *

There were things the Rogatchover was exceedingly particular about. He did not look at women, even unmarried women. When he walked to shul, he walked in the street and alleyways, instead of on the sidewalk. He did not discuss with yeshivah students those halakhot which pertain to man and wife. If a student went to him and wanted to talk about these topics, the Rogatchover would immediately ask him whether he was married or not.

He had to leave Dvinsk because of the war and moved to Petersburg, which became Leningrad, for ten years. He was certainly not happy about this and would sign his letters in those years, "Yosef Rosen, the Rav of Dvinsk, who is trapped in Petersburg." During these interim years, the hasidim adopted him as their rav, and enjoyed being with him very much.

* * *

The Rogatchover davened in the Planover shul, which was the hasidic synagogue. According to some, he would pray quickly, and if the *hazan* was singing the prayers for too long, he would yell out, "G-d understands you even without the song!"[33]

* * *

Rabbi Simhah Gorodetsky reported that he was in Petersburg for Shavuot in the year 1923. On the first day of Shavuot, in the late afternoon, the Rogatchover was studying the *Tashbatz*. He remarked to Rabbi Gorodetsky, "The *Tashbatz* was a great man. The whole Torah is included in a couple pages of his *sefer*." He also expressed his displeasure at the *minhag* that was spreading to read *Akdamot* before reading the Torah, saying that it is an interruption (*hefsek gadol*).

Rabbi Gorodetsky was sitting with the Rogatchover and Reb Shmuel Michel Tranin. As they were discussing something, Reb Shmuel took out a cigarette. Seeing this, the Rogatchover called to his wife to bring a coal. When she did not respond, he got up to go get a coal. As soon as he saw this, Reb Shmuel said, "It's okay—I don't really want a smoke. I just wanted to see the Rav's position on smoking on *yom tov*." The Rogatchover replied that he never smoked and thus did not know if it was a real need that would be allowed under the umbrella leniency of *okhel nefesh*. Reb Shmuel then said, "Indeed, it seems to me that it's permissible, since the Rebbe *Rashab* smokes on *yom tov*."

---

33   From Moshe Bloch as told in *Yahadut Latvia*.

"What?" exclaimed the Rogatchover. "You compare yourself to the Rebbe? The Rebbe is a saint and his smoking is on an entirely different plane!"

* * *

During the Rogatchover's stay in Leningrad, he came into close contact with a lot of Chabad hasidim, among them some of the most famed and distinguished of the time. Many interesting stories have trickled down to us from this time. Some of them are highly indicative of his outlook.

The *Rashab* was in Petersburg in the year 1917. One morning the hasidim saw that he was in an unusually good mood. One of the hasidim was brazen enough to ask the Rebbe about this. The *Rashab* replied, "This morning I received a blessing from the Rogatchover, who told me, 'I bless you with my power of Torah that you will be successful in all your endeavors.' Should I not then be happy?"

* * *

Shmuel Nimotin relates the following story. When the *Rayatz* wanted to move to Petersburg, he instructed his hasidim first to ask permission from the Rogatchover, who was considered the leader of the city at the time. Unfortunately, there were hasidim who thought they would be extra smart and take care of the matter in their own way. Apparently, they said something disrespectful to the Rogatchover and told him to leave. When the *Rayatz* heard about this, he immediately instructed these three hasidim to go beg for forgiveness from the Rogatchover, since they were "playing with fire." One of the hasidim went to the Rogatchover and asked for forgiveness, because his Rebbe had commanded him to do so. The Rogatchover forgave him, saying, "I see you are only asking forgiveness because your Rebbe told you to do so, but on your own, you would not have done so." One of the other two died within the year, and the other one, who had been a *lamdan* and devoted hasid, suddenly left Judaism, only returning to Orthodoxy many years later.

* * *

Shmuel Nimotin once came to the Rogatchover with a message from the *Rayatz* to come to a rabbinic conference. "The *nasi* calls? Let's go!" he said.

Reb Laizer Nannes tells the following story. "We once went to visit the Rogatchover in a group. We knocked on his door and his grandson opened it. When the Rogatchover heard guests entering, he called gruffly from the other room, "Who is it and what do you want?" We replied that we were students of Tomche Temimim, and he came out with a warm smile and invited us to sit down with him. First he wanted to know where we were coming from and whether we had access to a *sukkah*. We told him that we were using the *sukkah* of Shmuel Nimotin. "Incredible," he said. "You walk five kilometers to the *mikvah*, then another five to the Rebbe, then another five to Nimotin's *sukkah*! This contradicts the mandate to rest and take pleasure on *yom tov*. Why don't you just come to my *sukkah*? The truth is that one who is traveling to their teacher is exempt from the obligation to eat in the *sukkah*. But keep in mind that this is only if you are going to your Rebbe to hear Torah. Have you heard Torah from him today? Even if you did, do you think you fully understand it? At any rate, I think you are obligated in *sukkah*. Come to my *sukkah*!"

Later in that conversation, the Rogatchover inquired how we were making a livelihood, and where we got money to visit the *Rayatz*. We told him that we had borrowed the money for the train tickets, which was no small sum. "Wow, this is the power of Tomche Temimim, which produces Jews who are full of self-sacrifice. Borrowing money you do not have to travel to the Rebbe for *yom tov*. Let me ask you this, though—do you understand the greatness of your Rebbe? Do you have any comprehension to whom it is that you have traveled?"

One of the students there responded, "It seems from your question that you do have an understanding of the Rebbe's greatness. Perhaps you can tell us?"

The Rogatchover responded, "Comprehension of a Rebbe is not possible. One thing we can know for sure is that the Rebbe looks across the world, sees any Jew who is in trouble and pain, and prays for him. This is why a Rebbe is called *eine ha-edah*, the eyes of the congregation. It is because the Rebbe can see the whole congregation of Israel with his eyes."

* * *

Simhah Gorodetsky tells about a similar incident in which the Rogatchover asked him why he was in Petersburg for Sukkot. He replied that he had come to Petersburg to visit the Rebbe. The Rogatchover then asked him, had he come to Petersburg to see the Rebbe, or to the Rebbe to see Petersburg? He then added that there are seventeen differences and ramifications that hinge on this question. One of them was that if he had come for the Rebbe, i.e., if that was his conscious and sole motivation, then he was exempt from *sukkah*. He sent Gorodetsky off, saying, "the other sixteen differences I'll let you figure out yourself!"

The prison in which the *Alter* Rebbe was incarcerated was in Petersburg. It is told that when the Rogatchover passed the prison, he would always begin discussing whether he should make the blessing "who performed miracles for my fathers" (*she-asah nes le-avotai*) or whether the proper form was "who performed miracles for our teacher" (*she-asah nes le-rabenu*).

* * *

The *Rayatz* became deathly ill in 1921. He instructed the hasidim to send a *pidyon nefesh* to the Rogatchover and ask for a blessing for his recovery. The Rogatchover began his reply with the heading "To the leader of Israel, a commander in Judah, the shoot of ancient ones" (*nasi Yisrael, aluf be-Yehudah, geza tarshishim*). He wrote to the *Rayatz* that this sickness would soon go away and that it was merely a transitional and necessary refinement to induct him into the role of a Rebbe and leader.

Zevuluni relates the following. "Every day, I would enter his house to talk to the Rogatchover. Once, Nachman Bialik came to visit. The Rogatchover then gave him a copy of his book, the *Tsafnat Paneah*, at which point Bialik left.

Bialik later wrote that from the mind of the Rogatchover could be carved out two Einsteins. Legend has it that when the Rogatchover heard this statement, he dryly remarked, "And from the leftover specks, one could create numerous Bialiks."

* * *

The *Rashag* once asked the Lubavitcher Rebbe, during a *yom tov* meal, if hasidim have the custom to read the Book of Ruth on Shavuot. The Rebbe replied, "In Ekaterinoslav, the custom was to say it, but hasidim generally do not do it. As everyone knows, the Rogatchover was very against reading the *megillot*."

* * *

The Rogatchover was very fond of grapes, and would reportedly eat a breakfast of milk and grapes. Once a student came in the morning to ask him a question. The Rogatchover was in the middle of eating, but the minute the student asked his question, he started firing off sources and building his theory. "Certainly you are aware of the Tosefta regarding this…the implications there are very clear. But of course, the Yerushalmi argues with this. *Tosafot*, however, have a possible answer," and on and on. The whole while, the grape was bulging out of his cheek, completely forgotten, as he swirled about in his excitement and scholarship.

* * *

One time the Rogatchover received a letter from a yeshivah student in Israel. He was astounded at the mastery and depth that the young student exhibited. He was so impressed that when he next saw the *Or Sameah*, he told him excitedly about this young prodigy. But when he showed him the letter, the *Or Sameah* said, "It is an old letter from Reb Meshulam Igra." The next letter that yeshivah student received from the Rogatchover was a single page filled with hundreds of sources. The Gaon had listed every place that the Talmud speaks about thieves and forgeries!

The Gemara says "once Rabbi Akiva died, the honor of the Torah ceased". The commentaries explain that Rabbi Akiva would exert himself to explain every nuance in Torah down to the last crown on the letter yud. This is the honor of the Torah that people understand that there are no superfluous or unnecessary elements in it. From this perspective we can say "once the Rogatchover died, the honor of Torah was again removed from the world."

Chapter Two

Technical Conceptualizations

One of the most prominent Talmudic scholars and rabbis of the twentieth century was Rabbi Yosef Rosen, commonly known as the Rogatchover Gaon, the Genius of Rogatchov). He is also often referred to as the *Tsafnat Paneah*, "Decipherer of Secrets," the title of his main work.

The Jewish nation has not lacked in scholars over the last two thousand years, yet perhaps one would not be out of his depth to assert that no one has revolutionized Torah study quite as the Rogatchover did. He did not merely add knowledge and clarity to a vast corpus of scholarly literature developed over thousands of years. Beyond that, he challenged and restructured some of the most basic and axiomatic assumptions of Torah analysis in such a way as to show the Talmud in an entirely new light.

To understand the innovations and impact of the Rogatchover Gaon, it will be helpful to begin by considering the nature of the Talmud. In some six thousand pages, the reader engages with thousands of facts and arguments about almost every topic under the sun. Written as a series of conversations, the Talmud is fluid and tangential, jumping from topic to topic, unconstrained by subject or order. A conversation in Tractate *Shabbat* can be revisited in Tractate *Sanhedrin*, and an argument touched upon in Tractate *Pesahim* may only be fully explained in Tractate *Rosh Hashanah*, despite their being many volumes apart. Besides the lack of a structured, sequential progression of ideas, the Talmud's content is itself complex and often intimidating, lending itself to multiple interpretations of any given point. The Talmud's very structure therefore demands careful scholarship and much additional commentary. Yet, as centuries of Jewish scholars have discussed and debated the Talmud, its complex and fractured nature has only expanded.

This can, I think, be split broadly into three eras of further fragmentation. The first period is the era of the *Geonim*, the second of the *Rishonim*, and the third of the *Aharonim*.

While the Talmud usually discusses only one specific case, the *Rishonim* and the *Aharonim* often discuss what the law would be in related instances not recorded in the Talmud. This frequently generates many more arguments, as the commentators debate how similar the related instance is to the Talmud's recorded case, and the significance of differences between them.[34]

---

34   For example, the Talmud in tractate Yoma (74a) records a dispute about *chatzi shiur* (a half-measurement). There are many cases where the Torah forbids the eating of a particular food-item and records a penalty for an infraction. For instance, the Torah declares that the consumption of *cheilev* (certain forbidden fats of an animal) is punishable by *malkot* (lashes). According to the oral tradition, we know that one is only culpable if one eats the minimum *shiur* (measurement) of a *kezayit* (roughly 3.3. ounces). If less than a *kezayit* is consumed, one is not punishable under Biblical law.

However, what is the status of one who ate less than the minimum *shiur* (i.e. *chatzi shiur*)? Has he infringed upon the prohibition or not? We know he is not liable to punishment by the court, but does this mean that he has not done anything wrong, or does it simply mean that we are not able to punish him since he did not eat the minimal amount necessary to be judicially liable in court?

The Sages dispute this. Rabbi Yohanan says that even though it is not punishable, it is still Biblically prohibited. His reasoning is, that although it is only a half-measurement, it can potentially be combined with more of the same forbidden food, completing the full measurement. Therefore he says that even before it is combined with any other food it is still Biblically prohibited. Rabbi Lakish on the other hand, says that it is Biblically permitted. He argues that the Torah forbids "eating", which implies a significant amount. According to Rabbi Lakish, consumption of less than a *kezayit* is not considered "eating". He

Another way in which the complexity of the Talmud has developed is in the analytical scrutiny of the essential nature and status, the *geder*, of the law. This form of expansion is found more in the works of the *Aharonim* than in the works of the *Rishonim* or *Geonim*. The *Rishonim* and *Geonim* tend to discuss unrecorded or new situations that arise, and then debate what the law should be, and how similar the current case is to those cited in the Talmud.

The *Aharonim*, on the other hand, often do not deviate from the plain case in the Talmud. Instead, they focus their discussions on the precise nature of the prohibition or commandment. Often these two approaches mesh together. For example, in order to be able to rule on a new situation, the original recorded case needs to be reanalyzed, given broader parameters and scope. The level of attention paid to the minutest and subtle differences among various approaches in the *gedarim*-ridden world of the *Aharonim* is astonishing and often overwhelming in its subtlety and nuance. In short, the vast corpus of Talmudic literature can be seen as an ever-evolving system, branching further and further out, with constantly increasing knowledge and subsequent fragmentation of said knowledge.

In the world of the Rogatchover, however, a Talmudic dispute is never just what it seems to be on the surface. The dispute recorded in the Talmud itself is simply the result of a long stream of more primary disputes. This approach has numerous profound consequences for how one views the Torah. If one were simply to read the entire Talmud from cover to cover, one would come away knowing thousands of facts and arguments, yet they would all seem to be independent and disparate items of information and disputes.

The Rogatchover radically alters and reconstructs the way one views the body of Torah knowledge. From his perspective, all of the fractured and disparate items of knowledge and disputation

---

therefore says that as long as one does not eat the minimum requirement he has not transgressed a Biblical prohibition.

On the surface it seems to be a very straightforward dispute with clearly defined parameters. Yet in the writings of the commentators I have found some 29 (!) disputes that are directly related to this argument, with myriads more ramifications and abstractions that are indirectly related.

in the Talmud are simply derivatives of more basic and inclusive concepts. In field after field of Torah, the Rogatchover took numerous debates on seemingly disconnected subjects and showed how they are all predicated upon one core concept. All of the argumentation is simply ramification and extension of the core conceptual thread running through them all.

The Rogatchover is reported to have said that he could refine and abstract all of Torah knowledge into ten ideas. Thus, in the eyes of the Rogatchover, the Torah is a unified, interconnected, and harmonious body of knowledge, with all the apparent disparity being merely an outer, superficial layer of thought. In a similar vein, the Rogatchover is fond of saying that the whole Torah, from the *bet* in *"bereshit"* to the *lamed* in *"le-eine kol yisrael,"* is one long word.

A *mishnah* in *Uktsin* regarding apple stems, a *mishnah* in *Shabbat* concerning perfume, and a *gemara* in *Bava Kama* discussing property damages are all, in the Rogatchover's analysis, expressions of the same idea. The coherency and cogency that he brings out in the Torah is so pervasive in his work that one is hard-pressed to find a single piece of his writing that does not show how numerous, apparently unrelated laws are, in fact, one and the same.

To further understand this, consider the following example. A staunch libertarian and a fervent communist are debating whether government should have the power to compel a person to live in a specific place. The libertarian rejects such a notion, while the communist embraces it.

Is this really what they are debating? If asked why he rejects this proposal, would the libertarian simply say, "Because this is what naturally seems right to me?" Of course not. The libertarian would reply that the government does not have the right to infringe upon individual self-determination and freedom of movement.

The communist would then reply that the government most certainly does have the right to limit people to specific zones of activity. Since it is for the good of the country to have an ordered, controlled society, this restriction is within the rights of the government.

If we then pressed the libertarian further about why he believes this, he might reply that in his worldview, an individual has a fundamental right to be completely free from the constraints of authority. This is an inborn, primal right, not one to be earned or deserved. The only justification for government is as a necessary evil. Thus, the more limited the powers of authority, the more just is the system.

The communist would then, in all probability, retort that there is no such essential right of self-determination; the individual is simply a cog in a machine. Because he is only one component of a vast and populous society, certain of his freedoms are justly negated for the well-being of the whole.

The libertarian might then respond that an aggregate cannot possess something that its individual components do not.[35] That is, if we can negate individual well-being, then why not negate the well-being of society, if a society, at the end of the day, is merely a collective of individuals? And if the individual does not have a right to well-being and self-determination, then on what basis does a collective of individuals have that basic, essential right?

The communist could reply that an aggregate of individuals is indeed distinct from the individuals taken separately, and thus has different properties and characteristics. A collective is not just disparate people in a group, but rather is a new entity governed by its own set of rules and rights.[36]

Consider what just happened: we take a debate about whether a government can allocate homes to people, abstract it one layer, and discover that, in fact, the debate about homes is simply an expression of a deeper, more basic dispute about the limits of the rights of government. We then abstract that dispute in turn,

---

35   *"Ein bichlal ela mah she'biprat"*
36   Certain applications of this concept have a basis in Torah. See the *k'lallei ha'torah ve'hamitzvoth* from the Rogatchover Gaon, *erech tsibur,* which discusses several unique dimensions of a communal entity. See also the chapter in this book "Klal Uprat—Collectivist Constructs and Individualistic Integration".

realizing that it also is just an expression of a more primal and basic argument about individual versus collective rights.

We then discover that this basic argument about essential rights, and its two resultant arguments about the limits of government and assigning homes, are all predicated somewhat upon an entirely different debate, whether aggregates of individuals form a new entity with new characteristics.

Exactly in this fashion does the Rogatchover view every argument and law in the Talmud. He sees arguments as simply resulting from a series of more abstract and inclusive differences of opinion. Minute technical laws about animal hides and candles are his building blocks for grand, sweeping theories of the nature of life, religion, and reality.

A debate about grass fibers becomes a debate about the very existence of our world, and whether *halakhah* views physicality or spirituality as the primary determinant. An argument about slaves and converts is transformed into an argument about the ability of an entity to change its intrinsic identity. A prophecy about the wolf lying down with the lamb becomes a conceptual construct for discussing the advantages of quality versus quantity.

The finesse and grace with which the Rogatchover abstracts seemingly innocuous and technical *gemarot* was and is unparalleled. The Rogatchover does not just excel in Torah. He creates an entirely new field in Torah study, not dissimilar to what Einstein does in helping to create the theories of quantum physics and relativity.

His style differs somewhat from that of the schools of *lomdut* (systematic analytical study), which were prevalent in his day and which still enjoy widespread dominance in the *yeshivot*. Although an analysis of the differences between Reb Chaim, the father of modern *lomdut,* and the Rogatchover is beyond the scope of this work,[37] I think it might captured somewhat by the following analogy. Reb Chaim is a microscopic scholar. He takes laws and delves into their complex, ambiguous depths to discov-

---

37   But see later: "Reduction or Refinement" for a brief overview of the broad differences between them.

er their inner identity, their molecular structure, if you will. He splits hairs, refining each element of a law until the differences among all the parts were as clear as day.

The Rogatchover, on the other hand, is a telescopic scholar. In each law he sees the universe of Torah reflected therein. In his mind, each subject of Torah orbits around the others until they are all intertwined and fused together. He abstracts each law until it takes on massive proportions and gains immense applicability to all other fields of Torah.

The following quote from Rabbi Hillel Zeitlin[38] is somewhat in line with this characterization:

זכורני, שגדולי הלמדנים החב"דיים שבעיירתי, פעם—תוך כדי שיחתם בגדלותו הע־
צומה של "העילוי מרוגצ'וב"—אמרו זה לזה בלחישה: אבל בלימוד "על אתר", בזה
הוא לא כל-כך "איי-איי-איי"... כלומר, כל הגדלות שלו מתבטאת בבקיאות וביכולת
להקים בנין מורכב ממאות אבנים מהבבלי, ירושלמי, תוספות, רי"ף, רא"ש ובעיקר—
רמב"ם. אבל לימוד "על אתר" היה נקרא, אצל הלמדנים שלנו: להתעמק בסוגיא
כלשהי, לדייק בכל מלה ומלה, לחדור יותר ויותר לתוכה ופנימיותה עד שמגיעים
לשורשה, ואז להצמיח משורש זה אילן, ענפים, זלזלים, עלים ופירות.

ולא פעם היתה ההעמקה בסוגיא גדולה כל-כך, עד שהיו מסתבכים ותועים בה כבש־
בילי יער עבות.

"I remember that the greatest Chabad scholars in my town were once describing the exceptional greatness of the genius of Rogatchov. All of a sudden, they whispered to each other: 'But his localized knowledge of each *sugya* is not so exceptional.' In other words, all his greatness was expressed in his breath and scope and in his ability to construct a tower comprised of hundreds of pieces from Bavli, Yerushalmi, *Tosafot*, the *Rif*, the *Rosh*, and, most importantly, the Rambam. But localized learning meant to delve into the depths of the *sugya* as is. To be precise with every single word, to drill deeper and deeper into the internal structure of the *sugya* until reaching its roots. And then to grow from the roots a beautiful tree with branches, twigs, foliage, and fruits. And it was not uncommon to delve so deeply into a *sugya* that we would stroll and wander [in the *sugya*] as if we were on a path in a gigantic forest."

---

38   His article can be accessed at: http://www.shturem.net/index.php?article_id=64&section=blog_new

Once in a while, a brilliant mind descends upon a school of thought, and does not just digest and understand the information, but brings added clarity and order to the field. Even rarer is the mind that can innovate entirely new dimensions and nuances within a field. Yet rarer still, however, is the man who can create an entirely new school of thought. Such a man is the Rogatchover.

As a means of conceptualizing halakhic minutiae, the Rogatchover generally uses nine analytical frameworks to extract the core concepts from *halakhot*. I will briefly define them here, while in Section Three, four of the frameworks are explained in depth. These nine frameworks are:

1. *Homer* vs. *Tsurah*—Tangible vs. Intangible

2. *Ekhut* and *Kamut*—Quality and Quantity

3. *Klal u-Prat*—Individualism and Collectivism

4. *Zman*—Time

5. *Shloshah Gedarim* – Three Dissections

6. *Hiyuv u-Shlilah*—Positive versus Negative

7. *Peulah Nimshekhet*—Continuous Loop

8. *Harkhavah Mizgit* and *Harkhavah Shechnit*—Essential vs. Incidental Connection

9. *Nekudah ve-Tsiruf*—Core and Accumulation

Homer vs. *Tsurah*

Homer and *tsurah*, translated literally, mean "matter" and "form." *Homer* denotes the tangible spectrum of reality, as well as the *halakhot* and Talmudic perspectives that are rooted in a physical and material viewpoint. *Tsurah* means the spiritual, intangible spectrum of reality.

For example, the Talmud in *Hagigah* 12a states: "The school of Shammai says that the heavens were created first and then the earth. The school of Hillel says that the earth was created first and then the heavens."

What does this argument revolve around? Is there an underlying theme?

Indeed there is.[39] [40] Shammai says the heavens were created first. By "heavens," Shammai means spirituality and the intangible. In Shammai's view, spirituality is the primary determinant in *halakhah* and is the main barometer of reality. Therefore, as the dominant reality, it was created first. Spirituality, in this context, does not have any sort of otherworldly implication. It simply means something that exists in our universe, yet is immaterial and lacking concrete substance.

Hillel, on the other hand, says that in our physical world, material considerations are of primary importance, and one must use the physical spectrum as the dominant deciding factor in *halakhah*. Therefore the earth, meaning physicality, was created first.

The Rogatchover also occasionally uses these terms as a way of separating the outer tangible dimension of a *halakhah* from its inner intangible core. The *homer* of a *halakhah* is what the Rogatchover understands its essential principle and logic to be, its meat and potatoes, if you will, while the *tsurah* is the specific and temporary form that this principle was expressed in.

Ekhut and Kamut

Ekhut and *kamut*, translated literally, mean quality and quantity. The Rogatchover uses these terms to show how the tensions in

---

39   In Michtevei Torah letter #289:

וזה שיטת ב״ה בחגיגה דף יב

דחומר נברא תחלה ואח״כ הצורה היולית, אך ב״ש ס״ל

להיפך, דצורה היולית נבראת תחלה ואח״כ חומר, וזה

באמת בכל התורה דעיקר צורת הדבה.

40   In Mahadura Tinyana page 180:

וזה הגדר דפליגי בחגיגה

רף יב, דשמים נבראו תחלה לדעת ב״ש, ור״ל דהצורה

הוא העיקרית, ע״כ. ובשו״ת צ״פ (ווארשא) סי׳ נ

במחלוקת ב״ש וב״ה בחגיגה יב, שמים נבראו כוי, ר״ל

אם המציאות הוא הצורה או החומר,

certain *halakhot* have their origins in the balance between quality and quantity.

For example, there is a discussion in *Betsah* 22a[41] concerning burning incense. It was a common custom in Talmudic times to burn incense to waft a fragrance in the air. Another custom was to place clothes over a pit in which incense was burning in order to give the garments a scent. The Talmud states that burning incense on *yom tov* in order to have a pleasing smell in the room is permitted, while kindling incense in order to scent clothes is not.

What is the difference between the two? The Rogatchover explains as follows:

Fire is not within the tangible spectrum, and thus *halakhah* does not give it a legal relationship to a person. However, in cases where it can be grounded and "tied" to some sort of physical item, it does indeed reenter the halakhic scene. This is precisely the situation here. When one burns incense to scent a room, the kindling and the fire are burning to generate a smell in an area, but do not have a substantial direct relationship to any particular physical item. Burning incense for this purpose is thus permissible. Because fire has no quantity, and thus *halakhah* generally does not accord it any legal status, it is as though the act of kindling the flame is not seen in the eyes of the law, since there is no physical substantiation of being and presence to the flame.

Not so in the case of scenting clothes. When one lays the garments over the pier in which the incense is burning, one has "tied" the fire to a specific, tangible item. There is a concrete item to which the flame is directed. In doing so one has, in effect, grounded the flames in the physical spectrum, and thus *halakhah* acknowledges the burning and forbids it. In the same way, grounding the tongue of flame on a coal renders it valid for the Temple service.

41

אמר רב אסי מחלוקת להריח אבל לגמר אסור

"Rabbi Yosi said- it is a dispute whether one can perfume clothes but to have fragrance in a room, everyone agrees that that is permissible."

Klal u-Prat

Klal and *prat,* translated literally, mean the collective and the specific. The Rogatchover uses these terms to explain and explore the delicate balance between the individual and society within *halakhah.* More generally, he uses this framework as a springboard for theories that balance generalities and details.

For example, the Talmud in *Berakhot* 50a states:

"It is the same whether there are ten or ten myriads... If there are a hundred he says, 'let us bless the Lord our God'... If there are a thousand he says 'let us bless the Lord our God, the God of Israel'... If there are ten thousand he says, 'let us bless the Lord our God, the God of Israel, the God of hosts, who dwells among the cherubim, for the food which we have eaten.'"

The Talmud then asks whether there is an inconsistency here. First the Mishnah says that the liturgy (*nusah*) is the same whether there are ten people or tens of thousands. But immediately it goes on to say that there are differences in the *nusah* for ten, a hundred, a thousand, and ten thousand people.

The Talmud answers that the issue is in dispute. The former statement, that there is no difference once there are ten people present, belongs to Rabbi Akiva, while the latter statement of the Mishnah, that there are differences, is attributed to Rabbi Yosi the Galilean.

What are the reasons underlying this difference of opinion? What motivates Rabbi Akiva to say that once we cross the "ten threshold," there is no further differentiation of the blessing, while Rabbi Yosi asserts that there is?

Presumably, Rabbi Yosi feels that a larger group warrants a more prestigious blessing, because the assembly is a greater one. Therefore, with a hundred, we add "the Lord," with a thousand we add "the Lord, G-d of Israel," and the *nusah* reaches its climax with the group of ten thousand, where we add "the Lord, G-d of Israel, the G-d of hosts, who dwells among the cherubim."

Rabbi Akiva's position, then, is the puzzling one. Does he not acknowledge that the larger the group, the more prestigious the assembly, and thus the more significant should be the blessing?

While there are other more conventional approaches to defending Rabbi Akiva, the Rogatchover has a unique view on this issue. He sees in this technical liturgical argument an ontological and philosophical backdrop against which the technical disputation springs forth.

Rabbi Akiva holds that the collective unit formed when ten Jews are together is a *tsibur* (congregation), i.e., a group of the *klal*-centric variety. Therefore, there is no difference in quality between a group of ten and a group of a hundred, for once there are ten and the collective is formed, there is no longer recognition of the individual components. After the *klal* is formed, a greater quantity does not add any additional quality, since the greatest degree of quality that can be formed through individuals coming together has already been achieved.

As such, the "ten threshold" concept is a radical departure from the incrementally increasing quantitative approach that characterizes the *shutfut,* i.e., *prat*-centric concept, advanced by Rabbi Yosi. From Rabbi Yosi's point of view, a collective is of the *shutfut* or *prat* variety. Because the individual components that make up the collective are not negated and nullified therein, but rather are extant and discernible factors, the greater the number of individuals, the greater the collective unit becomes, and hence more prestigious blessings are required.

Zman

Many of the *mitzvot* of the Torah are time-dependent. The concept of time and its precise definition are thus of great importance. The Rogatchover questioned the very nature of time and explicated two different understandings of it. He claimed that there are two different ways of understanding time: as incremental and accumulative, or *shetah*, or as an essential, isolated point, a *nekudah*.

For example, the Torah requires a circumsion to be on the eighth day after birth. What precisely is the nature of this time-sensitive mandate? Does the Torah want the ceremony on the eighth day, to be understood as an isolated point in time? Or does it require that seven days should pass before the circumcision, and thus time should here be understood as accumulative?

Another example of understanding time-related mitzvot through these two very different conceptions can be gleaned from Sukkot. Using the model of *nekudah*, we would say that the fifteenth of Tishrei is a *gorem* or *sibah*, a catalyst. So the arrival of this day is the stimulus or active agent that creates the onset and operational status of *lulav*. Obviously, the mitzvah is not applicable on the fourteenth day, because it is caused and created by the arrival of the fifteenth.

Using the model of *shetah*, however, the arrival of the fifteenth of Tishrei means instead that a certain amount of time has passed since the last time we performed the mitzvah of *lulav*. In other words, the mitzvah is operational and active, to a degree, all year. The fifteenth of Tishrei is merely a *siman* (sign), as as opposed to a *sibah,* that a year has passed and the *mitzvah* can now be acted upon. All year, the mitzvah increases in strength and impact, until it reaches its climax on the fifteenth of Tishrei, possessing its full weight and legitimacy, and becoming strong enough that the Torah mandates one to act upon it and perform the mitzvah. Put simply, the difference is whether the mitzvah is active and present all year, yet is acted upon for only one day, or whether the mitzvah is only active and present when it can be performed.[42] [43] [44]

---

42   T"P Mahadura Tinyana page 55:

בגדר זמו המציאות אם כוונתה תורה השטח הזמן שיש עד יום

זה או רק נקודת הזמו ונ"מ דאם מחמת שטח אז הוא דבר מצטרף ,

ואיכה דבר קודם רק עדייו לא בא אבל אם הכונה רק

לנקודה של זמו פלוני אז קודם זה עדייו ליכא

43   The question can be raised more philosophically as well: what is the greater more powerful reality? The future or the present. See *hadranim al ha-shas hadran al masechet makot* where the Lubavitcher Rebbe develops the idea that this issue is a point of contention between the Babylonian and the Jerusalem Talmud.

44   Until the twentieth century, the question was if Time is one indivisible unit measurable in "units of time arbitrarily chosen" (Newton), or if it is composed of a myriad of "time atoms" (see Rambam, Moreh Nevukhim, I 73). With the advent of Einstein's theory of relativity, the debate has centered on Einstein's assertion that "absolute time does not exist and ... its rate of flow, that is to say, the measure of time differences and increments, is not necessarily

Shloshah Gedarim (Three Dissections)

The style of Reb Chaim Soloveitchik is well known, especially his *modus operandi* of splitting *halakhot* and Talmudic disputes into two elements. The Rogatchover, however, went further, often splitting ideas into three elements. For example, he dissected the commandment of circumsion into three parts. These are as follows:

1. The actual act of cutting the foreskin.

2. The mandate to not have a foreskin.

3. The mandate to be one who is circumcised.

With tremendous scope, he showed that there are many instances where just one of these elements would apply to the exclusion of the others. For example, if one is born circumcised already, he has fulfilled the second and third elements of the commandment, but is still lacking the first one, the act of cutting the foreskin. This is why one who is born circumcised must still undergo some form of cutting and drawing blood, because he must fulfill the first imperative as well.

The same analytical construct was applied to a *get* (divorce document). The Rogatchover posited that there are three different elements to this document.

1. To write on paper a kosher *get,* according to all its halakhic requirements. It should be written with specific intent for this man and woman (*lishmah*), with all the numerous details that apply.

2. The actual divorce, or the severance of the bond between these two people.

---

equal in different coordinate systems." In short, this means that the concept of simultaneity is relative. The Torah implications of this controversy are discussed by Rabbi M.M. Kasher in Talpiyot Vol. V (1952). The Rogatchover's without concerning himself with the discussions of physicists, mathematicians and philospohers expounded in incredible detail these problems purely in the context of halacha. See Rabbi Kasher's Mefaneach Tzfunot, pp. 87-112, and Rabbi Moshe Grossberg's Tzfunot HaRogatschovi, pp. 1-25. Rabbi Kasher also wrote a footnote on page 73 where he rejects R. Grossberg's characterization of the Rogatchover's theory of time.

3. A document of proof (*shtar reiyah*), to serve as proof should the single status of the divorcée ever be challenged.

With this dissection, he explained and clarified myriad difficult and confusing ideas in the Talmud.

Another place where he applies this three-tiered analysis was concerning the law of forbidden foods. There is a law that one who eats forbidden food in an unusual manner (*achilah shelo ke-arkhah*), such as eating raw meat, having food injected into the body, or swallowing food whole without chewing) is exempt from the Biblical prohibition. This, too, is dissected into three separate elements:

1. Instances where the unusual manner of eating removes the prohibition from the food. In other words, the Torah sees the person as eating pork, but permitted pork.

2. Instances where the food loses its status *qua* food. In other words, the Torah views the person as eating something, but not pork, nor any other food.

3. Instances where the status of the prohibition is intact, as well as the status *qua* food, but the unusual manner of consumption is not considered "eating" by the Torah. The pork is still considered pork, and eating pork is still prohibited, but injecting the pork into the body is not considered eating by the Torah, which only forbids eating pork.

With wondrous command of the Talmud, the Rogatchover brings a vast amount of proofs and examples to support his three-tiered analysis.

Another place where he uses this approach is regarding the laws against serving idols, *avodah zarah*, which encompass the following prohibitions:

1. The command not to serve idols.

2. The command not to create an idol.

3. The command not to own any idols

Obviously, each dissected element is elaborated with sources, supplementary information, and practical ramifications.

The Rogatchover innovated several key halakhic elements of marriage, and refers to this analysis often. Marriage, too, is dissected into three distinct layers.

1. Application of *kidushin* onto something (the woman).

2. The act of marrying.

3. The fact that the woman becomes *mekudeshet* (consecrated).

The first two elements the husband effects, while the Torah establishes the third.

Similarly, with divorce, he asserts that the witnesses on the *get* bring about three distinct processes.

1. The paper takes on the status of a divorce document.

2. The divorce and separation occurs.

3. The woman becomes a divorcée.

Here, too, he expounds at length on each element, finding support from both Talmuds and the *Rishonim*.

The same construct he applies to the concept of *ratson* (desire).

1. One can desire.

2. One can concede and agree.

3. One can simply not protest.

He posited that the *halakhah* requires the man to actively desire the woman in order to affect marriage, while the level of desire required from the woman is merely not to protest.

Hiyuv and Shlilah

Another favored method of analysis is the Rogatchover's approach of dissecting a *halakhah* into two different spheres. He often inquires whether a *mitzvah* was a positive mandate or a prohibitory negation. For example, a *kohen* (priest who serves in the Temple) must perform the Temple service, yet we can understand this in two ways. Either the Torah mandates a *kohen* to perform the service, or it simply prohibits anyone who is not a *kohen* from performing the service. Similarly, does the Torah require us to be in a state of pain on Yom Kippur (by not eating or drinking, not having relations, not wearing leather, etc.), or does it just require us to avoid pleasurable things?

Another example of this is regarding a widow's permission to remarry. The Rogatchover dissects the death of the husband in order to clarify what precisely is the permitting agent that dissolves the husband's claim on the wife. Is it the actual death, or simply the absence of the husband from this world?[45]

He debates this intricately, from many places in the Talmud, and leans toward the second, less intuitive, view. With this idea in mind, he interprets the Gemara in *Kidushin*,[46] which states: "It is not the husband who releases her with his death, but rather it is heaven who affects her release." It is not a decree of Torah that releases her, but rather, the nature of the world is such that when there is no husband, there is no hold on the wife, and thus she is released from any connection to him.

He applies this analytic construct to a vast array of issues, clarifying and categorizing field after field in Torah. This idea will be developed at length in Volume Two.

Peulah Nimshekhet

Yet another method of analysis is to define whether an obligation is a static one-time event or an ongoing, continuous process. For example, the Rogatchover investigates whether dipping (*tevilah*) in a mikvah is a one-time action of removing impurity or an ongoing state of being. Is a person a *mutbal* (one who is currently engaged in the dipping or purification process) at all times?

---

45   See siman 34 and 36
46   2b

Harkavah Mizgit and *Harkavah Shechnit*

This is a construct that the Rogatchover uses to explore the nature of different ways of combining things together. For example, the prohibition of building on *Shabbat* is fundamentally different from the prohibition of kneading dough on that day. When one builds by putting two bricks together, he has only created an incidental combination of the bricks, one that can be later undone. However, when one mixes water and flour together, he has created an essential combination, in which the two entities have mingled to the extent that they are now one in waythat they cannot be separated. The Rogatchover uses this concept to explain many seemingly conflicting *halakhot*. This idea will be developed at length in Volume Two.

Nekudah ve-Tsiruf

This is a method of determining whether something was one core element or whether it was an accumulative and incremental element. For example, the Torah's prohibition to not eat a *kezayit* (a minimum amount) of forbidden food can be understood in two ways. If the measurement is accumulative, one who eats even a speck has infringed the prohibition, but the transgression is not actionable until he has consumed a *kezayit*'s worth of forbidden food. The other way we can understand this is that the Torah's directive is predicated on one core point. It is forbidden to eat a *kezayit*, but the Torah's command does not pertain to anything less. This idea will be developed at length in Volume Two.

* * *

Graceful Abstraction

In this section, I will bring several examples of the beautiful and attractive abstraction of thought that the Rogatchover brings to *halakhah*, as well as elucidate several key elements of his interpretive style.

But first a couple words from Rabbi Zevin:

"The story of the Rogatchover is unique and does not fit into the normative narrative of Torah leaders and scholars. He was not just different in degree but different in kind. I do not just mean the amount of greatness, that is, the breadth and scope of his knowledge. Nor even is this because of his depth of thought. Rather, it is because he simply does not fit in with other Torah giants. He had an exceptional breadth, an exceptional depth and an otherworldly perspective.

Even his breadth of knowledge was superior, not just to those of his generation, but even to those of many preceding generations. When one looks in his books, one's head starts to become dizzy from all the sources cited. The same holds true with his incisive analysis and his original commentary. He stands alone, both in the sheer amount of his categorical and intellectual legal dissections, as well as in his creative and original explanations to the Torah of the *Tanaim* and *Amoraim*.

But all this still does not begin to describe his essential character. His core personality and unique value cannot be counted, measured or weighed. One can only measure someone in context to others. However he stands in total isolation from all other scholars. We are therefore left bereft of any means of starting to define his greatness.

His was a unique cognitive grasp, a unique discerning eye, and a unique perspective. When he brings a vast amount of sources to buttress his theory, one is amazed not just at the scope of his knowledge, but more importantly, at the way that he perceived these sources. He draws comparisons and contrasts that the normal mind does not see. I should say rather, that the mind sees, but does not appreciate. The same is true with his way of comprehension and development and the paths of his explanations and commentary.

Everything is sealed with his personal stamp.

We are used to exaggerated descriptions in our community especially at times of mourning or milestones. So much so that even the term "there was only one like him in the generation" (*chad be'dara*) rings in our ears like a poem or exaggeration.

The Rogatchover, however, was truly one upon whom we can say "there was only one like him in the generation," not in a poetic or exaggerated way. There was no one second to him in his time; nor in many generations before him in terms of his vast and wondrous command of the entire Torah, in all its principals and details and minutia."

The word "breadth," in truth, does not describe the measure and manner of the command of breadth exhibited by the Rogatchover. The normative understanding of what it means for a person to have scope and breadth is that he knows by heart a large amount of the Talmud. One who is greater knows even more Talmud by heart and has more of it at his fingertips, until the ultimate, where someone literally has the entire Talmud at his command. However, there are two different forms of breadth. One is simply knowing the material well and being able to recall it a moment's notice, yet not mastering the depth of the matter. Then there is another sort of breadth that might, in fact, be called "depth-in-breadth." This is a degree of knowledge where one possesses not only the material, but also a deep understanding and comprehension of it, with a sharp analysis and satisfying explanation.

Yet even both forms of breadth, the simple one and the integrated one, do not describe the Talmudic character of the Rogatchover. His breadth and command is itself an original ingenious thing.[47] It is a scope that astounds and surprises the learner with the concealed secrets of

---

47   See "The Analytic Movement" page 104 where Solomon portrays one of the differences between Reb Chaim and the Rogatchover as constituting a tension between a *charif* and a *baki* i.e. between depth and breadth. As I will demonstrate in the section below about Reb Chaim I do not think his portrayal holds water.

the Torah. It reveals expansive new fields of thought that no one imagined. When the Rogatchover dissects a concept in *halakhah*, when he splits it up into its different parts and assigns each one a unique character, he astounds, not just with his sharp and incisive analysis, but also with copious amounts of supplementary sources from the Talmud, the *Geonim* and the *Rishonim* that, when he explains them, precisely mirror his central premise.

For an innovative new theory that with its very being indicates it is an entirely new thought, he spread forth his fist and came back with handfuls of proofs, parallel cases and comparisons from the depths of the treasure chest which is the Sifra, Sifri, Mechilta, and both Talmuds.[48] To this one can only say:

'And you will say in your heart "who gave birth to all this…and these things—who raised them?"'[49]

I do not know if the Torah has a minister, for does it not say 'the Torah and G-d are one' (and how can one be a minister over G-d), but it is a fact that great and saintly people nicknamed him 'the Minister of Torah.' This is a name that fits him well. The Minister who ruled over all the infinite treasures of the Torah.

The moment you begin to delve into his books which are short and long at one and the same time (short insofar as the style and text is concerned, but long insofar as the content and depth is concerned), you feel that before you stands a ruler and minister over all the pearls of Torah; the revealed as well as the concealed. A man who deals in Torah as if it were his personal acquisition. And not in the manner of forcing Torah to suit his theories as one who makes forced decrees that compel. Rather all sources that he used appeared to come of their own goodwill and with pleasure to decorate and buttress the astounding and awe-inspiring towers that this wondrous craftsman built."

---

48   Zevin ad. loc.
49   Yeshaya 49:21

The interpretive style of the Rogatchover is truly unique. I would like to elaborate on it. Not just his wondrous creativity or brilliance, but who he was as a commentator on the Torah. With this I think that I will do a great service to those who delve into the Torah. We speak constantly about this incredible man, but many people do not know him or his style at all.

It is very hard to immerse oneself to the proper depth in his books, and, assuredly, more than a surface understanding is all but out of the question. Furthermore, his interpretations are usually nestled among his writings in a manner that is indirect and subtle. They come in the middle of discussions about other matters, sometimes seemingly as an afterthought. We therefore tend to talk a lot about the man without truly experiencing his worldview.

Sometimes, the supports and cases cited in his writings are tenuous, and the associations abstract. One would think that at these times, the Rogatchover's theories may appear weak. But it is not so. The sheer amount of material that he cites, the vast number of connections drawn, all point towards the strength of the theory. It is impossible for the chance and happenstance to occur consistently. Thus, all the supports erected may be slender on their own, but in conjunction with the others, create a thick base for the theory.

If we see one idea drill through multiple sources and concepts in Torah, it is indicative of its truth. This very notion, that the strength of an idea can lie in numbers, is itself a halakhic operating principle. Is this not the whole idea, when we consider the kashrut of a liver, of two indicators of invalidation? Either one of the signs, taken by itself, does not make the animal *treif* (not kosher), but as they work together, each one supports and lends strength to the other.

This fundamental idea is also utilized in the area of testimony. Two signs, or pieces of evidence, that by themselves are not enough can together sway the verdict.

This idea is rampant in the writings of the Rogatchover. Understandably, he only needs to invoke it when the associations he makes are so abstract that the reader is astounded to the point of disbelief.

I am right now focusing purely on the interpretations themselves, not on the conceptual backdrop against which they appear, nor the scores of supplementary sources brought alongside them. I wish to isolate the nucleus of his interpretative style.

Not always do his interpretations seem to be simple *peshat* (basic and literal understanding). Sometimes they seem unnecessary in the degree of depth and abstraction he conjures forth. Wherever he comments, there are usually other commentators who seek to explain the difficulty. However, these others are generally forced and strained interpretations. The Rogatchover does not ever reference them. He simply has no business with others. He says what he wanted to and moves on."

Several important features of his system are as follows:

Harmonic Interconnectedness

Halakhah is famous for its vast amount of detailed minutiae. There is an obsession with precision and categorization. In field after field of Torah, a single verse will break down into thousands and often tens of thousands of differentiated individual laws. The Rogatchover conceptualizes all these myriad laws. In his world, every legal position is indicative of an idea or conceptual background. Instead of reconciling contradictions and placing the text as the central basis, he does the opposite. The concept and the idea are given prominence, with laws and data serving to support and uncover the profundity of thought concealed within the halakhic minutiae. The Rogatchover unites and intertwines a vast array of details and technicalities into a rich tapestry of ideas. He shows how multiple seemingly unrelated *gemarot* really all derive from one concept. But his starting point is the idea. Although one might argue that the Rogatchover does not relate to the text as the supreme authority, but instead bends it to his concepts, the truth is that one who studies his works is astonished at his obedience and submissiveness to the text. He never searches for conceptualization. It comes naturally and intuitively, with any tension between idea and the text always swinging the pendulum in the direction of the text.

As a result, there is an incredible harmony in his works between the nuances of the text and the abstractions he posits within it. Many of his theories are balanced on the precise wording of a *halakhah* in the Rambam or the Talmud. While other Talmudic theoreticians get lost in the richness of the concepts being used, the Rogatchover never deviates from his primary calling: obedience to the text of the Torah. He therefore never seeks consciously to innovate. If a *halakhah* makes sense and fits in its context, he does not seek to bring conceptualizations to it. One who reads his works gets the sense that he naturally sees the systemic analysis instead of actively searching for it. Additionally, he is one of the only theoretical Talmudists in our tradition who is also a *posek* (halakhic decisor). In other words, he does not have the safety of the intellectual acrobatics of the *yeshivot*. People come to him with questions concerning real situations, so he has to apply his scholarship to real-world scenarios. Yet he adheres faithfully and consistently to his systemic analysis. Just as seeing only halakhic minutiae is limiting, so too is only seeing abstraction. The true scholar sees both, and attempts to let the text approach him and patiently observing what is required, instead of actively imposing a hermeneutical and intellectual preference onto the text.

Natural Resolution

Another facet of his innovative approach is that contradictions and tensions are resolved internally and comfortably. Throughout most of Jewish tradition, whenever there is a problem with the text, the Talmudist has to clarify and resolve the problem, either by bringing in more information, showing how the two contradictory texts are stated in different contexts, or reinterpreting the original source. There is a strong and consciously felt agenda of working with the text to clarify the issue. Yet, in the Rogatchover's world, there is no such agenda, or if there is, it is never consciously perceived. A tension within the text is merely an indication that one has not yet probed the depth of the issue. What the Rogatchover does is to zoom outwards and abstract the local issue into one of global dimensions. A contradiction amongst the Rishonim about the validity of a certain method of *shehitah* is really a discussion on the merits of quality versus quantity. A nuance in the laws of Shabbat is simply an indication that *halakhah* has a unique view on the creative power of art.

Generalized Concepts

In the system of the Rogatchover, concepts are extracted from the text and thus gain independence from it. In other words, throughout the history of Talmudic interpretation before the Rogatchover, when one walked away from the Talmud, one was usually left with no intellectual richness to be generalized and understood independently. But with the Rogatchover, a whole system of ideas takes shape, taking flight from the text and existing beyond the text, with the text serving merely as an anchor for the discussion. In other words, all the disparate parts take shape into one cohesive, unified form. This was embodied in many ways, not least of which is that often the Rogatchover resolves a problem in *hilkhot Shabbat* without referencing any of the literature on the laws of Shabbat! Not the Talmud, *Geonim*, *Rishonim* or *Shulhan Arukh*. Instead, he redeems the specific question from its textual trappings and abstracts it into a generalized conceptual idea which he then resolves via other areas of Torah that pertain to this concept.

Holistic Integration

One of the most striking features of the Rogatchover's unique scholarly character is his complete integration of all facets of Torah into one consistent and harmonious body of knowledge. The intensity that he brings to this holistic view of Torah is astonishing as well as highly suggestive.

From his vantage point, there is no difference between canonical text of the five books of Moses and a Rashi in *Yebamot*. Everything is viewed with the same serious, intense, and patient analysis. Whether it is a piece of the Talmud Bavli or Yerushalmi was irrelevant. A local custom and a story in the Midrash all take on the same gravity when he scrutinizes them. The Rogatchover operates on the principle that the whole Torah is one integrated and intertwined body. He buttresses this assertion from a *Tosefta*[50] which says:

"One who asks a question from a different area of Torah must state, 'I am asking a question which is not directly related.' So says Rabbi Meir. The Sages dispute this. 'This is not necessary, for the entire Torah is one idea.'"

He also breaks down the traditional wall between Talmud and Kabbalah, as well as Hassidut. In middle of a rigorous analysis of a Tosefta, he is apt to reference a Kabbalistic or Hassidic concept without breaking stride; as though it were the most natural thing in the world. Many of his metaphysical and philosophical concepts seem to be loosely drawn from Hassidut and Kaballah.[51][52][53]

Even legal walls that the Talmud itself set up, such as mamona me'issura lo yalfinan or, one cannot derive civil laws from religious laws, he disregards.[54]

---

50   Sanhedrin Chapter Seven.

51   Uri Meitlis, unpublished doctoral dissertation, Hebrew University. See also Yehoshua Mundshine "ledmuto haHasidut shel haRogatchover" Migdal Oz p.98

52   For some examples, see Tsafnat Paneah Mahadura Tinyana 12b; Tzafnat Paneah Trumot page 6; Tsafnat Paneah Mahadura Tinyana 89a

53   The Lubavitcher Rebbe wrote the following to R. Kasher: "The Rogatchover studies Kabbalah. And it is well known to many of those who spoke to him. This, notwithstanding the fact that he rarely cites explicitly Kabbalistic sources (though I have found such a case in his hidushim to hilhot avoda zara 12:6). But in general, absence of evidence is not proof and it would be worthwhile to look through the original manuscripts of his hidushim on the Torah." —Igrot Kodesh volume 18 letter # 6,993. Indeed a year later, the Tsafnat Paneah on the Torah was printed and it contains several citations of kabbalistic content as well as a quote from the Arizal. The source in avoda zara is highly illustrative. The Rambam writes that there is no clear measurement for pe'ah (the prohibition of shaving the corners of the head) but, "we have heard from elders that it is, at a minimum, forty hairs." The Kessef Mishneh writes: "The Tur wrote in the name of our teacher [the Rambam] that it is four hairs instead of forty and it would appear that that was the version he had of the Rambam". The Rogatchover rules leniently that the minium is four hairs, like the version of the Tur, since: "it is explained in sifrei kabbalah that pe'ah of primordial man [adam kadmon] contains four hairs. See the Mafteah Olamot." So strongly did the Rogatchover not see the hierarchies and walls between the different sections of Torah that he is deciding a question of law based on kabbalah. {Uri Meitlis pointed out this source to me.}

54   sihot kodesh 1976,p. 140

One could argue that there is a certain implicit understanding, developed over centuries of rabbinic writing, with which a hierarchy of importance has been formed. This means that a Rav and *posek* do not see a Yerushalmi or a *midrash* as having the same gravity as the Talmud Bavli. Also, certain *Rishonim* and *Geonim* are understood to be more authoritative and final then others. From the Rogatchover's viewpoint, however, no such hierarchies seem to exist. Everything is questioned with the same intense intellectual spirit and everything needs to fit with all the other parts of Torah. Complete integration and inclusion is his signature style.

This approach is even extended to secular knowledge. The Rogatchover believes that there is complete harmony between Torah and all forms of knowledge, and that everything is included within the canon of Jewish Torah literature. Certainly this attitude is shared by many scholars, but the Rogatchover could actually see the places in Torah that parralel secular knowledge.

His daughter Chana relates: "My father did not know how to read or speak Russian. He would sign his name in Russian only because he memorized the shapes for his name, but he had no comprehension of the language of the land. I once asked him how he knows so much secular knowledge. 'Everything is in Torah. That is not the wonder. The wonder and shock is that other people do not see it.'"

The Rogatchover himself says: "There is a clear proof from the Talmud that the world is round. Rav and Shmuel debate [Megillah 11a] whether the verse that states Ahashverosh ruled from Hodu to Kush means that Hodu and Kush were adjacent to each other or were at opposite ends of the world. Only if the world is round is there room for both possibilities, that they are both a) next to each other and that b) they are at opposite ends of the world. For a circle has no beginning or end and can be looked at both ways."

Another aspect of this wondrous integration is his ability to find strong textual support for local customs that do not seem to have any firm basis. To him it was simple and clear as day that they enjoyed a solid basis in the authoritative text of the Bavli. He could not understand how others did not see it. Not only did he find authoritative sources in the Talmud for mere customs, he also found sources for philosophical inquiries, especially concepts from the *Moreh Nevukhim*. He was an expert in the *Moreh* and brought vast amounts of examples, proofs, and comparisons in *halakhah* and both Talmuds to back up the statements of the *Moreh*.

The Rogatchover built on the statement in *Moreh Nevukhim* that "any change is external to the core identity" and innovated with it many novel insights into various *halakhot*. He has in his writings a full volume on the *Moreh* in which he explains all the Rambam's words through the prism of *halakhah*. Holistic integration of many different conceptual frameworks was his specialty.

Rabbi Zevin writes:

> "Academics would converse with him and take great pleasure in hearing his perspectives on different matters. He would dissect a secular field of knowledge from the Talmud's framework and they would listen with tremendous pleasure. Nothing was hidden from him. A great Rabbi once told me that he met with the Rogatchover and was astonished at his intimate geographic familiarity of every inch of Israel, simply from his command of the Talmud. While describing his travels, the Gaon remarked "why did not you take this road and save yourself an hour?" This was despite the fact that he had never been to Eretz Yisrael."

Keeping in tune with his style the Rogatchover sees no disconnect between *halakha* and *aggadah*. In the books of the Rogatchover, we bump into many places and numerous comments where he weaves together various halakhic sources. The integration between *halakhah* and *aggadah* is holistic and complete in an astonishing manner. Sometimes, with these comparisons, he sheds new light on *halakhah,* and sometimes the converse is true—a new perspective on *aggadah* is produced.

One small example:

Avot de-Rabi Natan (chapter 31) enumerates many things that are true both about the world and about man. "Wind in the world and wind in man—this is the nostrils of a person...the Angel of Death in the world and the Angel of Death in man—this is the heels of a person."

This statement is simply incomprehensible. Why are the heels of a person seen as the Angel of Death in man? The commentators explain with various forced and convoluted theories. But every honest reader feels that this is a stretch, very far from the simple intent of the words. The Rogatchover, in the middle of dealing with a *halakhah* about reading the *Shema*, sheds light on this enigmatic concept by explaining the statement via a revolutionary approach.

In *Nazir* (51a), the Gemara asks if the decomposed earth from a corpse's heels is impure (*tamei*) and causes those who touch it to become *tamei*. *Tosafot* explains that there is a strip of skin in the heel which has no vitality, no nerve endings, and thus no feeling of pain. Therefore, since it has no life, perhaps when it rots it is not dead, and thus does not become *tamei*. This, then, is the explanation of the statement in *Avot de-Rabi Natan*. Because the heels of a person contain a place without life force, this is the angel of death in man. This is also a great place to see the Rogatchover's cryptic style. All the innovative, creative, original understanding in this piece of *midrash* is encompassed in one indirect line elsewhere in his writings on a totally different topic. Now go and consider the amount of treasure and depth in his theories on the Rambam that extend for pages!

Another way of seeing his holistic integrative style is from his letters. It is the Rogatchover's style to mix Torah sources even into personal letters. A letter does not leave his hands without a string of Talmudic sources cited. Although we do not have his letters concerning personal matters, we can see his penchant for this from the headings on many of his letters. In one letter he begins:

"*Erev Shabbat Kodesh* [Friday], the eleventh of Tishrei. The day that they did not allow Bava ben Beta to bring his sacrifice, as it states in *Keritot* 25 and *Meilah* 14b. 1928, Dvinsk."

An exception that proves the rule is one letter that he sent to the United States regarding a certain individual who wanted to allow for the possibility of divorce by using a proxy during the *hupah*. He omitted any reference to a source in the Talmud on purpose.

"Today I received your letter, which was accompanied with foolishness and stupidity. All you desire to do is permit adultery and increase the [number of] illegitimate children born to the Jewish nation. I do not even want to engage with you on this from the halakhic perspective, as is explained in Sanhedrin."

The reference to Sanhedrin is the statement[55] "Know what to respond to a non-believer. Rabbi Yohanan said this is only talking about a non-Jewish scoffer. But as for a Jewish scoffer, on the contrary, ignore him."

Another story that illustrates this point is as follows. Once a woman came to him for help with her baby. She related a bizarre story—her infant refused to nurse on *Shabbat*. Without a moment's hesitation, he counseled her to wear her weekday clothing when nursing the infant on *Shabbat*. A few days later, the woman's husband came back beaming. "Rabbi, your advice worked!" he exclaimed.

The Rogatchover responded lightly: "This matter is explicitly recorded in a *Tosafot* in Bava Kama 37a. The Mishnah states that an ox can be considered a *mu'ad* [an animal that needs a special measure of protection because it has gored a number of times] on *Shabbat*, but not on weekdays. *Tosafot* explains that, on *Shabbat*, an ox may not recognize those usually familiar to him because they are wearing different clothing. We see from *Tosafot* that animals sometimes identify people by outer factors such as color and shape. This poor woman had changed her garment in honor of *Shabbat*, and her particularly sensitive infant mistook the change of clothing for a change of person."[56]

This story is illustrative. For the Rogatchover, this is not an issue into which one needs to delve. Right away, he sees the *Tosafot* in front of him. In other words, his framework of Torah analysis is not separate from his other cognitive processes, but is part and parcel of him. The first time he learned that *Tosafot*, he ab-

---

55   70b
56   Heard from Tovia Preschel

sorbed that entities having only a primitive consciousness can be disturbed, or can otherwise change their behavior, due to a different color in their surroundings. That piece of information is not forgotten—it is digested and internalized. As we stated in Chapter One, the Rogatchover's memory was not simply phenomenal—it was fully integrated with his knowledge of Torah. His system of Torah was one with him, so it was natural, when the woman came before him, to see the logic of *Tosafot* applying to her situation.

Another angle on this can be gleaned from the following story:

Once, word of a wandering anti-Semitic band reached the community. Major towns and villages had already suffered great damage to life and property, and local rabbis decreed a fast day because of the dangerous situation. The entire Jewish community hid in the mountains. In the flurry of activity, it was several hours before the Rogatchover's absence was noticed. Two brave young men volunteered to search the abandoned city for the Gaon.

Going directly to his home, they found him deep in thought before the ever-present Gemara and Rambam. When he noticed the young men, he laughed and said: "Is not it odd that the rabbis have declared a fast day? Undoubtedly, they were thinking of the Gemara in *Taanit*… and the Rambam… but, of course, you realize that they forgot the Yerushalmi and *Tosefta*…" The young men realized with a jolt that the Rogatchover was not thinking at all of his personal safety, but of the halakhic implications of the situation.

There were many great and saintly scholars who also delve into the halakhic subtleties of the fast day, but do so from the safety of shelter. The Rogatchover lacks, to the point of eccentricity, a this-worldly material orientation. Certainly one could challenge his behavior—if the Torah itself demands that he run to protect his life, how could he stay behind when danger was present? But this question misses the point. It is not a conscious choice to remain behind. He simply observes reality through the framework of Torah. A fast day and roving bands of murderers are only real to him insofar as *halakhah* and Gemara have something to say about them. This is who he is—someone for whom the Torah,

Talmud, *halakhah,* and *midrash* were merged into one system, and from within this system, he experienced reality.

Another story illustrates his ability to see all secular knowledge in Torah. The Rogatchover was very knowledgeable in medical matters, based on his expertise in Talmud, where all sorts of illnesses and cures are mentioned. During the end of the illness that claimed his life, his personal doctor, the famous surgeon Professor Mintz of Riga, examined him and advised him to have an operation. The Rogatchover tried to argue with him by quoting a Yerushalmi about the nature of the illness. He protested that according to the Yerushalmi, the surgery needed to be performed elsewhere in the body, not where the doctor had said it should be done. Professor Mintz got up and said: "Obviously, I do not argue with the Yerushalmi. I suggest that the Yerushalmi operate on the Rav, and not I." The Rogatchover eventually acquiesced, and passed away a few days after the operation.

Philosophy

An important feature of the Rogatchover's system is his use of philosophical ideas to explain Talmudic nuances and subtleties. In this venture, the *Moreh Nevukhim* was his guide. In truth, this element of his system can be seen as just another facet of the general integrated approach elucidated above. Yet it is so pervasive and prevalent in his works that it does indeed deserve its own focus.

It is said that traditionalists view the Moreh in the shadow of Mishneh Torah while the haskalah movement and its offspring view the Mishneh Torah in light of the Moreh. Yet, the Rogatchover innovated a third path. One in which there is no tension between the two. Not just did he explain the Moreh from an Orthodox traditionalist position, indeed he saw it as a book of halakha. He used it as a helpful tool to use for dissecting and clarifying halakhot. In his world the Rambam wrote two halakhic works, the only difference being, one was conceptual the other technical.

In a fascinating essay[57] R. Kasher asserts that the Rogatchover increasingly quotes from the Moreh as he gets older. How did

---

57   Mefaneach Tzfunot page 32.

the Rogatchover understand the Rambam studying Greek philosophy? Certainly he was no admirer of Aristotle. In a letter[58]
he writes "Aristotle may his name be erased". Yet to him it was
resolved simply and halakhically. The prohibition to study he-
retical disciplines is only when they are prevalent and command
obedience. See Section Three for more on this.

Hillel Tzietlin also asserted that the Rogatchover's use of the
Moreh was as a halakhic book.[59]

Style of Responsa

The Rogatchover is known through his books, especially the
Tsafnat Paneah on the Rambam. But he is also one of the most
important *Poskim* (legal decisors) of his generation, in terms of
the sheer number of requests for him to decide matters of *halakhah* and *hashkafah* (Jewish thought).

His letters number in the tens of thousands. His style is to answer any question that comes his way. He does not distinguish
between a great *Rav* and a simple Jew. Each and every day, he
responds to many letters without looking in a *sefer* and without
any pause for thought. Instantly, the very second he reads the
letter, he dips his pen into ink and starts writing.

A Rav once asks him a question, and upon receiving a response,
continues questioning based on the new information he has just
received, until he has written the Rogatchover five letters on one
concept. The Rav is hesitant because he thinks perhaps the Rogatchover feels bothered and harassed by his repetitive inquiries.
The Rogatchover, in his next letter, writes: "You should not hes-
itate to write to me and request of me, for this is the essence of
learning Torah. On the contrary, I am very pleased by all this."[60]

We can see how important his responding to questioners was
from a letter he writes three months before his passing on the
fifth of Kislev, 1936. He was already very sick from the illness

---

58   Shut HaChadashot page 491 in a letter sent to Rabbi Dovid Putch.
Originally printed in Kovetz Kerem Shlomo # 135.
59   See his essay (translated by Yehoshua Mundshine) in Kfar Habad 893
page 60
60   Shu"t #106

that would take his life and complains: "I received your letter and I am so bothered that I am sick in bed …do not bother me because I am sick."[61]

Nonetheless, in that same letter, he does in fact answer the question. Admittedly, the answer is short, accompanied by only five Talmudic sources.

Rabbi Zevin writes:

"It appears that the Gaon wanted to publish his letters in a book form. In one of his Teshuvot he wrote:

"G-d should help me to have my halakhic letters published and then I will elaborate on this point."[62]

It did not come to pass. The book of letters that we have today is a compilation by a publishing house. They just gathered whatever letters they could find. They did indeed receive permission from the Rogatchover to do this, but he himself did not participate in the editing or ordering process. So far, there are three hundred twenty letters in four volumes. If not for the tragedy of the war, the publisher would have been able to print more. There is no conceptual or chronological order to the letters. What a pity that the publisher did not even put in an index!

"In all areas of Torah" is how the publisher described the scope of the letters. He did not exaggerate. Even if one turns to the Rogatchover with a specific question in a niche field of Torah knowledge, the answer usually comes from an entirely different field. So many people turn to him with different types of requests—this one with a request to resolve a family dispute, that one with a problem that had been bothering him for years, another one wants a unique interpretation on some *gemara*, and the fourth simply wants to converse with this great man.

The elaboration that one finds in the *Tsafnat Paneah* is absent from his letters, but the same astonishing novelty is there just as strongly. He never deals with the question on the questioner's

---

61   Shu"t #288
62   Shu"t #15

terms. Right away he zooms out to the abstraction of the question and deals with it on his own terms.

For example, someone asks him whether one who does work on a *yom tov* (Jewish holiday) that falls out on Shabbat would be liable for breaking *yom tov*. The Torah permits us to do work on *yom tov* if it is part of preparing food. However, this special dispensation does not apply on Shabbat. The question then is whether one who does indeed break Shabbat would also be breaking the *yom tov*, or whether he only breaks Shabbat.

The Rogatchover deals with this question at length, but not using any of the sources one would think he would use. *Masechet Betsah* is not cited, nor is *Masechet Shabbat* or *Shulhan Arukh*. Instead, he is fascinated by the underlying conceptual frontiers embedded in the question. As he phrases it, when the Torah grants a dispensation and overrides a prohibition, is the dispensation operational only when performed in exactly the way the Torah delineates? Or is it constantly active in other contexts as well?

In other words, perhaps the Torah's permission to work on *yom tov* is valid only when it does not fall on Shabbat. From this perspective, if one tries to use the dispensation in a situation that the Torah does not intend, the dispensation simply does not apply. Since this is the nucleus of the question for him, he does not care to start analyzing *hilkhot shabbat* or *hilkhot yom tov*. Instead, he starts drawing parallels from all over the body of Torah. Any case that he can relate to the issue at hand becomes a launchpad for further halakhic discussion.

For instance, one of the cases he cites in that letter is in the Yerushalmi,[63] which records a dispute regarding whether one who is included in a group for *korban pesah* (the sacrificial lamb offered on Passover), but who is given only the marrow of the bone, is legitimately a group member, and whether he fulfills his obligation. The Talmud[64] explains that the whole idea of belonging to a group for *korban pesah* is an innovation. Additionally, breaking the bone of a *korban pesah* to get at the marrow is prohibited, even though, after the fact, one who indeed breaks the

---

63   Pesahim chapter 7
64   90a

bone and eats the marrow has fulfilled his obligation. This then plays into our question, for we can formulate the data as follows:

If the whole idea of belonging to a group is an innovation, perhaps it only works when performed in a way that fits precisely with the Torah's intent. Or do the Torah's dispensations work in all scenarios, even when done in ways that conflict with other laws?

In this letter, the Rogatchover does not decide the *halakhah* unequivocally. This is, I believe, for two reasons. First, it is not a practical question, but rather a theoretical one. Second, it is a dispute in the Yerushalmi, in which the Rogatchover perhaps does not want to take sides.

When a practical question comes before him, however, he makes his opinion known. Whether anyone would follow his line of reasoning and plumb its depths is a different story, but the ruling itself is clear. He does not use the *poskim* and never mentions the *Shulhan Arukh*. Except for a few *Rishonim*, the contents of his letters are solo flights of abstraction through the sea of Talmud.

I do not think that he lacks respect for the author of the *Shulhan Arukh*. In two places, he defends the *Kesef Mishneh*, another work by Yosef Karo. But to find *Shulhan Arukh* referenced in a letter is quite a feat. In *Tsafnat Paneah* he also quotes the *Kesef Mishneh* several times, but never the *Bet Yosef* or the *Shulhan Arukh*."

In one letter he states: "And I know that you will find many contradictions against my theory from the *poskim*. However, I am merely as one who sifts through the Talmud Bavli and Yerushalmi and develops his theory from the original material."[65]

He writes another letter in even stronger terms: "Our job is only to delve into the Gemara and Yerushalmi and *Tosefta* to understand their words. We are not ever beholden to anyone else."[66]

Sometimes he brings strong proofs to the words of the *poskim* and *Aharonim* without mentioning them. For example, the *Rama*

---

65   Shu"t #104
66   Shu"t #105

writes in *Yoreh Deah*[67] that if one finds a hole in an animal's liver, there is a sure way to know whether the hole was there when the animal was alive, or whether the hole came about from the *shohet's* (ritual slaughterer's) knife. If the hole is round, one can be certain that it was there when the animal was alive—thus the animal is *treif.* If it is not round, then we know the movements of the slaughterer are what made the hole. The Rogatchover, as is his wont, does not bring the *Rama*, but sources the Yerushalmi on this.

Another instance of this phenomenon is where the *Aharonim* write that even if the hole is round, if there is any indication that there were worms in the animal, we can say that the worms made the hole. The animal did not develop it naturally, so the meat is kosher. The Rogatchover, without mentioning any of this, supports this with a Talmudic source (via a *Rishon*). Rashi writes in *Shabbat,*[68] "those worms make a small hole in curtains," and then adds at the end "that the holes are round."

The question of whether a suspect liver is indeed kosher is presented to him many times. Yet—and this is truly astonishing given the vast amount of literature on this very question—not once does he bring up *Yoreh Deah* or the *poskim* that deal with this subject. Even when someone explicitly asks a question based on *Aharonim*, he finds a way to deal with it directly from the Talmud and not mention the *Aharon*.

He is asked about a red *sirhah* in a question following directly from an *Aharon's* rulings. His answer starts with a *gemara* in *Nidah*[69] concerning red flesh, which is a sign not to worry about blood. He continues with a *gemara* in *Hulin*[70] regarding the solidity of blood. If the blood is thick, the animal is not kosher, while if the "blood" is thin, this indicates that it is merely sweat. He then quotes a *gemara* in *Shabbat*[71] which states that blood is thick and wine is thin. Connected to this, of course, is the *gemara* in *Gitin*[72] which tells a story about sick animals exuding reddish sweat. He then concludes that with a *sirhah*, there is no

---

67	Siman 36
68	75a
69	21a
70	112b
71	77a
72	67b

cause for concern if the liver itself is exuding blood, unless it is dripping, about which the *gemara* in *Nidah*[73] raises concerns.

It boggles the mind. Consider how much ink the *Aharonim* spilled on this issue, how much sweat and tears they exerted on it. The Rogatchover, in two lines, solves the issue in his unique style, with strange and novel proofs from all over the Talmud.

Obviously, this same *modus operandi* applies in many different areas. This is his style in questions of *nidah* and questions of *mikvaot*, questions of *shlihut* and questions of financial disputes, questions of *gitin* and names in a *get*, an area of *halakhah* with few textual roots and many branches of questions. Here, too, he skips mention of any of the *poskim* who deal with the issues.

His specialty and expertise come out the most in halakhic questions that arise due to new developments. Can birds grown in an incubator be eaten?[74] Can one boil and *kasher* non-kosher pots using heat from an electronic source?[75] Can one insert semen from a husband into his wife?[76]

He also deals at length with purely theoretical questions. Our tradition teaches that the manna was able to take the taste of whatever the person eating was imagining. Would a Jew be permitted to imagine a non-kosher taste and eat the manna in such a state?[77] Or is it forbidden, since a taste is like the actual thing (*taam ke-ikar*)? If someone comes forward voluntarily and admits that he accidentally killed someone, do we force him to escape to a city of refuge (*ir miklat*)?[78]

Perhaps the most incredible facet of his responsa is the consistency and uniformity of the analytical system that runs through it. Generally speaking, the level of significance and authoritative voice is different in halakhic responsa than in Talmudic analysis and commentary. There is an element of grave responsibility running through rabbinic responsa. There is the sense that, at this moment, it will not help to be sharp and crafty with one's

---

73   10b
74   Siman 273
75   Ibid.
76   Siman 238
77   Siman 2
78   Siman 215

thinking. The imperative and desire to be analytical and creative for the sake of beauty or intelligence is missing. The need to decide and adjudicate actual law forces the Talmudist to become practical.

Is this person guilty or innocent?

Is this food kosher or not?

Brilliant, delicate, cerebral towers of thought built from the stones of many sources carried over from the sea of Talmud will not help you here.

For the Talmudic commentators, the opposite is true. Here the decisive, important elements are the timeless and the foundational. There is no imperative to focus on a specific time-sensitive scenario. There are no happenstance occurrences before the commentator. There is no enslavement to practical and specific details that change by the month and year.

The stark, astonishing truth is that this difference in authorial voice simply does not exist for the Rogatchover. He has only one way, which runs through his books on the Rambam, his commentary on the *Moreh*, his commentary on the Torah, and his halakhic responsa. He has the same approach, the same command of scope, the same incisive dissection of Talmudic categories, and the same astounding creativity. It was all the same, whether he is writing a long analysis of a nuance in the Rambam or answering a practical question which needs tangible arbitration.

This is all only further amplified by the fact that the Rogatchover was trailblazing a new path. One who treads the beaten path of the *poskim*, availing himself of those who came before him, is, generally speaking, more at ease. He finds the information he needs in the earlier authorities, in the *Shulhan Arukh* and its commentaries. If he cannot find what he needs there, then he formulates his opinion hesitantly and with caution, carefully avoiding ruling in opposition to any earlier authority.

The Rogatchover does not even deign to mention earlier authorities, let alone rely on them! The weighty responsibilities that fell on him were squarely on his shoulders alone.

Another element of his responsa is that he does not like to respond in a specific manner. In one letter he writes:

"I cannot respond to you, answering what each person should do, because my style is only to write the matter as it appears to me how to rule. But the responsibility of getting the details right I do not accept upon myself, for who knows if the writer got them down precisely. Also this style I have is in keeping with the *Tosefta* in *Demai* which rules that one should answer a regular person in a general manner saying, "if this is the case then it is pure. If this is the case then it is impure," instead of saying you may eat or not eat…I also do not know the character of the person writing to me, and therefore I set my status such that I only respond in a general manner, stating the contents of the case, without the specifics of the story as it played out."

Do not mistakenly think that the Rogatchover does not account for the details. On the contrary, he is meticulously sensitive to the tension of all the various details and any changes that occurred in them. In fact, in nine letters (nos. 95-103), he writes nine different answers to the same question, because there were subtle differences in the letters that he received from the Rav who was asking. The Rogatchover writes back sharply: "Believe me that I was trembling, I could not believe what was happening. I received from you four letters and each one tells a different story! I sense a plot here…"

When the Rav asks the Rogatchover why he regrets an earlier decision, the Rogatchover responds:[79] "G-d forbid—I did not retract my ruling! I only wrote the law as I saw it in its general concept. But I was not ruling in regards to the actual story which took place. There was much ambiguity among the testimonies, therefore I wrote again, but G-d forbid to say I retracted."

There are usually three partners in producing a work of rabbinic responsa: the author, the organizer, and the publisher. The author who merits to publish his own rulings has the luxury of choos-

---

79   Siman 32

ing the nicest and most prestigious examples. Not every letter written for a temporary and chance occurrence is fit to be published, given the permanent nature of a book. But many of the most famous books of rabbinic rulings have been published by the printer without any selection or ordering. Whatever comes into the printer's hands first is what goes in the compilation.

An organizer, though he cannot choose which letters are the most appropriate, can at least bring some order and logic to the letters, either by concept or by content. The Rogatchover, however, did not get to publish his own responsa.

The Rogatchover's letters spread by the tens of thousands all over the globe, but they are not compiled in a single volume, even though he very much desired this. Between 1935 and 1938, four volumes of responsa from the *Tsafnat Paneah* were published in Warsaw. The edition that we have today has been worked over by an organizer, Rabbi Yisrael Safran, who ordered them by content. He also inserted, at the beginning of each letter, the question asked.

His first four letters deal with civil marriage, a problem that troubles Torah scholars and adjudicators. Usually the rulings are lenient in the sense that a civil marriage is considered non-binding. The Rogatchover, however, rules stringently on them. He elaborates at length on this with many different arguments. One notable idea he posits is that the marriage is binding because the man and woman consider themselves husband and wife. Furthermore, he rules that this is not a question of clarification (*biur*) on which one could say that since they do not believe in *halakhah*, their perspective is non-binding. Instead, he posits that living together itself creates the marriage. Against such a claim, no rationalization will help.

In his discussion of this, he writes, "Rashi and *Tosafot* erred here and misunderstood the *peshat*." Yet in the same letter, he states, "I cannot argue with *Tosafot*"! He feels comfortable arguing with the *Rishonim* in explanation and commentary, but he does not dispute *Tosafot* when it comes time to issue a ruling.

In a different context, however, he writes,[80] "Even though our great masters and also the Rambam did not agree with me, and I am but dust under their feet, nonetheless the bottom line is as I wrote and ruled." Perhaps he allows himself to argue with the *Rishonim*, even in halakhic rulings, as long as his ruling is stringent and not lenient—or perhaps the explanation lies elsewhere.

Other questions arise from the opposite angle, regarding marriages with witnesses, but not for the sake of living together, rather, for citizenship or visas. When the Rogatchover is asked his opinion on this, he writes:[81]

"According to the law, they are married, since there were witnesses. We find this same phenomenon in the times of the *Tanaim*, as is explained in the Yerushalmi in *Yebamot* (ch. 4), *Tosefta* in *Ketubot* (ch. 5), and Rashi in *Kidushin* (71), that Rabbi Tarfon married three hundred women to *kohanim* in order to allow them to eat sanctified food, since it was a year of terrible famine."

Regarding the permitted status of a widow, he dissects the death of the husband in order to clarify what precisely is the agent ending the husband's claim on the wife. Is it the actual death, or simply the absence of the husband from this world?[82]

He debates this intricately, from many places in the Talmud, and leans toward the second, less intuitive, oath. With this idea he interprets the *gemara* in *Kidushin*[83] which states: "It is not the husband who releases her with his death, but rather it is heaven that affects her release."

It is not a decree of Torah that releases her, but, rather, the nature of the world is such that when there is no husband, there is no hold on her, and she is released from any connection to him.

Often his answers would starkly contrast with the simplicity of the question. An example:

The those fat in keilim states the following:

---

80   Siman 34
81   Siman 5
82   See siman 34 and 36
83   2b

"Rabbi Shimon the humble one said to Rabbi Eliezer, 'I entered into the temple in the space between the alter and the hall without performing the required washing of my hands and feet'. He [Rabbi Eliezer] replied, 'who is revered? You or the Kohen Gaddol'? Rabbi Shimon was silent. Rabbi Eliezer then proclaimed, 'you are embarrassed to say that even the dog of the Kohen Gadol is more revered then you.'"

The questioner asked the Rogatchover the meaning of this enigmatic statement concerning the dog of the Kohen Gadol. Most people would reply it was a common expression in those days or such similar explanations. Not the Rogatchover. To him there was no incidental or arbitrary statements in the Talmud. He explained as follows:

In general, cases of capital punishment require twenty three judges instead of the usual three. The Kohen Gadol however, requires the full grand court of seventy one judges if he comes before the court.

In Sanhedrin the Gemara entertains the idea that the ox of the Kohen Gadol as well, if bought before the court for killing a person, would require the full grand court of seventy one judges.

This then is the meaning of Rabbi Eliezer's bizarre statement to Rabbi Shimon. Rabbi Shimon if brought before the court would require twenty three judges while the dog or animal of the Kohen Gadol would require a grand court!

Biblical Interpretive Style

Another intriguing aspect of the Rogatchover's scholarship is his commentary on Biblical verses. In his books, especially the later ones, we find him explaining verses in his unique style. From the perspective of *peshat*, obviously, his interpretations are a bit far from the simple meaning of the verse. But from a Talmudic and halakhic angle, they are compelling and fascinating.

Thus, in his commentary on *Humash*, no "story" is interpreted simply in humanistic or even moral terms. Every sentence, word, and letter in the Torah is related to the eternal verities of *halakhah*. The fate of Sodom and Gomorrah is understood in the light of the laws of *ir ha-nihdat* (the totally corrupt city that earns destruction). The serpent's curse, being the eternal enemy of mankind, is reflected in the *halakhah* that a snake can be put to death without a *bet din* (court proceeding), unlike other animals. Jacob set up stones on which to sleep because he was legally laying claim to the land; in order to do so, it is not enough to simply sleep there, but one must "make the bed" as well (*Bereshit* 18:21-24).

In *Bereshit* 22:6, before the *Akedah* (binding of Isaac), Abraham piled the wood on Isaac, but not the knife, because there is a disagreement between the Talmud Bavli (*Pesahim* 66a) and the Yerushalmi (*Pesahim* 6:1) regarding whether it is permissible to lean the knife on the sacrifice once it has been sanctified. Abraham wanted to make sure that every detail of his precious *korban* was perfect, and was scrupulous to fulfill all halakhic opinions.

When Yosef's brothers went to Egypt, the Torah (*Bereshit* 48:8) tells us that he recognized them, but the brothers did not recognize him. Rashi explains that when they had separated, Yosef, unlike his older brothers, had not yet grown a beard. Another reason might be that Yosef's brothers did not gaze directly at his face because the Talmud (*Hagigah* 16a) states that staring directly at a monarch is damaging to the eyes.

In the prophet Isaiah's descriptions of the age of Moshiach (ch. 11), we find the passage, "And the wolf shall dwell with the lamb, and the leopard...with the kid, and the calf with the young lion...and a little child shall lead them." These last words are often taken to reflect the state of utter docility which will prevail during the Messianic Era. Yet, there are no mere metaphors in the Torah. In truth, only "a little child" would be allowed to lead these combinations of animals, for their joining constitutes the prohibition of *kelayim* (forbidden combinations), and no older person, even a child of educable age, is allowed to do this.

Attitudes towards Minhag

It would be possible to think that an authoritative and strong man like the Rogatchover, who does not accept any authority besides the Talmud and *Rishonim*, would be skeptical of and devalue the different customs of different Jewish communities. But this is not so. The Rogatchover blazes an individual path. For every custom, he finds sources in the Talmud Bavli and Yerushalmi, incredibly innovative ones. In truth, it is almost certain that those who instituted the customs never dreamed that their decrees would one day enjoy such substantial textual support.

For example, there is a custom that before the reader of the Megillah reads all ten names of Haman's sons, the community reads the verse out loud in unison. The *Haye Adam* writes that this custom is ludicrous and "is not a legitimate custom." The Rogatchover proves that not merely is the custom a valid one, in fact, without it, one has not fulfilled the obligation of hearing the Megillah! This is because it is explained in the Talmud that the ten names of Haman's sons need to be read in one breath. Building on this, the Rogatchover proves with multiple sources that halakhically, whenever one is fulfilling their obligation for a mitzvah by hearing words from someone else, one can only legally "hear" and fulfill the obligation insofar as actual words are concerned. However, the manner in which words are read is not transferable from the reader to the listener; any halakhic conditions that are laid onto the words cannot be fulfilled by listening to someone else read those words. (The Rogatchover does not concern himself with directly explaining this in *Hilkhot Megilah* in the Rambam. This explanation is found in passing in his supplements to *Hilkhot Gerushin*.)

With this explanation, he clarifies with ease a question that perplexed the Vilna Gaon. The ten names of Haman's sons are written in large letters by the scribes. The Vilna Gaon, in his glosses to *Shulhan Arukh*, declared his confusion regarding this. The Rogatchover brings the words of a *Tosafot* in *Berakhot* (2a), who states that words which are read by the community are written in large letters. With ease and simplicity, he resolves tensions and knots that perplexed giants.

This custom, reading the ten names of Haman's sons out loud, is not sourced in any primary or even secondary text. It is a custom that is written in *Shulhan Arukh* and that *Rishonim* practiced as well, and yet no one has ever found a source for it. The Rogatchover states simply that it is, in fact, a clear *mishnah*.

On the contrary, those customs for which the Rogatchover does not find a Talmudic source are discarded. He simply does not perform them or endorse them. Nonetheless, he does not mind if others do. A Lubavitch Hasid once entered the Rogatchover's home on the first day of Sukkot to use the Rogatchover's etrog for the mitzvah. This was during the years the Rogatchover spent in Petersburg. Since one needs to perform the mitzvah before prayer, this was before *shaharit* (morning prayers).

"Here are the etrog and lulav," the Rogatchover told him. "Take them into the sukkah and use them, as the Gemara states, 'hasidim and men of worth would use the etrog in the sukkah.'"

"What about the Rav?" responded the Hasid.

"I am a simple man and not on such a level. I did it in the house."

For himself, he considers it adequate to perform the mitzvah in his house. For others, he encourages them to do according to their custom.

Once, on *Tisha be-Av*, the hazan was about to chant the *kinah* beginning with "*Eli tsiyon ve-areha*," which laments the fact that we can no longer perform *pidyon ha-ben* (redemption of the firstborn).

"Fool!" the Rogatchover called out from the back of the shul. "Do you not know that we do indeed perform *pidyon ha-ben*!"

Rabbi Simcha Gorodetsky walked over to the Rogatchover. "But that is what is written in the siddur." He asked him. "Why is the hazan a fool?"

The Rogatchover did not respond, and walked around the shul a couple of times before coming back to Rabbi Gorodetsky. "There is a *Ramban* that implies that we can no longer do *pidyon ha-ben*," he told him. "The hazan can continue."

Comparison to Reb Chaim: Refinement or Reduction?

As mentioned in Chapter One, the Rogatchover studied with Reb Chaim.[84] Both their chief works are on the Rambam and they share a similar analytic system. One can scarcely imagine the depth of learning and debate that surely raged between them. Yet, as we shall see, the divergence between them is also significant and not to be dismissed.

As a brief introduction, I will quote Rabbi Joseph B. Soloveitchik, who writes:[85]

> "Torah scholars used to denigrate those who studied the laws of kashrut. Only those who were about to enter the rabbinate would study this area of the law. Who could guess the day would come with the development of the Brisker approach, and these laws would be freed from the bonds of external and common sense explanations, and become transformed into abstract concepts, logically connected ideas, that would link together to form a unified system...suddenly the pots and pans, the eggs and onions, disappeared from the laws of meat and milk; the salt, blood, and spit disappeared from the laws of salting, the laws of kashrut were taken out of the kitchen and removed to an ideal halakhic world constructed out of complexes of abstract concepts....take for example what was done with the tractate of *Kelim*. At first reading, this appears to be little more than a catalog of household items....as if the entire purpose of the tractate is to describe the domestic objects of a second century household. But this is impossible. Reb Chaim

---

84   In writing this section I have drawn on several sources:

1.   "The Analytic Movement" by Norman Solomon

2.   "The Conceptual Approach to Torah Learning: The Method and its prospects" in "Leaves of Faith" by Rabbi Aharon Lichtenstein

3.   "Mi'rab Hayyim MiBrisk VeHaGrid Soloveitchik Vead Shiurei HaRav Aharon Lichtenstien; al gilgula shel masoret limud, 9 Netuim 51,64.

4.   Marc Shapiro, review essay, The Brisker Method Revisited, 31 Tradition 78,84.

5.   "Legal Theology: The Turn to Conceptualism in Nineteenth-Century Jewish Law" by Chaim Saiman.

85   Ma Dodech Midod 28 (Ha'Doar 1963)

unveiled the tractate's true meaning. He abstracted the ideas from their physical form, placed the concept in place of the fact, the logical connections over the material form, and ideal principles over concrete objects.

Reb Chaim invented the conceptual approach to Talmud study. He fashioned an ideal world and discovered independent halakhic constructs. If we understand a bit about conceptualization and quantification of the natural sciences, as it developed by the fathers of classical and modern physics from Galileo to Newton and down to our times, we will understand Reb Chaim's approach to halakhah, which is surprisingly similar to mathematical scientists' approach to the physical world…

Thus halakhah is purified from all exogenous influences. Based on this approach, one rejects the psychologization or historicization of halakhah…halakhic thinking follows a path of its own. Its rules and principles are not psychological/factual but ideal/normative, as is logical/ mathematical thinking. The historical and factual context does not impinge on truth or correctness of halakhic judgments, just as the validity of mathematical thought is not assessed through psychological analysis."

Although Reb Chaim is considered the father of the analytic and conceptual approach to the Talmud, the truth is perhaps more complex than that. It is my humble contention that, to a large degree, the Rogatchover eclipses Reb Chaim's system of analysis. First of all, on a practical level, the Rogatchover's *Tsafnat Paneah* was published long before Reb Chaim's *Hiddushe al ha-Rambam*, which was only printed in 1936, the year the Rogatchover died. Additionally, while Reb Chaim lived a semi-secluded life in his yeshiva, with his sole interactions being in the yeshivah, the Rogatchover was a global figure who corresponded with, and thereby exposed his analytical system to, a vast array of world leaders and scholars.

Several more points must be made. Reb Chaim deals with conceptualization by introducing analytical inquiry and categorical principles via the *hakirah* (two-sided query). It seems intuitive and natural for a dispute to be predicated on some underlying ideas-based divergence of opinion. In general, the idea that a commandment or object can be viewed in two different nuanced ways is very much in tune with the way we perceive the world. Indeed, it is very similar to the Rogatchover's mechanism of *hiyuv* (positive nature) and *shlilah* (negative nature) explained above. But this approach is still operating from a particular viewpoint. The Rogatchover takes this many steps further and introduced not just an intuitive two-sided query, but rather an innovative three-tiered dissection (*sheloshah gedarim*). He also introduces nine or ten different mechanisms for conceptualizing *halakhah*.

The nature of the *hakirah* is somewhat arbitrary as well, since all it really means is that one can split hairs conceptually with what appears to be a static piece of information. Yet the nature of this hair-splitting analysis is not explained in the slightest. The Rogatchover, on the other hand, introduces what we may perhaps call *hakirot* with personality and flavor. Each of his mechanisms for introducing profundity to technical *halakhah* is not just an empty mechanism awaiting the Talmudist's application, but instead stands on its own with a viable and firm nature. *Ekhut* and *kamut* have a self-sustaining logic and nucleus which gives them a personality. One who wants to conceptualize *halakhah*, therefore, has many self-contained mechanisms by which to uncover its depth. They can postulate a tension between quantity and quality, generalities (*klal*) and specifics (*prat*), a two-tiered conception of time (*zman nekudah* and *zman shetah*), and so on. (Of course, if they are actively seeking to inject depth, they are already somewhat out of line with the Rogatchover's system.)

Consider as well that Reb Chaim is limited to one mechanism. For example, the Reb explains that the injunction to get rid of one's *hamets* (leavened bread) can be understood in two ways. Either the prohibition is *bi-heftsa*, i.e., in the actual item, meaning that the bread is a forbidden item irrespective of man. Or perhaps the prohibition is *bi-gavra*, i.e., directed towards man, but the *hamets* essentially is a permitted item. The Rogatchover suggests a similar breakdown while instead framing the issue as *homer* versus *tsurah*.[86] Framing it as being whether the prohibition is related to the tangible form of the bread or the intangible allows the Rogatchover to build a complex theory that the two disputants in this case, Rabbi Shimon and Rabbi Yehudah, are in

---

86   Michtevei Torah p. 51

fact arguing in several cases concerning their intellectual leanings toward *homer* or *tsurah*. He then expands the whole analysis into another field, quality and quantity. He showed how, in this case, *homer* and *tsurah* are essentially the outer expressions of quality and quantity.[87] He then related the whole discussion to the time of *Moshiach*, asserting that Rabbi Shimon and Rabbi Yehudah are arguing whether *Moshiach* will be a quantitative difference from the time of exile or a qualitative quantum leap of a difference. Readers can see for themselves the vast divide that exists between the *hakirah*-centric model of Reb Chaim and the dynamic and multi-tiered system of the Rogatchover. Another way of postulating the dispute was as the tension between essential identity and peripheral identity *(etzem vs. to'ar)*.[88]

Brisker *gedarim* also have such limited language that it often is obtuse and confusing. Many times the only words used to convey delicate concepts are *din* (the law), *koho bi-heftsa* (the power of the object), *koho bi-gavra* (the power of the person), *halot hashem* (the activation of its name), *halot hadin* (the activation of its law), and so on. These terms are highly technical, confusing and not really clearly defined. This is perhaps due to a discomfort in using terms that did not originate from within the rabbinic canon. The Rogatchover, however, does not have this problem. This could be because he relies on the *Moreh* as his way-station for introducing terms not commonly used in rabbinic literature. A more daring approach (and, I suspect, the correct one) is that, in his world, everything comes from and is consciously seen in Torah. Therefore, even if he had never seen the *Moreh*, he would have innovated multiple mechanisms to explain the profundity that he simply sees shining through the text. Perhaps the Brisker hesitation with non-rabbinic terms is due to their system developing from a conscious, concerted effort to conceptualize

---

87   Shu"t Varsha Siman 50
88   Michtevei Torah p. 50

halakhah,[89] [90] whereas the Rogatchover is like a man describing things that no else sees or can describe in language.

Another major point to be made is that Reb Chaim postulates *halakhah* as theology. Everything exists via the analysis of Torah. As Rabbi Joseph B. Soloveitchik wrote in *Halakhic Man*:

> "When halakhic man comes across a spring bubbling quietly, he already possesses a fixed *a priori* relationship with this phenomenon: the complex laws regarding the halakhic construct of a spring... when halakhic man approaches a real spring he gazes at it and carefully examines its nature. He possesses, *a priori*, ideal principles and precepts which establish the character of the spring as a halakhic construct, and uses the statuses for the purpose of determining normative law: does the real spring correspond to the requirements of the ideal *halakhah* or not? Halakhic man is not overly curious and he is not particularly concerned with cognizing the spring as it is in itself. Rather he seeks to coordinate the *a priori* concept with the *a posteriori* phenomenon."

This is all well and fine. But why would the divine text be reduced solely to **legal** principles? Why would it not include theology, philosophy, agriculture, architecture, indeed all forms of knowledge? The whole idea that Talmud and Torah can be reduced to legal knowledge begs the question: why is the legal canon so privileged to be the final and only embodiment of the divine text and will? The Rogatchover answers this question by rejecting its very foundational premise. He refines *halakhah*, Talmud,

---

89   Rabbi Aharon Lichtenstein wrote in a similar vein: "Torah is perceived as grounded upon rational principles and marked by consistency and coherence. A Torah that is developed and perceived as an organic entity is nobler then one that is a potpourri of practical directives. As Einstein rejected Heisenberg's indeterminacy because he could not imagine G-d playing dice with the universe, so I believe, Reb Chaim espoused conceptualism because he could not imagine the words of G-d as a pedestrian amalgam of incommensurate detail...there is a power majesty and grandeur in Torah, conceptually formulated that a patchwork of minutiae largely molded by ad hoc pragmatic considerations cannot match" Indeed. The question is how concerted of an effort was made to grant Torah that conceptual grandeur and how much flowed naturally from Reb Chaim's viewpoint.
90   See Prof. Saiman for more on this.

Midrash and all Torah literature not just as legal categories, but instead as metaphysical and philosophical principles.

Yet Brisk is the school that popularizes the project of conceptualization. This is, I think, due to two reasons. First, the Rogatchover's concise and cryptic style of voluminous citations makes it hard for all but an elite few to access the profundity of his thought. Secondly, the Rogatchover does not have a *yeshivah*; his interaction is thus limited to rabbis and scholars without any influence on the next generation of Talmudists.

Yet another major, if not conclusive, point is that Reb Chaim and his followers are not *poskim* and indeed have a strong anti-*posek* bias. To them, being a *posek* is secondary to absolute immersion in the Talmud simply for the sake of intellectual study. As such, they have the shelter of the study hall to protect their intellectual pursuits. There is actually a certain cognitive dissonance here—one wonders if Reb Chaim would indeed rule based on his *hakirot*. But the Rogatchover is a famous Rav and posek who lives in the world of practicality and pragmatisms. A woman whose chicken has a suspicious hole in its lung, or a man who wants to know how much money he has to pay his disputant, need actual, tangible answers. This is the perfect test to see if the Rogatchover wholly and truly believes in his own system. He answers this challenge. As we noted earlier, the Rogatchover maintains a consistent and steady interpretive system. The same quantification of halakhic data, the same abstract profundity that is applied to a subtlety in the ordering of a particular *halakhah* in the Rambam, that very same system is applied to a real-world situation that confronts him.

In terms of differences in interpretive style, Reb Chaim seeks to distinguish and differentiate between laws and principles. The Rogatchover seeks to reduce, refine, unite, and intertwine as much of Torah as possible. Yet when the Rogatchover turns his considerable talents to splitting, he comes up with three dissections instead of the classical Brisker *hakirah*.

While Reb Chaim and his school are extreme traditionalists who have great difficulty confronting their own creative and novel system,[91] the Rogatchover was conscious of this shift and open about it in many ways. Indeed, the very fact that he basically ignores the entire canon of the *Aharonim* attests to his fiercely independent and self-concious original style.[92]

To be sure, I am not seeking to downplay Reb Chaim and his followers. But the picture painted for us is that the project of conceptualization of Talmud and halakha was created and owned by the Briskers. It is time to realize that that picture might have broader brushstrokes than we thought.

Rabbi Kalina

Regarding this amazing man and his correspondence with the Rogatchover, Rabbi Zevin writes:

"For four straight years a conversation lasted between the Rogatchover and Rabbi Mordechai Kalina. This exchange contains two hundred and ninety letters filled with deep and intricate discussion. The exchange jumped from one idea to the next reaching across almost every area of Talmudic analysis. It started in the week of Va'era 1932 and lasted until the week of Toldot 1936."

Who was this extraordinary man who kept up with the Gaon for four years?

I will admit that I did not hear of this man until writing this book. It appears that not many scholars are aware of this Rabbi Kalina. A cloud of graceful humility hangs over him. Suddenly he appears on the horizon and stands head and shoulders above the crowd, an awesome genius. The rapport between them is so

---

91   Many stories abound as to Reb Chaim asserting that he was only developing the Rishonim and not innovating anything new. See Prof. Saiman for more on this.

92   It is an open question if the Rogatchover influenced any of the Briskers. See "The Analytic Movement" page 193 where Solomon writes:

"What are the possibilities of the Analysts [his term for Briskers] having been unfluenced by Rozin? Unfortunately it is impssible to say with any degree of certainty. Many of them must have met him—Amiel even received ordination from him—but there is no evidence that any of them was his pupil. None of them, again with the exception of Amiel, quotes his written works..."

Amiel represents an exception from within the Brisk movement and requires further research. Yet all things considered, he was an aberration from within the Brisk system and not an extension of it.

abstract and quick that it is extremely hard to follow. Both have similar styles of thinking laterally from subject to subject. I do not think there is one area of Talmudic analysis that they do not touch on in these letters.

The whole exchange starts with one letter Rabbi Kalina writes in which he challenges some of the Rogatchover's theories in *Tsafnat Paneah*. This serves as a springboard for the ensuing discussions. For example, Rabbi Kalina posits, based on the *Ran*,[93] that the *hallel* said when bringing the *korban pesah* is not the usual praise and song to G-d, *shira*, but rather has the status of reading, *kriyah*.

With this distinction between *hallel* as song and *hallel* as reading, Rabbi Kalina resolves *Tosafot*'s question of how the Jews could have sung *hallel* when they sacrificed the *korban pesah* in Egypt, if the law is that one is not allowed to offer a song unless the ritual of pouring the wine libations (*nisakhim*) is performed. These libations were absent in Egypt, so how could they have offered up song to G-d with this *korban*? Rabbi Kalina resolves this by positing that only *hallel* as song is forbidden, but hallel as reading is permitted, even absent the wine libations.

The Rogatchover responds by pointing out that we must conclude that *hallel* said during the *korban pesah* has the usual status of song, since the Levi'im were the ones who sang it, as stated in the Yerushalmi and the *Tosefta*: "The Levi'im stand on the choir stand and say the *hallel* in song."

As is his way, he elaborates on ideas which are pertinent to the nucleus of his idea and which underlie the discussion, whether linearly or laterally.

Rabbi Kalina does not concede any ground with his next letter. He admits that the literary implication from the *Tosefta* is at odds with his theory, but he points out that the Mishnah's literary implication supports him, and a *mishnah* trumps a *tosefta*. He brings more support from the Gemara in *Pesahim*[94] which states: "Can it be that the Jews sacrificed their *korban pesah* and shook the *lulav* and did not sing *hallel*?"

---

93   Pesahim end of chapter 10
94   95b

The connection drawn by the Gemara from *korban pesah* to *lulav* is puzzling. Rabbi Kalina drives his point home by asserting that the connotation is that the same type of *hallel* applies to both. Since obviously there is no *korban* brought with the *lulav*, this proves that the *hallel* said on both occasions does not fall into the category of song accompanying a sacrifice. He then expands into an analysis of the Rambam's opinion about a *korban pesah*. From this base of proof, he clarifies when the *hallel* was said, whether it was when the sacrifice was killed, or whether it was when the sacrifice was being offered on the altar.

The Rogatchover responds again and these two giants are off, spinning around each other and jumping from one field to another, while the discussion become larger and more intricate all the while.

The tone in the letters is not that of a debate. One who glances at them would never imagine the titanic struggle going on before his eyes. All the sharp stabs and jabs usually present in an intellectual debate are absent. Each side presents material and makes his point without preamble. In fact, each one helps the other. We find that whenever one of them thinks the other makes a good point, he would strengthen his opponent's theory, even to the detriment of his own argument.

Another theory the Rogatchover has about marriage is that when a woman marries, two halakhic forces are activated. One is her connection to her husband, and the other is her forbidden status, or removal from all other men in the world. Correspondingly, the *get* has to negate both forces. Now, if the husband gives her what is called the "scent of a get" (*reiah ha-get*), which means that he writes "you are separated from me, but you are not permitted to any other man," such a *get* is not valid. Yet according to the Rogatchover, the husband has indeed removed one force, namely, his connection to his wife. Only her forbidden status to the world has not been removed. Therefore, it makes perfect sense that *Tosafot*[95] write that if the husband then dies after giving her this unusual *get*, she can still perform a levirate marriage with his brother. This is because, according to the Rogatchover, the imperative to marry her husband's brother stems from the second aspect of marriage, her removal from all other men in

---

95   Gitin 82b

the world. This force is still extant even after the *get,* since the *get* her husband gave her did not negate this force. Rabbi Kalina likes this idea very much and brings proofs for it, even though it weakens an aspect of his own argument.

There is no study without a novel ruling. From this exchange emerged several astonishing halakhic rulings, for example:

Witnesses see a person kill someone. They grab him and do not let him go until they come to the courts. In such a case, since there is no doubt of this person's guilt, the court cannot kill him.[96]

A half-slave, half-free woman (*shifhah harufah*) who was married to someone can never be divorced.

These novel rulings and many others are the pearls these giants leave us, the precious stones that fall unnoticed from their battle.

---

96   Letter #180. See also T"P Mahadura Tinyana page 28.

Chapter Three

Kamut and *Ekhut*

This section is about the dual spectrums by which we measure reality: quantity and quality. While these terms have fallen out of popular use, the concepts they denote are still firmly entrenched in our psyche and thought processes. We are constantly gazing out into the world, and our gaze often branches out to a two-tiered perspective. The first way we measure the world around us is in terms of the actual: tangible, quantifiable, present reality. The very word "quantifiable" has "quantity" as its root.

The second way we perceive the world is in terms of quality. Quality means a certain broadening of scope to appreciate the intangible qualities of the object of our gaze. The quality of an item is not often immediately discernible. For one thing, the quality of an item is often subjective and lends itself to a myriad of opinions. Besides, the idea that there is an intangible spectrum of reality means that when we try to measure things on that intangible spectrum, we are dealing with an analysis of an entirely different sort from that of the easier tangible and quantifiable spectrum.

As you might guess, the terms "quantity" and "quality" will often overlap with "tangible" and "intangible." Consequently, it is useful to lump these concepts together. Originally, when I was in the initial planning stages of this book, I discussed these two concepts in two different chapters, because the Rogatchover often uses them separately, and they are usually understood to be disparate concepts.[97] But their similarity and resemblance is so striking that in many places where the Rogatchover uses "tangible" (*homer*) and "intangible" (*tsurah*), "quality" (*ekhut*) and "quantity" (*kamut*) can be substituted without disturbing the conceptual structure of the analysis. In addition, the Rogatchover himself, in several places, delineates a concept in terms of quality and quantity, but then ends by using the words "tangible" and "intangible." This subtle transition is often immediate and effortless. Indeed, it is sometimes instinctive and intuitive to the reader. I therefore, with some reservations, decided to discuss these two concepts in the same chapter. The few areas where there is some tension between tangible and intangible versus quantity and quality I have noted and placed at the end of the chapter. Additionally, throughout the chapter, I will generally use the terms "quality" and "quantity" to denote both sets of concepts.

To understand the relevance and application of these terms, it will be useful to consider several areas of human life that we naturally, if not consciously, divide into quality and quantity. Consider the story of Apple and Microsoft. These two companies have long battled for supremacy in the computer market, but have recently settled into an uneasy truce of sorts. Each company has chosen a different path to achieve their goals, indeed, a different philosophy. Apple chose the quality path, while Microsoft chose the quantity path. Apple decided to pursue a closed system. This was extraordinarily revolutionary at the time. Instead of pursuing a cross-platform interface and operating system, so that the maximum number of people could use their products with the maximum variety of devices and applications, Apple chose to have a closed system, in which their products could only be used with their operating system and applications. This led to Apple choosing to not have Adobe Flash work with their products. Why was this? Put simply, it was to maximize the quality and integrity of their products. By choosing a narrow

---

97   The Mefaneach Tzfunot as well

focal point, they were able to build a product that didn't just work, but set the fashion and style within the PC world. It took foresight and patience to trust the intangible quality of a closed system over the much more immediate value of an open platform that interfaces with all types of systems and programs. To be sure, Apple came under much criticism. Customers said that they could not do the things that an open computing experience allows. They could not connect the hardware they wanted, develop or run the software they wanted, or have the open-ended experience other computers provided.

Microsoft, on the other hand, chose to pursue a path predicated on the tangible quantity of multiple options and cross-platform capability. Time will tell which path was wiser, but certainly these are very different philosophies. One is entrenched in quality and future value, and the other is embedded in quantity and the tangible present value of a product.

Another area which is essentially a debate between quality and quantity is the advertising industry. All day we are bombarded with mass advertising. It is on our buildings, cars, clothes—even in public bathrooms! This is the quantity philosophy of advertising. Throw out an enormous amount of exposure to a product, and eventually, a small minority of people exposed will respond. The other philosophy is a much more quality-based one. People like Seth Godin, Timothy Ferris, and others have advocated for "permission marketing" schemes. Target a small amount of people with a small amount of ads. But make your ads highly specific and relevant to your niche target group. Counterintuitively, these smaller-scale advertising waves have been extremely successful.

Nassim N. Taleb has shown that when we increase the number of elements in a system, thus increasing its complexity, there is often a decrease in quality control. The interaction between the quantity of work and the quality of output is a nuanced and often counterintuitive one. As he says, "When you increase from 100 workers in a factory to 200, you either exponentially increase the quality of the company or exponentially decrease [it]." Thus we see that the relationship between quality and quantity is not a linear one.

We can also apply these dual quantity and quality categories to a tenet of Jewish faith. The idea embedded in the *Shema* is one of the central beliefs of Judaism, that there is no other God besides the one true Lord. However, according to Kabbalah and Jewish philosophy, the essential meaning of the verse is that there is no other true existence besides God. Herman Cohen phrased this as follows: "The claim of the unity of God is not a quantitative one, but rather a qualitative one." Indeed, we often relate to God as a quantitative entity, i.e., the being who pervades all existence, without limit, who transcends the limits of time and space. The problem is that some people conceive of God as a superhuman entity, as if God were simply a bigger, better, and more perfect version of a human being. Often this is formulated as follows: "Humans have intellect, but possess a narrow and deficient intellect. God, however, has a perfect, sublime intellect. Humans can do kindness in a limited and sporadic fashion, but God is the ultimate possessor of kindness. He embodies perfect kindness and compassion." This was a major theme in Jewish philosophy and Kabbalah,[98] as some scholars understood the concept of the ten *sefirot*, the idea that there are ten unique attributes that God possesses, to be saying just that. This is what I call the quantitative God.

The qualitative God is one whom we understand to have a completely and utterly different quality of existence than ourselves. He is not just bigger, better, more perfect, and all-encompassing. He is God. He is an entirely different type of entity. From this standpoint, we do not say that God is everywhere. Rather, God is God; his nature necessitates, by definition, that He be everywhere and all-encompassing. His quality of being is such that he exists without limit. Therefore, naturally and automatically, he is everywhere and eternally present. This is what I call a qualitative perspective of God. The terminology employed by Kabbalah is that the *sefirot* express God's essence, and He invests himself in them, yet they do not ultimately define him. His essence transcends even his expressions and characteristics.

There are numerous and myriad areas to which this dichotomy can be applied. Is it better for a child (or an adult, for that matter) to study a small amount of material in depth, or to amass

---

98   See the footnote in Tanya chapter 2 concerning the dispute between the Rambam and the Maharal regarding this very issue.

a superficial understanding of large swaths of information? Should one buy an expensive, high-quality item that will last a decade, or a cheap made-in-China item that will wear out in a few years? What should our work ethic be? Small amounts of highly charged and effective time, ala *The 4-Hour Workweek*, or a slow and methodical pace? Maybe the choice is subjective, depending on personality types. Are some people inherently more suited to a quantity perspective then a quality one?

I have brought these examples to show the prevalence and relevance of these terms in the present day. They enjoyed much usage in the era of the *Rishonim*, with the Rambam, Kuzari, Saadya Gaon, Alshich and others using them as conceptual constructs to discuss various issues. They underwent a renaissance and reinvention in the early era of *pilpul*, as well as the later schools of the *Aharonim*, because they are a useful and creative way of understanding categories and laws within two separate frameworks.

Though the more traditional philosophical terms—quality, quantity, intangible, and tangible—that the *Rishonim* employed have fallen out of common usage, the ideas and perspectives they express have not.

In this chapter we will explore the concepts of quality and quantity and their complex relationship.[99]

Our analysis starts off with questioning whether halakhah creates an obligation with respect to quality alone, distinct from quantity. This entails discussing the various laws that concern fire, since fire is a prime example of an entity that has quality but lacks any tangible quantity. We then turn to dissecting the essential identity of fire, on which all the legislation regarding it is founded. The discussion will then turn to the area of prohibitions (*isurim*). The Rogatchover explores the idea that certain prohibitions are operating from a framework of quality, not quantity. This same idea is applied to the area of ritual impurity

---

99   It is important to note that many of the terms the Rogatchover uses are somewhat interchangeable. This means that a conversation about quality and quantity can transform into a dialogue about the spiritual spectrum of reality (*tsurah*) versus the tangible (*homer*), or the tension between essential identity (*etzem*) and peripheral identity (*to'ar*). This is an important, if sometimes confusing principle in the Rogatchover's writings.

(*tumah*). The next issue we discuss is whether G-d's perspective is primarily colored by quality or quantity. Lastly, the interaction between the two, and the temporary supremacy of quantity, is explained.

To begin, we must look at the perspective halakhah takes with respect to quality and quantity. The Talmud[100] raises the question whether a flame can be regarded as an entity at all. If someone takes a flame from a house to the public domain on Shabbat, are they liable for carrying an item on Shabbat? The Rogatchover sees in this legal query a conversation about the place of quality within the body of Jewish law.

It all depends on how we view a flame. The actual flame is intangible and does not take up any physical space. It is truly an anomalous existence, in the sense that it does not share any of the conventional properties of physical matter.

That being the case, we are faced with a legal problem. What are we to make of a flame insofar as *hilkhot Shabbat* are concerned?

The Rogatchover frames the question as follows:[101]

Can there be quality without quantity? In other words, can we view the flame as an entity in its own right, possessing a quality of existence, while at the same time lacking any quantity, or tangible breadth and width? Even if we can, does halakhah concern itself with this, and obligate a person with respect to items that lack tangibility and corporeality?[102]

---

100   Betsah 39a:

המוציא גחלת לרשות הרבים חייב ושלהבת פטור: והא תניא המוציא שלהבת כל שהוא חייב אמר
רב ששת כגון שהוציאו בקיסם

101   See Mefaneach Tzfunot who quotes a letter from the Rogatchover (page 200):

עיין ביצה דף לט,
דהוצאת שלהבת בכל שהוא והוצאת פחמין מבואר בתוס'
שבת דצריך שיעור, וכן הפתילה ושאר דברים, גם נ"מ
לעושה שלהבת או למכבה שלהבת, עיין ביצה דף לט
גבי הוצאת שלהבת, וברכות דף נב' חה תליא אם יש
איכות בלא כמות

102   A similar issue is the question surrounding microscopic phenomena. For example, at Sukkot time everyone checks their *etrogim* for blemishes. What is the status of an *etrog* that has no noticeable blemish, but, when viewed

The Rogatchover understands the answer to be in the negative. Halakhah is a framework that generally only concerns itself with the tangible and the measurable.

This issue is given more parameters in the Gemara in *Pesahim* (75b[103]), which has a lengthy discussion regarding types of coals and flame in the context of the halakhot of Yom Kippur and incense (*ketoret*). The Talmud is analyzing what types of coals are kosher to be used in burning the incense. The discussion clearly expresses the view that coals with flames visibly burning are entirely different from a tongue of flame in isolation from a coal. There is a massive qualitative difference between the two, to the extent that one is valid for the service in the Temple and one is not.

Why is there such a gulf between the two? The difference seems to be superficial at best. Both are burning and exuding heat. The only difference seems to be whether the flame is attached to a physical item or not.

The Rogatchover;[104] however, sees an unbridgeable gap between the two. Since halakhah does not deal with entities that lack quantity, a flame cannot be said to halakhically exist if it is not grounded in a physical item. Therefore, it is invalid for the Tem-

---

under magnification glass or a microscope, one can perceive imperfections? Similarly, if one can ascertain a problem in the script of a Sefer Torah only via a magnifier, would that invalidate the Sefer Torah? The most common question though, arises when checking produce for insects. If one cannot detect any sign of bugs in the produce, but they may perhaps be visible through magnification, is one allowed to eat the produce? And if not, is one required to use such a magnifying device to check to ensure that there are no lurking insects? Other applications are concerning issues of fertility and In Vitro Fertilization.

See the Ya'avetz (Shu"t Sheilat Ya'avetz vol. 2, 124) and the Sefer HaBrit (cited in Binat Adam 38). See also Shu"t Tuv Ta'am V'Daat (Tinyana, *kuntress acharon*, 53), Arukh HaShulhan (Y"D 84, 36), Shu"t Igros Moshe Y"d(vol. 2, 146 s.v. *umah),* Rav Shlomo Zalman Auerbach (Shu"t Minchat Shlomo, Tinyana 63, 2 s.v. *uma'attah)* and Halichot Shlomo *Moadim* (vol. 2, Pesah Ch. 7, 25).

103   ת"ל אש אי אש יכול שלהבת ת"ל גחלי הא כיצד מביא מן הלוחשות אלמא גחלים לא איקרי אש

104   See Mefaneach Tzfunot page 200:

וכן שלהבת, עיין

ב"ק דף כב, ופסחים דף עה ע"ב ע"ש, וזה הגדר דהדלקה,

ונדלק, דהיינו לעשות אש אסור אלא ביו"ט כמבואר ביצה

דף לג, להוליד דבר, ועיין כיצד, דף כב, גבי ריח, וזה

גדר לאו דלא תעשה מלאכה בפסחים דף מז ע"ב'.

ple service, since its existence is not grounded in the tangible and quantitative dimension of reality.

A flame that is attached to a piece of physical matter, however, is substantiated, or given a quantity of being. It is grounded in the tangible spectrum and thus halakhah accords it significance.

The same conceptual base can be found in the Talmud's understanding of one's relationship to a fire that he himself started. If someone lights a fire in their own backyard that spreads and burns down a neighboring house, he is liable and obligated to fully pay for all damages.

The precise formulation of this obligation is a subject of dispute in the Gemara (*Bava Kama* 22a).[105]

Rabbi Yohanan says that fire is considered as one's own active force. It is as if the person is actively shooting flaming arrows at the house that burns down. Resh Lakish, however, says that the fire is not considered as the person's own force, since it spreads on its own and is no longer under his control. The rationale underlying his culpability is that the fire is considered as if it were his property. Just as when an animal damages, its owner is liable, so too with fire.

When Rabbi Yohanan is asked why he does not agree with Resh Lakish, he responds that fire cannot be understood as property since it lacks physical being (*leit beih mamasha*). An animal is physically present, and thus it makes sense to speak of proprietary relationships. Fire, however, does not have a tangible presence, so we cannot assert a proprietary relationship between the

---

105

אתמר ר' יוחנן אמר אשו משום חציו וריש לקיש אמר אשו משום ממונו וריש לקיש מאי טעמא לא אמר
כרבי יוחנן אמר לך חציו מכחו קאזלי האי האי לא מכחו קאזיל ורבי יוחנן מאי טעמא לא אמר כריש לקיש
אמר לך ממונא אית ביה ממשא הא לית ביה ממשא

"It was stated: R. Yohanan said: Fire [involves liability] on account of it being his arrows [i.e. the human agency that brings it about]. Resh Lakish, however, maintained that the liability is from property [i.e. the fire is considered as his property and just as one would be liable for his ox that damages, so too is he liable for 'his' fire]. Why did Resh Lakish differ from R. Yohanan?—His contention is: Human agency must emerge directly from human force whereas fire does not emerge from human force [because it spreads on its own]. Why, on the other hand, did not R. Yohanan agree with Resh Lakish? — He may say: Property contains tangible properties, whereas fire has no tangible properties."

flames and the one who kindled them. Here, too, we see a perspective in halakhah that affirms that concrete quantity is necessary for an item to fall into the spectrum of law and obligation.

A similar question can be formulated regarding carrying scent on Shabbat. Can the scent of something be viewed as an entity insofar as carrying on Shabbat is concerned? According to the Rogatchover, this is also essentially a question of whether halakhah recognizes quality without quantity.

Consider the Talmud in *Shabbat* 62b,[106] which states the following:

A woman may not go out on Shabbat carrying a spice bundle (an ornament worn around the neck in which spices are placed to create a fragrance) or a flask of balsam oil. If she did go out, she has transgressed Shabbat, and is required to bring an atonement sacrifice in the Temple (*korban hatat*). This is Rabbi Meir's opinion.

Rabbi Eliezer disagrees, saying that she has not transgressed Shabbat and is exempt from a *korban*. The reason she is exempt is because a pendant containing spices or a small flask containing oil are considered to be in the category of *takhshit* (ornament). Items that are categorized as a *takhshit* are Biblically permitted to be worn on Shabbat, since it is not considered carrying when going out with them. Just as wearing a shirt on one's back is not considered "carrying," so too, items with aesthetic or secondary uses and benefits are allowed to be worn on one's person, even if they are not essential.

Rabbi Eliezer then qualifies his ruling, stating that she is only exempt when the spice bundle contains spices or the flask contains oil. But if they do not have spices or oil inside, she is obligated to bring a *korban*, meaning she has transgressed Shabbat. Since it is not the norm to wear a pendant or a flask when it is emp-

---

106

דתניא לא תצא אשה במפתח שבידה ואם יצאת חטאת חייבת דברי רבי מאיר רבי אליעזר פוטר בכובלת ובצלוחית של פלייטון כובלת מאן דכר שמה חסורי מחסרא והכי קתני וכן בכובלת וכן בצלוחית של פלייטון לא תצא ואם יצאה חייבת חטאת דברי רבי מאיר רבי אליעזר פוטר בכובלת ובצלוחית של פלייטון במה דברים אמורים כשיש בהם בושם אבל אין בהם בושם חייבת אמר רב אדא בר אהבה זאת אומרת המוציא אוכלין פחות מכשיעור בכלי חייב דהא אין בה בושם כפחות מכשיעור בכלי דמי וקתני חייבת רב אשי אמר בעלמא אימא לך פטור ושאני הכא דליתיה לממשא כלל

ty, they are not considered ornaments when empty. Therefore, since they are not able to be classified as ornaments, they revert to *masa* (carrying) status.

To facilitate a fluid, smooth understanding of the next part of the Gemara, it is necessary to mention the following principle about carrying on Shabbat. In order to transgress Shabbat, it is not enough to simply carry something in the public domain. One must carry a certain minimum quantity in order to be Biblically culpable. Each item has its own minimum requirement, or *shiur*. For example, one who is carrying food must generally carry an amount equal to the size of a dried fig before he is liable.

The minimum amount for other objects may be less or more, depending upon the item in question. For example, one who carries a vessel such as a jar would be Biblically liable even for carrying a tiny jar, since he has carried a whole, complete vessel. With food, however, it depends on the amount, not on the completeness of the item.

The Talmud, later in *Shabbat* (93b), discusses an intriguing case concerning one who takes out a jar containing a small quantity of food, where the food does not satisfy the minimum requirement, yet the jar, as a complete vessel, does. There should seemingly be no question as to his culpability. For the jar he is liable, but for the food he is not.

Yet the situation is more complex than that. Since the jar is being used as a receptacle for the food, it is viewed as not having its own independent existence; it is merely an accessory of the food. Thus he cannot be liable for carrying the jar, since it is not its own halakhic entity. Rather, it is an extension of the food. Yet for the food he also cannot be liable, since the amount of the food is less than the minimum. Thus, counter-intuitively, though he carries more (the food as well as the jar), he ends up not being liable. If he had carried only the jar without the food, he would have been liable.

The Gemara attempts to deduce something from Rabbi Eliezer's opinion. Rabbi Eliezer said that when the flask is empty, she is liable, since then it is not a *takhshit*, because it is not the normal custom to wear an empty flask. But what about the scent of the balsam oil that still emanates from the flask? Is that not comparable to the case where one carries less than a *shiur* of food in a vessel?

Here, too, she is taking out two things: the scent that is wafting from the flask, which is less than the *shiur*, since there is no substance to which to assign a *shiur*, and the flask itself, which satisfies the *shiur* because it is a complete vessel. But still Rabbi Eliezer holds that she is liable in this case! Is he not arguing on the Mishnah on 93b and forming his own opinion? According to the Mishnah on 93b, she is exempt, since the scent lacks a minimum *shiur*, and for the flask she is also not culpable, since the flask is merely an accessory of the scent.

The Talmud answers that these two cases are not conceptually parallel. Smell, unlike food, has no tangibility *(leit bei mamasha)*. Since there is no substance to the scent, the flask is considered to be empty, and cannot be said to be an accessory of the scent.

What is the essential discussion here in the Gemara? The Rogatchover sees it as being predicated upon the tension between quality and quantity. The question is whether halakhah addresses objects that lack any measurable quantity and instead possess a certain quality of presence.

Scent here is classified as belonging to the spiritual realm. It is not tangible or concrete, and halakhically is viewed as being the only sense that is a sensory faculty of the soul, not the body.[107]

However, we can posit that scent does exist from a qualitative perspective. Smell has a presence, can be detected, and has an effect on the physical realm. However, it lacks any tangible quantity.

Thus, this Gemara regarding carrying scent on Shabbat becomes a discussion on the nature of quality as it exists in isolation from quantity.

---

107   This is why on Saturday night at the closing of *Shabbat* we smell spices to comfort the soul as we head into the lesser holiness of the week.

Another place where we see this issue discussed is in *Betsah* 22a.[108] The discussion there concerns incense. It was a common custom in Talmudic times to burn incense so as to waft a fragrance in the air. Another custom was to place clothes over a pit in which incense was burning in order to give the garments a scent. The Talmud states that burning incense on *yom tov* in order to have a pleasing smell in the room is permitted, while kindling incense in order to scent clothes is not.

What is the difference between the two? The Rogatchover explains as follows:

As we have seen, fire is not within the tangible spectrum, and thus halakhah does not give it a legal relationship to a person. However, in cases where it can be grounded or "tied" to a physical item, it does indeed reenter the halakhic scene, as was shown in the Gemara in *Pesahim* regarding the coals and the flame on Yom Kippur.

This is precisely the situation here. When one burns incense to scent a room, the kindling and the fire have no particular locus of activity. That is to say, they are burning simply to generate a smell in an area, without a substantial direct relationship to any particular physical item. Therefore, this is permissible. Since fire has no quantity, and halakhah generally does not accord it any legal status, it is as though the act of kindling the flame is not seen in the eyes of the law, since the flame is not substantiated. But when one is scenting clothes by laying the garments over a pier in which incense is burning, one has "tied" the fire to a specific tangible item. There is a direct concrete item into which the flame is being funneled. In doing so, one has grounded the flame in the physical spectrum, and thus halakhah sees it and forbids it, just as grounding the tongue of flame in a coal validates it for the Temple service.

Yet another instance where this comes up is in the laws of kindling fire on *yom tov*.[109] On *yom tov* it is permissible to light a

---

108

אמר רב אסי מחלוקת להריח אבל לגמר אסור

"Rabbi Yose said- it is a dispute whether one can perfume clothes but to have fragrance in a room, everyone agrees that that is permissible."
109   See Betsah 33b.

candle from a flame that has already been burning since before the beginning of the festival. Yet it is forbidden to strike a match and create a new flame. This seems to be a perplexing law. When one lights a candle from a pre-existing flame, one has still created fire, since this second fire did not exist before. The fact that the the new flame came from another flame, not a spark or a match, should be a slight, insignificant difference. Yet it is the basis for the halakhah; from flame we can create more flame, but from a match we cannot. The fact that in both cases we are creating a new flame does not seem to be addressed.

The Rogatchover understands this to be an expression of the unique place fire possesses in halakhah. Since fire lacks quantity, it generally does not fall within the spectrum of halakhah. Here, this is a redeeming lenient factor. Because flame has no quantity, if one lights a candle by touching it to a pre-existing flame, one has not created new flame, since the first flame has merely transferred some of its existence to a new location.

In other words fire, lacking corporeality, has a fluid, flexible existence. Normally, an entity is concretely defined, with specific dimensions that cannot be exceeded without adding to or changing the entity. However, a tongue of flame does not exist on the tangible spectrum. It can therefore exceed its prior boundaries and extend onto another candle.

Another interesting application of this concept is related to a legislative dispute about the precise nature of fire. Regarding the forbidden act of kindling fire on Shabbat, there is a debate among the codifiers about what is included in the scope of "fire." The question is whether one is liable for merely creating fire, such as lighting a candle, or whether one is only liable when the fire destroys something. This debate is in turn predicated on whether fire should be understood as a flame in isolation, or rather as the effect of combustion and destruction of physical matter.

The *Shulhan Arukh ha-Rav* rules (*Kuntres Aharon, siman* 495:2) that fire should be defined as creating fire. The *Avne Nezer* (*Orah Hayim* 138) and others disagree, ruling that fire should be defined as the combustion of a substance.

Some of the implications of this dispute are whether one can use incandescent bulbs for Shabbat candles (*hadlakat nerot*), or whether heating up metal until it is red-hot falls under the umbrella of forbidden kindling on Shabbat. If one holds that the halakhic definition of fire is only when there is combustion of concrete matter, then heating up metal is not be classified as fire. If, however, one understands fire to be a flame in the abstract, there is a flame being kindled once the metal starts to glow red-hot.

The Rogatchover's analysis can help shed light on the philosophical or conceptual basis for this dispute. If fire, which lacks physical substance, cannot be addressed halakhically, then the only way it can be understood is in relation to its effect on the physical spectrum, that is, its combustion and consumption of material substance. If, however, it can be understood in the abstract, then it can be seen as merely a tongue of flame, without regard to physical consumption.

Another source that the Rogatchover shows to depend on these concepts is the Talmud in *Yoma* 74a. The Talmud there records a dispute[110] about *hatsi shiur* (a half-measurement). There are many cases where the Torah forbids the eating of a particular food item and records a penalty for an infraction. For instance, the Torah declares that the consumption of certain forbidden fats of an animal (*helev*) is punishable by lashes (*malkot*). According to the oral tradition, we know that one is only culpable if one eats the minimum *shiur* (measurement) of a *kezayit* (roughly 3.3 ounces).

But what is the status of one who eats less than the minimum amount, i.e., *hatsi shiur*? Has he infringed upon the prohibition or not? We know he is not liable to adjudication by the court, but does this mean that he has not done anything wrong, or does it simply mean that we are not able to punish him?

Regarding this there is a dispute. Rabbi Yohanan says that even though it is not punishable, it is still Biblically prohibited. His reasoning is that, although it is only a half-measurement, it can

---

110

גופא חצי שיעור רבי יוחנן אמר אסור מן התורה ריש לקיש אמר מותר מן התורה רבי יוחנן אמר אסור
מן התורה כיון דחזי לאיצטרופי איסורא קא אכיל ריש לקיש אמר מותר מן התורה אכילה אמר רחמנא
וליכא

potentially be combined with more of the same forbidden food, completing the minimum amount. Therefore he says that even before it is combined with any other food, it is still Biblically prohibited. Resh Lakish, on the other hand, says that it is Biblically permitted. He argues that the Torah forbids "eating," which implies a significant amount. According to Resh Lakish, consumption of less than the minimum amount is not considered "eating." He therefore says that as long as one does not consume the minimum amount, one has not transgressed a Biblical prohibition at all.

The Rogatchover forges a novel path in understanding this part of the Talmud. He explains[111] [112] that this dispute hinges upon the balance between quality and quantity. Rabbi Yohanan understands the minimum requirement of a *kezayit* to be a statement about the quantity of the prohibition. The Torah is simply giving a quantity of consumption necessary for the sinner to be liable in court, but the quality of the prohibition is the same, from before the *kezayit* until after the *kezayit* requirement is met. Resh Lakish, however, understands the minimum requirement to be a statement pertaining to the quality of the prohibition. If one eats less than the minimum amount, the quality of the prohibition is nonexistent. In other words, the minimum amount is a threshold that must be crossed in order for the prohibition to exist at all.

According to this, the issue of combinations of food, with which Rabbi Yohanan buttressed his position (*khivan de-hai lehitsaru-fi*), explains why each mouthful of forbidden food has the same degree of *issur*. The argument could be made that eating less than the minimum amount, which is not subject to judicial review, is

---

111   Mahadura Tinyana page 140:

כבר הארכתי

אם חצי שיעור אסור מן התורה, ר"ל דיש ב' גדרים בשיעורים, א' נקרא שיעור המצטרף,
גדר הצטרפות או גדר גקודה

112   Hilkhot Teshuva Chapter 1 halakhah 5:

ועיין תוס' יומא דף פא ע"א, ועי' בירושלמי פ"א דפאה
ובכ"מ בזה, וכך דכל שיעור המצטרף פחות מזה נמי שמו
עליו, רק שצריך לצרף, וזה בעצם המחלוקת דר"י ור"ל
גבי חצי שיעור אם אסור מן התורה, דריש לקיש ס"ל
דהשיעור הוא עצם ופחות מזה לאו כלום הוא, ור"י ס"ל
דהוא מצטרף ופחות מזה ג"כ שמו עליו,

not the same quality of prohibition as when one eats more than the minimum amount, which is in fact judicially liable. If this is the case, we cannot combine what he eats before he reaches the *kezayit* threshold with what he eats after reaching that threshold. This is because of the legislative principle that we do not combine prohibitions of different degrees of severity.

Thus, only after he eats the minimum amount, and has entered the realm of judicially liable consumption, are we able to start counting another *kezayit*, which makes him liable to adjudication.

Therefore, Rabbi Yohanan stated his opinion, noting the principle of combination in order to stress that all amounts of forbidden food have the same quality and degree of prohibition. The Torah requires a minimum quantity for the consumer to be liable to judicial adjudication, but that threshold does not pertain to the nature of the prohibition at all. Rabbi Yohanan views the minimum requirement as a ruling regarding the quantity of the prohibition, while Resh Lakish sees it as a ruling regarding the quality of the prohibition. According to Resh Lakish, without the minimum requirement, there is no prohibition at all. It is only once one eats the full *kezayit* that the prohibition is created.

Consider the ramifications of this. The commentators discuss the case of one who eats less than the minimum amount during the last few seconds of Yom Kippur, when we are commanded to fast. Is this forbidden or permitted? Some reason that it is permissible because the halakhah is in accordance with Rabbi Yohanan. Eating even less than a *kezayit* is prohibited because more food can always be eaten in combination with the initial amount. But in this case, by the time one eats that additional food, Yom Kippur will already have ended, and all food will revert to a permitted status.

Therefore, one group of scholars holds that there is no Biblical prohibition on eating less than a *kezayit* in the last few seconds of Yom Kippur. This group includes, but is not limited to, *Rivash, Pri Megadim*, Reb Akiva Eiger, *Hatam Sofer, Maharsha, Tslah, Shevuot Yaakov, Maharits Hiyut, Tiferet Yisrael*, and *Magen Avot*.

The group opposing them vehemently disputes this. They say that even when the potential for a later combination does not exist, Rabbi Yohanan would still hold that less than a *kezayit* is prohibited. This group of scholars includes, but is not limited to, *Avne Miluim, Sede Hemed, Kovets Shemuot*, Maharam Schick, *Barukh Taam, Shaagat Aryeh, Hikre Lev, Arugat ha-Bosem*, and *Shem Aryeh*.

How do they explain Rabbi Yohanan's own statement that less than a *kezayit* is prohibited because of the combining factor? They do so in a variety of ways, but the defining feature of them all is that they are struggling to reconcile a core statement of Rabbi Yohanan that seems to be in conflict with their legislative position.

The uniqueness of the Rogatchover's approach is that it frames the issue in a way that there is no conflict in the first place. This is because, according to his theory, Rabbi Yohanan views the minimum requirement as a statement purely about the quantity of the prohibition, without reference to quality. With this in mind, the supplementary statement about combination was meant as a proof of his position, not a justification for it. Rabbi Yohanan was simply stating that if we consider all food in combination, both before and after a *kezayit* is eaten, this implies that all this food has the same degree of prohibition. Otherwise, it could not be considered together.

Thus, even at the end of Yom Kippur, when there is no time to eat a *kezayit*, and combination does not come into play, Rabbi Yohanan's position would be the same.

The Rogatchover's approach will also naturally resolve a legal discrepancy in Rabbi Yohanan's position. In the rules of forbidden carrying (*hotzaah and haavarah*) on Shabbat, there is a principle that one must perform two acts to be liable. One must both pick up an object in a private domain (*akirah*) and set it down in a public domain (*hanakhah*).

Rabbi Yohanan rules that picking up an object from a private domain without putting it down later in public (*akirah be-lo hanakhah*) is permitted. But what happened to the principle of combination? Seemingly there is an issue of combination here, since one must combine picking up with a later putting down to complete the forbidden act. Therefore, just as he did with forbidden food, shouldn't Rabbi Yohanan also apply this principle in the matter of carrying on Shabbat?

The theory above resolves this simply.[113] Merely picking up an item without putting it down (*akirah be-lo hanakhah*) is not forbidden. Picking up without putting down is not half-forbidden, but rather is not forbidden at all. Only both in conjunction are forbidden. As such, there is no potential combination to reckon with, since the degree of prohibition is not the same in this case, in contrast to that of forbidden food case, where it is the same. In fact, there is no prohibition here at all. [114] [115]

Another advantage of framing Resh Lakish's position in terms of the quality of the prohibition is that it resolves with ease another difficulty facing the classical commentators. Resh Lakish concedes[116] that one who eats *hatsi shiur*, but with the intent to eat an entire *shiur*, a full *kezayit*, is indeed liable. How can this be? If eating less than the minimum is not liable, then why is the mere intention to eat more enough to incur liability? Simply put, we never punish motivation in halakhah; only action is judicable. Yet according to Resh Lakish, if one eats less than the minimum amount, with the intent to eat a *kezayit*, then he has still infringed upon the Biblical prohibition, even if he does not ultimately eat a *kezayit*.

However, according to the Rogatchover's theory, this is resolved in an intuitive and precise way. We have just explained that Resh Lakish's entire position is fixated on the quality of the prohibition. That being the case, we can indeed take into account the eater's motivation, because motivation is an element that per-

---

113   See Likkutei Sichot Volume 7 page 110-111.

114   For conventional understandings of the differences between *chatzi shiur* and *chatzi melacha*, see *maharitz chayot* and *korban netanel* on Shabbat 74a. See footnote 18.

115   See the Torah Shleima Parshat Yisro page 76 footnote 260 who brings several Aharonim regarding the formulation of this concept as constituting *chatzi melacha*. The problem that these commentators will face is that they still have not explained why we do not apply the potential for combination to *chatzi melacha*. According to the Rogatchover it is because the two acts are fundamentally different in degree and nature and thus do not lend themselves to combination.

116   Yerushalmi Trumot Chapter 6 halakhah 1

tains to the quality, not quantity, of the act. Since quality is of critical concern to us, motivation can and should be considered. Thus, Resh Lakish's position on intention to eat a *kezayit* aligns perfectly with his notion of the nature of the minimum requirement itself.

Another of the Rogatchover's interesting lines of analysis is whether there is a direct relationship between quantity and quality. Can one change the inner quality of something by adding more quantity to it?[117]

The texts he uses as a springboard for this discussion are the laws of *taharah* (ritual purity) and *tumah* (impurity), which are deservedly known as one of the most complex and confusing areas of Torah. There are extensive and exhaustive laws concerning the types of impurity that can contaminate food and liquid, and there is an intricate hierarchy of ascending levels of impurity.

Impurity is also infectious. If a *tame* (impure) piece of food touches a neutral piece of food, the impure food confers on the pure food item a secondary degree of impurity. There is a caveat, however: in order for a food item to be able to infect something else with impurity, it must be of a certain minimum size (*kebetsah*), or about the size of an egg.[118]

In Tractate *Eduyot* (chapter 3, *mishnah* 2), there is a dispute regarding a case where one gathered many pieces of food together to collectively satisfy the minimum size requirement.[119] Rabbi Dosa says that in order to meet the minimum size requirement of a *kebetsah*, the food must be one single item. Pushing many crumbs together does not satisfy the requirement because they are all different pieces. The Sages, however, say that this form of

---

117   The Mefaneach Tzfunot (199) brings a thought-experiment by the Otzar Hachochma regarding the molecular makeup of matter. Many physical items that have very different properties are on the molecular level differentiated by only one or two molecules. So by changing the quantity of something from two hydrogen (water) to three, we now have an entirely different item (hydronium).

118   There are those who hold that a food item must be the size of a *kebetsah* to even be able to contract impurity from something else in the first place.

119

אוכל פרוד, אינו מצטרף, דברי רבי דוסא; וחכמים אומרין, מצטרף

meeting the minimum size requirement is sufficient. What is the core of this dispute?

The Rogatchover[120] sees the issue as whether the *kebetsah* requirement pertains to the quantity or the quality of the impurity. The Sages, who say that pushing so many different pieces of food together is sufficient, hold that the minimum requirement is merely about quantity. We need a certain amount of *tamei* food in order to contain enough impurity to project it outward onto other items. There being no connection among all these pieces does not disqualify them as a *kebetsah*. If one needs a certain amount of moisture to moisten something, the more moist pieces of cloth he gathers, the more moisture in aggregate he has, and he can use it to moisten something else.

Rabbi Dosa,[121] however, understands the size requirement to be a statement about the quality of the impurity. In order to contaminate others, a food item must be possessed of a certain quality or type of impurity, one so powerful that it can expand onto other items. The quantity of the *kebetsah* is not the point. The size requirement is merely a benchmark to measure the potency and quality of impurity. In merely bringing together disparate

---

120   See the glosses on Moreh Nevukhim (Part 1, Chapter 74):

עיין מ"ש
בירושלמי ערלה פ"ב גבי אם ב' חצאי ביצה שחברן אם
מטמאין אחר, אם הא דאין פהות מכביצה מטמא אחר
משום שיעור עצמי או דלא קיבל [טומאה] כל כך שיהא
אפשר לטמא אחר, עיין זבחים דף לא, ומ"ש בתוספתא
פרה [הובא בר"ש פרה פ"ח מ"ז] גבי כזית שמילא, ועיין
בהך דמנחות דף נז, וירושלמי תרומות פ"ב ה"ב, ע"ש
בזה

121   See the Mishneh Torah Hilkhot Tumat Okhlin Chapter 6 halakhah 17 where the Rambam seems to rule like Rabbi Dosa:

אוכל פרוד שהוא כולו מכונס ודבק זה בזה אע"פ שאינו חיבור להתטמא ואינו כגוף אחד כמו שביארנו הרי הוא מצטרף לכביצה לטמא טומאת אוכלים אחרים ואם לא כנסו אלא הרי הוא מפורד כמעשה קדירה והקטנית אינו מצטרף עד שיקבצם ויעשם גוש אחד

"When separate foods are all collected in the same place and are clinging to each other, even though they are not considered as joined with regard to the contraction of impurity, and they are not considered as a single mass, as explained, they are still combined to produce the measure of an egg-sized portion to impart impurity to other foods. If the foods were not collected as one mass, but instead were separate like cooked food and legumes, they are not considered as a combined entity even in that context until they are collected and formed into a single mass."

See also the Raaved.

items of food to meet the size requirement, one does not thereby enable this collection of foods to contaminate others, since there is no incremental increase of impurity. This is like bringing two slow runners to a sprinting match and saying that their combined speed will make them win the race. Quantity is irrelevant within this framework; quality is key.

This issue gains another dimension when we reflect on the following question. Consider an impure food item, larger than a *kebetsah*, that breaks in two. Both of these two separate pieces touch a single pure food item. Will Rabbi Dosa say, in this case, that the pure food item does indeed become impure, even though each half of the impure item, on its own, is less than a *kebetsah*?

The Rogatchover explains[122] that, in such a case, everyone would agree that there is no need for the impure food item to be one single piece. The fact that it is now two (or more) disparate pieces is irrelevant. This is because the size requirement is of an essential nature. Since this food item once possessed this level and degree of impurity, it retains it, even when broken into two. The dispute between the Sages and Rabbi Dosa thus only applies in a

---

122   See Tsafnat Paneah Trumot Chapter 7 page 29a:

הנה לענין טומאת אוכלין בכביצה שאם נגע במקצתו
שיהיו גם האחרים טמאים, מבואר בתוספתא וטהרות,
ובפרה דף יז, ובדברי רבינו בהלכות טומאת אוכלין פ"ו
דלא מהני חיבורי אדם וכו׳, אבל זה לכולי עלמא אם
היה מתחלה כביצה שלם ונטמא ואח"כ נחלק ואח"כ נגעו
ב׳ החלקים בדבר אחד מטמאין אותו אף שאינם מחוברים
כמבואר בסוף פ"א דטהרות הובא בזבחים דף לא ע"א
וזהו מה דאמר שם התם איתא לשיעורא, ר"ל דהשיעור
לטמא אחרים כבר חל עליו, אך היכא דמתחלה לא נגע
רק לפחות מכביצת, בזח פליגי ר׳ דוסא ורבנן בפ"ג
דעדיות דר׳ דוסא סבר דכיון דלא היה עליהם לעולם הך
דין דלטמא אחרים אי אפשר לחול עליהם אח"כ ע"י
חיבורין, דס"ל דהך דמטמא אחרים הוא דבר עצמיי, לא
מטעם הכמות. ולכך כיון דלא היה עליהם לעולם הדין
לכך לא מצטרפי, כו׳, אך אנן לא סבירא לן כנ"ל גבי
כביצה לטמא טומאת אוכלין דזה לא הוה בגדר עצם רק
בגדר שיעור ולכך מצטרפין אף אם לא היה בהם שיעור
לטמא אהרים מעולם, ועיין ברכות רף ג ע"א גבי זימון
כה"ג, ובירושלמי שם פ"ו ה"א דהוה בזה מחלוקת

situation where all the disparate pieces never had been part of an impure food item that exceeded the size requirement.[123]

This discussion is very similar to the way the Rogatchover understands the dispute between Resh Lakish and Rabbi Yohanan about eating forbidden foods less than the minimally judiciable amount of a *kezayit* (*hatsi shiur*). In that case, the Rogatchover shed light on what precisely the dispute was about. Is the *kezayit* a qualitative threshold that creates the prohibition, or is it simply a marker for the courts to be able to act on the infraction. Here we have a similar proposition. According to our theory, the dispute between Rabbi Dosa and the Sages is structured in an analogous way. Rabbi Dosa holds that the *kebetsah* requirement indicates a difference in the quality of the impurity. Therefore, single food items over a *kebetsah* contaminate others. Conversely, the Sages hold that all we need to contaminate others is a certain mass and quantity of any impure food item, which the *kebetsah* satisfies.

Another place where the concepts of quantity and quality intersect is embedded in an interesting *midrash*[124] (*Torat Kohanim*). In *Vayikra* (26:6), the Torah states regarding the Messianic era:

"And I will destroy all marauding creatures from the earth."

The precise meaning of this prophecy is a matter of some contention. Rabbi Yehudah says it means that G-d will literally destroy all wild animals in the Messianic era, while Rabbi Shimon says it means that G-d will simply destroy their marauding nature, but

---

123   This essentially is the discussion in the Talmud in Zevahim 31a:

דתנן כביצה אוכל ראשון וכביצה אוכל שני שבללן זה בזה ראשון חלקן זה שני וזה שני הא חזר ועירבן ראשון הוי

124

והשבתי חיה רעה מן הארץ, ר' יהודה אומר מעבירם מן העולם, ר' שמעון אומר משביתן שלא יזוקו, אר"ש

אימתי הוא שבחו של מקום בזמן שאין מזיקים, או בזמן שיש מזיקים ואין מזיקים, אמור בזמן שיש מזיקים ואין מזיקים סוכן הוא אומר וגר זאב עם כבש

"And I will be *mashbis* marauding creatures from the earth" Reb Yehudah says it means G-d will literally destroy them, remove them from this world. Reb Shimon however says, G-d will remove their marauding nature. Said Rabbi Shimon "when is the praise of the Allmighty greater? When he destroys the marauding creatures or the marauding nature within them? Clearly it is when he merely removes their nature. As it says "the wolf will lie with the lamb".

not the animals themselves. The Rogatchover understands[125] the dispute as one of quantity and quality.

Rabbi Yehudah interprets the verse literally, since his primary perspective is that of quantity. From that perspective, when G-d says he will remove an animal from the earth, He means just that, actual physical removal, so that zero such animals are found in the world. Rabbi Shimon's main perspective is one of quality, which is why he understands the prophecy to be the removal of the marauding quality of these animals, not their physical removal.

Another instance where Rabbi Yehudah debates this point is regarding the laws of Passover. There is a commandment to destroy all leavened bread (*hamets*) before the onset of the festival, but we find a dispute concerning the precise nature of the destruction.

The Bible states[126] "destroy *hamets* in your house," employing the word *tashbitu*, which is the same root as *mashbit*, used concerning the removal of maurauding creatures in *Vayikra*.

The Sages say[127] that one can destroy his *hamets* by throwing it in the sea, where it will decompose in the water, or crumbling it into the wind. Rabbi Yehudah says that there is only one option—burning it.

Rabbi Yehudah is consistent in his overall approach. The concept of destruction, as embodied by the word *mashbit* or *tashbit*, means the utter destruction of the item under question, i.e., the breakdown of its quantity of mass and volume. The Sages, however, posit that merely destroying its quality, or its current form of existence, is sufficient.[128] By crumbling the bread into the

---

125   See Tsafnat Paneah Vayikra 26:6:

הנה בתו"כ פרשת בחוקותי על קרא דוהשבתי חיה כו' מביא שם

פלוגתא דר' יהודה ור"ש אם ההשבתה ר"ל כמות הדברים, וס"ל לר' יהודה

ואזיל לשיטתו דאין ביעור חמץ אלא שריפה ר"ל צריך שלא תהא

כמות, וכמבואר בירוש' פ"ב דפסחים השבתה שיהא בלא יראה

אבל ר"ש ס"ל דהשבתה הוי ג"כ ביטול איכות הדבה

126   Shmot 12:15
127   Pesahim beginning of Chapter Two.
128   A practical legal difference between the two is offered by the Rogatchover. If one must destroy the very bread itself, then that means that the

wind or decomposing it in water, one has effectively destroyed its current form of existence. Thereafter, it is irrevocably and absolutely unrecognizable, and thus its presence and quality of former being has been destroyed.[129] [130]

Another area where we find quantity and quality intersect is in the opinions of Rabbi Gamliel.

The Talmud[131] relates that Rabbi Gamliel, who was the leader of the generation (*nasi*), had very strict acceptance standards at his *bet midrash*. You might say that he ran an early version of Harvard University insofar as difficulty of admission was concerned, though his standards were slightly more subjective. His policy was that only students who possessed integrity and whose "external behaviors reflected their inner convictions" (*tokho ke-baro*) were admitted to his study hall.

After he was deposed,[132] the new leadership instituted more flexible and open admissions standards, and as a result, "many

---

prohibition is laid onto the very essence of the bread. That in turn mandates that *hamets* that one forgot to get rid of on Passover, after Passover is still forbidden and must be destroyed. The reason being that its very identity has had a prohibition drilled into it by Passover. Therefore that prohibition is still contaminating the bread after the festival expires which in turn necessitates its subsequent destruction.

If however the destruction is only to remove the breads outer form of being, its shape and texture, then one understands the prohibition to be only on the breads outer and peripheral identity. That would compute into the bread that was inadvertently maintained over Passover being permitted after the festival since the prohibition was a secondary characteristic that was being forced onto it by the festival. Therefore once the festival is over the prohibition naturally dissipates.

129   This is a classic example of the multi-varied usage of terms that the Rogatchover is liable to use for the very same concept. This tension between Rabbi Yehudah and the Sages (or Rabbi Shimon) that he describes as being predicated upon the conflict between quantity and quality can also be explained (Tsafnat Paneah Kuntres Hashlama side 65) as the conflict between essential identity (*etzem*) and peripheral identity (*to'ar*), substance (*homer*) and form (*tsurah*)(Michtevei Torah #110 26a), objective category (*cheftza*) and subjective application (*gavra*)(Hilkhot Maachalot Assurot Chapter 15 halakhah 9). See further appendix 1.

130   See Likkutei Sichot volume 7 page 190 and on where the Lubavitcher Rebbe expands this approach of Rabbi Yehudah into the realm of Hilkhot Shabbat. Rabbi Yehudah's positions on *melacha she'eina trzicha le'gufa* and *davar she'eino miskaven* can be collapsed into the overall scheme outlined above.

131   Berakhot 28a

132   See Berakhot 27b for the details on this rabbinic coup.

questions that had not been resolved in a long time were solved that day." I raise this point because clearly Rabbi Gamliel was convinced that the quality of students should be the overriding concern in building a scholarly institution. The other rabbis vehemently opposed him, subscribing to the view that quantity should be the guiding metric of the yeshivah.

We find Rabbi Gamliel's quality-oriented approach rearing its head yet again in the laws of prayer. The Talmud[133] records a dispute between Rabbi Gamliel and the Sages concerning the nature of communal prayer. Rabbi Gamliel holds that the essential obligation of communal prayer is for one representative (*shaliah tsibur*) to pray while everyone else listens, while the Sages hold that the obligation is for people to come together to pray, but with each individual still retaining his own independent obligation.

How is this related to the battle for dominion between quality and quantity? The Sages who assert that every person prays individually understand the power of a group to be in its quantitative number. More people means more talents and energies coming together and being focused into one cohesive unit. The religious importance of communal prayer can be understood as an affirmation of the social and human power of a community in general.

Rabbi Gamliel, on the other hand, perceives a group as being fundamentally different in kind from disparate individuals; it is one indivisible unit. As such, the power of the group can only be represented by one individual who comprises and symbolizes the internal unification of all the people in the group. As *Shulhan Arukh Ha-Rav* states,[134] "he is the representative of them all…his utterances are as if they are all uttering."

Yet a further expansion of Rabbi Gamliel's quality-oriented approach can be seen in his legislative position concerning the Talmudic principle of *modeh be-miktsat*, or partial admission.

Partial admission is when the plaintiff claims that he lent the defendant one hundred dollars and demands payment. The de-

---

133   Rosh Hashana 33b
134   Orach Chaim Chapter 213 paragraph 6.

fendant then admits half the claim and claims that he only owes fifty dollars. In this situation, the defendant is required to take an oath on the fifty dollars that he denies. The Talmud[135] raises the question of the scope of partial admission.

If the plaintiff claims that the defendant owes him one hundred sacks of wheat, and the defendant states that he in fact owes the plaintiff one hundred sacks of barley, which is worth about half the price of wheat, does this count as partial admission? Rabbi Gamliel asserts that it does, while the Sages take issue with this claim.

According to our theory that Rabbi Gamliel is committed to his quantity-tinted legislative glasses, we see that his position here is in line with his overall scheme. This is illustrated as follows.

Every claim made by the plaintiff is comprised of two elements. The first is the quantity and specifics of the claim—how much money is owed, in what currency it was lent, etc. The other element is the quality of the claim. That is to say, irrespective of the details, the plaintiff is claiming the defendant owes him a certain sum of money. In our situation, the plaintiff is asserting that he is owed one hundred sacks of wheat, valued at one hundred dollars. When the defendant rejects this claim, stating that he in fact owes one hundred sacks of barley, valued at fifty dollars, he has committed a partial admission from a quality-based perspective. The details, i.e., the quantity, do not match up, since in the specifics the defendant completely rejects the narrative of the plaintiff. But in the overall understanding of the quality of the rejection, we can understand that the claim of the plaintiff has not in fact been entirely rejected.

Can the fluctuation of the quality of an item change its quantity? It appears that the answer is yes.[136] [137] Consider the Talmud in

---

135   Shavuot 38b

136   See Sh"ut Warsaw Siman 50:

ועי' ב"ק דף צז,

גבי מטבע פסלתו מלכות כו', ומז, דאמר נשתנית צורתו

ר"ל הסכם הדמיוני

137   See Tsafnat Paneah Trumot:

אך כך דהנה גבי

פסלתו מלכות פסק פסק רבינו דאינו יכול לאמר הרי שלך

Bava Kama (97a),[138] regarding a thief who stole a coin which was later invalidated when the king issued a new form of currency. Can the thief return the now defunct coin and be exempt from any payment? The answer to this hinges upon whether the thief acquired the coin upon stealing it or not. In halakhah, a thief can acquire a stolen item; he can keep the stolen item and choose instead to financially reimburse the owner. However, in order to acquire a stolen item, the thief must physically change the item somehow. If the thief acquired the coin at any point by introducing a physical change onto it, then he must pay the owner the worth of the coin at the time of the theft, i.e., before it was invalidated by the king. If he did not acquire the coin, then he can return the now useless coin to the owner and declare, "What I have stolen is before you."

Rabbi Yehudah holds that because one can tell by looking that a particular coin is no longer valid, this is tantamount to a physical "change" in the coin. Since the coin has undergone a physical change, the thief has acquired it, and thus must pay the owner its value at the time of the theft. The Rogatchover extracts from this discussion the principle that a change in quality, the coin's being rendered useless, can effect halakhically a change in quantity. Since the coin is discernibly different from the new currency and therefore is acquired by the thief, it has undergone a "physical change."[139]

לפניך, והטעם משום דמטבע עיקר הדבר הוא הצורה

וההסכם, וכמבואר ב"מ דף מז, ע"ב, ומו ע"ב, וכיון

שנפסלה שוב אין זה הדבר ולא שייך לאמר הרי שלך

לפניך, ועי' מש"כ רבינו בפיהמ"ש ע"ז פ"ג דצורה נקרא

דבר הבדוי ושהוא רק י בגדר הסכמי, ע"ש

138

א"ל רבא לרב יהודה לדידך דאמרת פסלתו מלכות נמי היינו נסדק הרי תרומה ונטמאת דכי פסלתו מלכות

דמי וקתני אומר לו הרי שלך לפניך א"ל התם לא מינכר היזיקה הכא מינכר היזיקה

139   This is further amplified by the Rogatchover's contention that a coin can only ever have a secondary identity and never has intrinsic value per se. See Tsafnat Paneah Trumot side 13:

אד כד דהנת גבי

פסלתו מלכות פסק רבינו דאינו יכול לאמר הדי שלך

לפניך, והטעם משום דמטבע עיקר הדבר הוא הצורה

וההסכם, וכמבואר ב"מ דף מז, ע"ב, ומוי ע"ב, וכיון

שנפסלה שוב אין זה הדבר ולא שייך לאמר הרי שלך

לפניך, ועי' מש"כ רבינו בפיהמ"ש ע"ז פ"ג דצורה נקרא

דבר הבדוי ושהוא רק י בגדר הסכמי, ע"ש

An interesting and quite explicit application of the quantity versus quality discussion is the following discussion in the Gemara regarding the optimal way to learn Torah.

"Rabbi Shimon Ben Gamliel and the Rabbis debated. One said that *Sinai* is a superior quality in learning, while the other side said *oker harim* is a finer trait."

Sinai literally means Mount Sinai. Here, the Talmud uses *sinai* as a metaphor for the quality of vast knowledge and scholarship, as if to say, one who has the entire Torah at his fingertips, just as it was given at Mount Sinai.

Oker harim literally means a demolisher of mountains. The Talmud uses it for one who has sharp and incisive analytical skills. Although this individual may not know all of Torah by heart, he is possessed of superior intellectual abilities. Thus the Rabbis and Rabbi Shimon are debating what the more desirable and admirable trait in Torah study is.

"Who is a man embodying qualities of *Sinai*? Rav Yosef. Who is a man embodying *oker harim* abilities? Rabbah. They sent the debate to the east [*Erets Yisrael*] for a resolution and the answer sent back was: *sinai* is superior."

Sinai versus *oker harim* is essentially a debate on quality versus quantity. *Sinai*, which is broad global knowledge, equates to quantity of knowledge. *Oker harim*, which is localized, sharp thinking, equates to quality of thought.

In the final analysis, Sinai is superior, hence quantity is superior. Additionally, the Talmud in *Yebamot* (14a) records that *Bet Shammai* held the high ground in terms of superior thinkers and scholars, while *Bet Hillel* had a larger number of scholars and Torah legislators. However, *Bet Hillel* followed their own opinions. This was an astonishing phenomenon, when one considers that *Bet Hillel* knew and acknowledged *Bet Shammai*'s superior caliber of scholars and legislators.

Yet this is perfectly understandable once we realize that this was a conscious and philosophical choice. When resolving legislative disputes, what should be the primary orientation of the law?

Should we accord supreme weight to the quality or the quantity of the disputing sides? In according that weight to the numbers of *Bet Hillel* over the sharpness of *Bet Shammai*, halakhah is in effect saying that the tangible quantity of scholarship carries the day. *Aharei rabim lehatot,* or following the majority, is a mechanism that is at once easily discernible and given to easy use. Approximating the relative degrees of scholarship inherent in different people is a more difficult or impossible task. Therefore, for now,[140] the halakhah follows *Bet Hillel.*

---

140   But not in the Messianic era. See "Hillel and Shammai" for more on this.

Chapter Four

Homer and *Tsurah*

It is a fundamental belief in all religions that there is more to
reality than what meets the eye; the idea that there is an intangible or spiritual aspect of the universe. But while all religious
frameworks are built on this idea, not all of them share the same
perspective or degree of emphasis on spirituality. The central
theme of this chapter will be an exploration of the nuance and
hierarchy of the intangible spectrum as halakhah understands
it. The Rogatchover, in developing this theme, gives voice and
articulation to many ideas that have long been implicit in the
understanding of the Talmud, yet have never gained substantial
and concrete definition.

The Rogatchover posits that many areas of Torah and Talmud
can be understood as discussions about the balance between the
tangible and intangible realms.[141] As we see in Chapter Seven,
the Rogatchover suggests that the tension between tangible and

---

141   See Tsafnat Paneah Sh"ut, part 1 chapter 50:

מחלוקות רבות בתלמוד תוכנן היא הבעייה אם המציאות היא

הצורה או החומר

spiritual considerations is a major driving, and perhaps even defining, force in the debates between *Bet Shammai* and *Bet Hillel*
(hereafter "Shammai" and "Hillel"). Our analysis starts by pinpointing several instances where they debate the primacy of the
tangible and intangible spectra. After the first couple of sources
from these debates are considered, the discussion widens into
the broader sea of Talmud.

The schools of Shammai and Hillel, intellectual and scholarly rivals for hundreds of years, have greatly influenced the development of Torah. Between Hillel and Shammai themselves there
are only three, or possibly five, disputes. But three hundred sixteen[142] arguments between the schools they founded are recorded in the Talmud. Of these arguments, two hundred twenty-one
revolve around various halakhot, sixty-six are *gezerot* (preventative laws), and twenty-nine are discrepancies between Biblical
and legislative interpretations.[143] Despite Shammai's having a
tendency to be strict and Hillel's leaning towards the lenient, in
fifty-five, or fully one-sixth, of these disputes, Shammai rules on
the side of leniency.

The Talmud in *Hagigah* (12a) states, "The school of Shammai
says the heavens were created first and then the earth. The school
of Hillel says the earth was created first and then the heavens."

What does this argument revolve around? Is there an underlying
theme? Indeed there is.[144] [145] Shammai says the heavens were created first. By "heavens," Shammai means spirituality and the intangible. In Shammai's view, spirituality is the primary determinant in halakhah and the main barometer of reality. Therefore,

---

142   Jewish Encyclopedia, House of Hillel and House of Shammai.

143   Jewish Encyclopedia, Bet Hillel and Bet Shammai.

144   In Michtevei Torah letter #289:

וזה שיטת ב״ה בחגיגה דף יב

דחומר נברא תחלה ואח״כ הצורה היולית, אך ב״ש ס״ל

להיפך, דצורה היולית נבראת תחלה ואח״כ חומר, וזה

באמת בכל התורה דעיקר צורת הדבר

145   In Mahadura Tinyana page 180:

וזה הגדר דפליגי בחגיגה

רף יב, דשמים נבראו תחלה לדעת ב״ש, ור״ל דהצורה

הוא העיקרית, ע״כ. ובשו״ת צ״פ (ווארשא) סי׳ נ

במחלוקת ב״ש וב״ה בחגיגה יב, שמים נבראו כוי, ר״ל

אם המציאות הוא הצורה או החומר

since it is the dominant reality, it was created first. Hillel says, however, that in our physical world, material considerations are of primary importance, and one must use the physical spectrum as the dominant deciding factor in halakhah. Therefore the "earth," meaning physicality, was created first.

We see in the behaviors of Shammai and Hillel themselves an expression of this conceptual divide. The Talmud relates[146] that Shammai is fixated all week on the impending Shabbat. Each day, he is on the lookout for an especially nice delicacy. Upon finding said delicacy, he sets it aside for Shabbat in order to honor the holy day. If, however, he later finds an even nicer specimen of that delicacy, he declares the new item to be in honor of Shabbat and eats the former one.

Hillel however, typifies a different behavioral pattern. He does not set aside anything for Shabbat before Friday morning. If he finds a delicacy on any other day of the week, he eats it that day, since he relates to each day on its own merits, not merely as a preparation for Shabbat. As the Talmud states so eloquently, "baruch Hashem yom yom," or "bless G-d day by day." Each day is its own unit in time; we should not be fixated now on a later day, even Shabbat.

The different behaviors of these two Sages embody their distinct philosophical outlooks on life. Shammai's reality hinges on the spiritual spectrum, so the future, intangible day of Shabbat is the determining factor for him, outweighing the present day's realities. Hillel's world revolves around the physical, so the tangible, actual present is of far greater import to him than the intangible, hazy future.[147]

---

146   Betsah 16a

147   What's perplexing is that the halakhah here follows Shammai, instead of the usual accordance with Bet Hillel. Perhaps the rationale underlying this is that we are dealing here with questions of a spiritual nature. 'Should the honor of Shabbat outweigh the honor accorded to a regular day of the week 'is a query which is predicated on such spiritual ideas as "the honor of Shabbat" and "the service of G-d mandated by the current day". Therefore, since the question is firmly entrenched in the tension and balance between spiritual ideas themselves, the primacy of spirituality which is Bet Shammai's signature is more appealing.

A Scent of Separation

When a couple wants to divorce each other, the legal mechanism for doing so, the *get*, has certain requirements. One of these is that the document must make clear that there is a complete end to the relationship between husband and wife. As a result, a *get* containing a clause suggesting a separation that is not absolute is suspect, and will not be valid in certain situations.

A specific example is brought in the Talmud in *Gitin*.[148] A man divorces his wife and states that she is divorced from him, but is not permitted to everyone. Since he states that she is not permitted to everyone and forbids her to certain people, she is not divorced. There is a remnant of the marriage which is still extant, that is, the prohibition on marrying the individuals the husband specifies. However, even though the *get* is invalid, it is called a "scent of a *get*" (*reiah ha-get*), and prohibits the wife from eating consecrated food (*terumah*).

Why is this? And why do the Sages differ? The Rambam brings this very passage in the Gemara,[149] declaring that the prohibition on *terumah* that this *get* imposes on the wife is of rabbinic origin. *Tosafot*[150] disputes this and claims that the prohibition is Biblical. The Rogatchover suggests[151] that the dispute over whether the prohibition of *terumah* is Biblical or rabbinic is predicated on the struggle between the tangible and intangible. He frames it as follows.

The *get* discussed here is not very substantial. It possesses a serious flaw in its wording and thus is not considered to be fully operational. However, there is some semblance of legitimacy to it, which is why it imposes a prohibition on the wife. Thus the term "scent of a *get*" is precise. Scent is a sensory faculty of the soul, not the body, which is grounded in the intangible realm. We see the Talmud affirm this perspective in the discussion about

---

148   82b

149   In Hilkhot Gerushin chapter 8 halakhah 5 and in chapter 10 halakhah 1.

150   Gitin 82b s.v. "afilu lo".

151   T"P Ad loc.:

ומאוד הארכתי בזה בגדר ריח הגט אם פוסל מן התורה או רק

אסמכתא דזה רק צורה ולא חומר ע׳ ברכות מיג נשמה נהנה

בו דאין בו ממש

166

the *havdalah* ceremony,[152] where it states that the soul has pleasure from scent. In our situation, this *get* has some semblance of legitimacy. The only question is whether this intangible and insubstantial form of divorce should be accorded concrete legal standing. If one operates with a perspective from which intangible elements have primacy, then this *get* has concrete standing, and thus the prohibition imposed on the wife vis-a-vis *terumah* is of Biblical origin.

If one is operating from a perspective grounded in the tangible, then this *get* does not have standing, and the prohibition is only of rabbinic origin. Indeed, we see this very dispute between the Rambam and *Tosafot* mirrored in a different debate between Shammai and Hillel.

Imagine the following scenario. A man writes a *get* for his wife, but has a change of heart after writing it, so he does not give it to her. What does halakhah dictate in this case? Seemingly, there should be absolutely no legal standing to the *get*, since it was not given. Yet Shammai says that even though he did not give the *get* to his wife, just the writing of the *get* creates some form of prohibition.[153] This hazy prohibition is sufficient to prohibit the wife from eating *terumah*.

Another expression of this can be seen in the Talmud's discussion[154] of the legal obligations imposed on a watchman. A watchman is not allowed to use the item he is watching. If he does indeed use it, he incurs liability and responsibility for the item, even for freak accidents. What if someone merely thinks about using the item, but in fact does not? Does he, too, incur extra liability? Shammai, in keeping with the primacy of the intangible, claims that the watchman incurs liability just for thinking about using the item.[155] Hillel, of course, opposes such a claim. As long as the watchman does not actually use the item, he incurs no extra responsibility.

---

152   Berakhot 43b
153   See Gitin 81a
154   Bava Metzia 43b
155   This is in stark contrast to other areas of halakhic jurisprudence, such as thinking about doing *melakha* after Shabbat (see shulhan arukh harav orakh chayim siman 318), in which a person's thoughts do not fall under the scope of legal obligations.

The Rogatchover applies this two-tiered perspective not just to legal relationships, but even to physical objects.

What happens when a convert dies, leaving a large estate with no relatives? The Talmud declares[156] that the property is free to all comers on a first-come, first-served basis. In Jewish law, the only mechanism for taking possession of a house is through a process called *hazakah*.

Hazakah means that one has to display owner-like behavior while improving the property. The classic example is an owner-less field that is only partially fenced. If someone comes along and completes the fence, thus encircling the entire property, he has acquired it, because he has improved the property and displayed ownership.

A curious law exists within this field (of law). Suppose that someone dies without relatives, leaving his field ownerless, and then someone else builds a palace in this field. The palace, however, is not complete; doors are not hung in the doorways. This is the only thing missing, so one would expect that it does not make a substantial difference in the application of the law. But if a second man passes by this property, sees the palace, notices the missing doors, and hangs doors in the palace that he himself did not build, he has acquired the ownerless land of the deceased!

The rationale underlying this astonishing law is that, as we said, *hazakah* must include improvement of the property. But the construction of a house or palace without doors is not considered an improvement, because a structure lacking doors cannot serve its basic purpose of shelter. Therefore, since this palace is not usable, its builder has not improved the property and so does not acquire it. The stranger who merely builds doors has now rendered the palace usable and thus has improved the property, making him the owner.[157]

---

156   See Bava Basra 53b:

א"ר נחמן אמר רבה בר אבוה הבונה פלטרין גדולים בנכסי הגר ובא אחר והעמיד להן דלתות קנה מאי טעמא קמא לבני בעלמא הוא דאפיך

157   The Rambam brings another application of the importance of doors to a house in Hilkhot Mezuzah chapter 6 halakhah 1.

"There are ten requirements that must be met by a house for the person who dwells within to be obligated to affix a *mezuzah*. If one of the requirements is lacking, there is no obligation for a *mezuzah*. They are:

The Rogatchover adds nuance to this discussion by explaining[158] that a house exists on two planes. There is the actual material being used, like wood, stone, marble, the beams in their supports, and the gravel in the foundation. Then there is the essential identity and character of the house, without which it is merely so many pieces of wood and stone mashed together, without a cohesive identity. These are the *homer* and *tsurah* of the house, its tangible and intangible strata. The physical materials, their sizes and shapes, are the tangible factors, while the overall theme and identity is the spiritual or intangible aspect of the house.

Thus, a house without doors is not considered complete. It is not just deficient in utility, but even lacks the overall identity of "house." Anyone can enter at will, and thus the owner does not have control of the house. As the Talmud states, *"kama livni be-alma hu de-apikh,"* he has merely rearranged some bricks. The view implicit in the Talmud's words, that the so-called house is just a pile of disparate pieces of material without a cohesive identity, precisely aligns with the Rogatchover's contention that there is an elemental and overarching layer of intangible identity inherent in this structure.

Therefore, the one who affixes doors to the house, giving it the final blow and thus its overarching identity, is the one who becomes the owner. In effect, he has dealt the final blow to the intangible essence of the house, while one who renovates the kitchen has only worked on the tangible material of the house, without approaching its overall identity.

---

a) for the area [of the dwelling] to be four cubits by four cubits or more;
b) for it to have two doorposts;
c) for it to have a lintel;
d) for it to have a roof;
e) **for it to have doors;**
f) for the entrance to be at least ten handbreadths high;
g) for the dwelling not to be consecrated;
h) for it to be intended for human habitation;
i) for it to be intended to be used for a dignified dwelling;
j) for it to be a permanent dwelling.

158   See Tsafnat Paneah Mahadura Tinyana 6a:

יש בהבית שני גדריס עצם דהיינו אבנים ועצים ועפר זה הוי בגדר
תלושה ולבני בעלמא עי׳ ב״ב דבלא דלתות אין עליו שם בית
לקנין ור״ל דצורת הבית הוא נשלם בהדלתות והצורה יש עלי השם
מחובר דזה נעשית רק לאחר שבנה בית ולכך ס״ל לרבינו דבית
בלא דלתות פטור מן המזוזה דאין עליו שש בית מחובר

From this vantage point, one can resolve a discrepancy in the Rambam's rulings, where he seems to directly contradict himself. In one place[159] he writes that someone who lives in a consecrated house has infringed on its sanctity, yet in another place[160] he rules the opposite.

Yet once we understand that a house, or any object with an overall theme and purpose, is comprised of two strata of reality, its tangible material and its intangible identity, we can assert that there is a difference between the two cases the Rambam addresses.

In the first case, the owner rents the house to someone else, and then consecrates it to the Temple. Here we must consider the nature of rentals. When the owner rents the house, what precisely is he renting? He is not renting the actual wood and stone, for the tenant to use as he likes, but rather is renting the overall purpose and utility of the house, which is to give shelter to a specific person. Therefore we can say that when the owner consecrates the house, he does not consecrate its stratum of overall identity, because that has already been designated for the tenant. Instead, the owner consecrates the tangible layer of the house, its physical materials. If this is the case, then the consecration is successful, because the materials of the house are uprooted movable mate-

---

159   *Hilkhot Erkhin* chapter 6 halakhah 30:

המשכיר בית לחבירו וחזר והקדישו הרי זה קדש ופקעה השכירות ואם דר בו השוכר מעל

[Although a person] rents out a house to a colleague, if he retracts and consecrates it, the consecration is effective and the rental arrangement is terminated. If the tenant dwells there, he violates the prohibition against misappropriating sacred property.

160   *Hilkhot Me'ilah* chapter 5 halakhah 5:

אין מעילה אלא מן התלוש מן הקרקע אבל הנהנה בקרקע עצמה או במחובר לה לא מעל אפילו פגם כיצד החורש שדה הקדש או הזורע בה פטור נטל מאבקה ונהנה בה ופגמה מעל הדש בשדה הקדש מעל שהאבק שלה מועיל לשדה והרי נהנה באבק ופגם השדה וכן אם חרש שדה הקדש כדי להעלות אבק לעשב שנתן בה ונטל העשב מעל הדר במערת הקדש או בצל אילן או שובך של הקדש אע"פ שנהנה לא מעל וכן המקדיש בית בנוי הדר בו לא מעל אבל המקדיש עצים ואבנים ובנה בהן בית הדר שם מעל כמו שיתבא

The prohibition against *me'ilah* applies only to articles that have been separated from the earth. If, however, one benefits from consecrated earth or from consecrated articles attached to the earth, he does not violate the prohibition against *me'ilah* even if blemishes that entity... Similarly, when one consecrates a house that was built, a person who dwells in it does not violate the prohibition against *me'ilah*. When, however, a person consecrates wood and stones and builds a house, a person who dwells in it violates the prohibition against *me'ilah*, as will be explained.

rial, or what is called *talush* in halakhah. Only movable items are eligible for the degree of consecration in which benefitting from the item is forbidden, that is, only movable items can incur *meilah*. Real estate, not being movable, cannot be consecrated to this extent. But since the owner consecrated only the tangible material of the house, which is movable and not connected to the ground, the consecration is successful. The renter cannot benefit from the house without becoming liable for *meilah*. Thus, he must move out.

In *Hilkhot Meilah*, however, the Rambam rules that even if someone lives in a house that the owner has consecrated, this dweller has not infringed on the house's sanctity. The difference is that there is no renter in this case, which means we are free to interpret the owner's consecration as referring to either the tangible or intangible identity of the house. Therefore, we interpret the consecration as being of the intangible identity, not the physical materials. Therefore the consecration does not address the entire house, because items which are not movable, like the house's intangible identity, cannot receive the highest degree of consecration, in which benefit is forbidden. In the second case, the house is not one hundred percent consecrated, which is why the Rambam rules here that "when one consecrates a house that was built, a person who dwells in it does not violate the prohibition against *meilah*."

The implication of this is that the natural, default position of human consciousness is to consider the larger, more general outlook. We intuitively put many details together to perceive an ordered, cohesive whole. We do not see metal, knobs, windshield wipers, and glass; rather, we see a car, one single unit. Therefore, when there is no renter involved, and we are under no compulsion to interpret the consecration of a house in any particular manner, we instinctively revert to understanding the consecration as the intangible essence of the house, i.e., its larger general structure, not the individual disparate items from which it is constructed.

Another area where we see this two-tiered perspective is in the laws of *tsaraat* (ritual leprosy). There is an interesting field of Jewish law centered on this phenomenon, part of which concerns its effect on structures. If a blotch appears on a house, and through various methods is proven to be *tzaraat*, the house and everything in it becomes impure. However, there is a dispute[161] concerning the necessary minimum size of a blotch in order to make a house impure. One opinion asserts that even a small blotch the size of an olive (*kezayit*) is sufficient, while the other opinion claims that we require one full brick of the house to have the discoloration, no matter the size.

The Rogatchover[162] injects into this argument an understanding of the philosophical backdrop of this dispute. The argument is predicated on the above distinction between the *homer* and *tsurah* of a house. The opinion that a blotch is judged by its size, which must be at least a *kezayit*, accords with the perspective that a house is defined by its individual components, by its tangible spectrum. As such, we require a certain minimum size, regardless of whether this blotch is on two separate bricks or walls.

The other opinion, that we judge a blotch not by its size, but by covering "one full brick," comes from the viewpoint of perceiving a house through its overall cohesive identity. Here, a house is a sort of body, and thus we require one of its "limbs," its bricks or other parts, to be fully contaminated. We do not think of the house as a house-sized aggregation of material, and thus we do not think of the blotch as an olive-sized aggregation of mold. Just as with a dead body, we judge the impurity by the house's limbs, irrespective of the size of the limb.

The Rogatchover posits that a physical item, once altered, can never regain its prior intangible identity. This is true even if one restores the object back to its exact former tangible shape and size. We see this in the Talmud in various places. But first it is important to preface this point.

---

161   Nega'im chapter 13 Mishnah 3.

162   See Tsafnat Paneah Mahadura Tinyana page 6 and on:

אם זה הוי בגדר פרט בדבר חדש מן הבית והוי כמו אבר דאין

לו שיעור או כיון דזה נעשה מדברים מופרדים אין עליו שם הרבבה

מזגיית רק הרכבה שכוניית זה ס״ל לת״ק ור״א חסמא ס״ל כיון

דהגורם להטוגאה הוא רק צורת הבית בן ד׳ כתלים זה הוי כמו הרבבה

מזגיית וחלקים ממנו הם חלקים חדשים והוי בגדר אבר ולכך מטמא

כל שהוא

According to Jewish law,[163] a thief can acquire an item he steals if he effects a permanent change in it. For example, if a thief steals raw wool, then smooths and dyes it, then that wool becomes his property. This is because, in essence, the original item no longer exists, and thus cannot be returned to its original owner.[164] If, however, the change effected by the thief can be undone, then he has not acquired the item and must return it, because it is able to revert to its original form. The original stolen object still exists and must be returned.

The Talmud in *Bava Kama* discusses the following case.[165] If one steals a bar of silver and melts it into coins, he has not acquired the silver, since it is possible to melt the coins back into a bar. If, however, he steals coins and melts them into a bar, then a transfer of ownership has been effected, because he cannot remake those very same coins. Once he has bent the tangible form of the coins past a certain point, the silver is no longer considered the same entity. The conventional understanding is that this is because it is impossible to recast those coins in the exact shape and size that they were before the theft.

The Rogatchover uses this law as a support for his theory that a change in the tangible spectrum can affect the intangible spectrum of an object. We see that the prior identity of the coins does not return, even though the initial change takes place on the tan-

---

163   Bava Kama 79a

164   According to rabbinic law, even a change that can be reversed transfers ownership to the thief in order to encourage robbers to repent. See Bava Kama 95a.

165

אמר רב פפא האי מאן דגזל עפרא מחבריה ועבדיה לבינתא לא קני מאי טעמא דהדר משוי ליה עפרא
לבינתא ועבדיה עפרא קני מאי אמרת דלמא הדר ועביד ליה לבינתא האי לבינתא אחריתי הוא ופנים
חדשות באו לכאן ואמר רב פפא האי מאן דגזל נסכא מחבריה ועביד זוזי לא קני מאי טעמא הדר עביד
להו נסכא זוזי ועבדינהו נסכא קני מאי אמרת הדר עביד להו זוזי זוזי פנים חדשות באו לכאן

R. Papa said: If one misappropriated sand from another and made a brick out of it, he would not acquire it, the reason being that it could again be made into sand, but if he converted a brick into sand he would acquire it. For should you object that he could perhaps make the sand again into a brick, [it may be said that] that brick would be [not the original but] another brick, as it would be a new entity which would be produced.

R. Papa said: If one misappropriated bars of silver from another and converted it into coins, he would not acquire them, the reason being that he could again convert them into bars, but if out of coins he made bars he would acquire it. For should you object that he can again convert it into coins, [my answer is that] it would be a new entity which would be produced

gible physical spectrum. According to this theory, an intriguing passage in the *Midrash Rabbah* can be explained in a new light.

The Midrash states[166] that G-d created the Red Sea, the Sea of Reeds, with the condition attached that it split for the Jewish nation when they flee from Egypt. But why is this condition necessary? Why could G-d not simply create the sea and then command it to split when the time comes? According the above theory, we can resolve this question as follows. We know that once an entity changes its physical form, it can never regain its former intangible identity. We also know that G-d does not create anything new; everything that was created was called forth into being in the six days of creation. If this is the case, then the Sea's splitting must have been part of its character from the time of its creation. Otherwise, after it splits, it would become a new entity, and not the same sea that G-d created.

This whole discussion takes on new depth in the laws of conversion, the ultimate change of spiritual identity. The Talmud has a curious conversation[167] concerning the command to have children and how it relates to a freed gentile slave, who assumes the status of a Jew, and a convert.

The Talmud is discussing the case of a convert who had children when he was a gentile. The question is whether he has fulfilled his obligation to "be fruitful and multiply." The dispute regarding this is between Rabbi Yohanan and Resh Lakish. Resh Lakish says he has not fulfilled his obligation, since the law is that a convert is like a newborn baby, in that he has severed all prior familial relations to the extent that he is Biblically permitted to

---

166   Shemot Rabbah on 14:23.
167   Yebamot 62a:

איתמר היו לו בנים בהיותו גוי ונתגייר ר' יוחנן אמר קיים פריה ורביה וריש לקיש אמר לא קיים פריה
ורביה רבי יוחנן אמר קיים פריה ורביה דהא הוו ליה וריש לקיש אמר לא קיים פריה ורביה גר שנתגייר
כקטן שנולד דמי

.... אמר רב הכל מודין בעבד שאין לו חייס

It was stated: R. Yohanan said, If a man had children while he was an gentile and then he became a convert, he has fulfilled, the duty of propagation of the race; and Resh Lakish said: He has not fulfilled the duty of propagation of the race. 'R. Yohanan said: He has fulfilled the duty of propagation,' since he had children. 'And Resh Lakish said: He has not fulfilled the duty of propagation' because one who became a convert is like a child newly born.

marry his biological parents if they were to convert (though this is rabbinically prohibited).

Rabbi Yohanan says in response that since a gentile is also obligated to have children, the convert has still fulfilled the obligation, even though he did it before converting. Concerning a freed slave, however, both Rabbi Yohanan and Resh Lakish agree that he does not fulfill his obligation by having fathered children while still a slave.

This is puzzling. Why do they draw such a distinction between a slave and a convert, to such an extent that everyone agrees that there is no transfer of his past to the present? With a convert, Rabbi Yohanan at least asserts that there is (some) transfer of his past identity and actions into the present.

The answer[168] lies in the difference in degree of control that the convert and the slave have on the metamorphosis they are undergoing. The convert undertakes this reworking of his identity by his own will, and thus retains some semblance of his former identity, just enough, according to Rabbi Yohanan, that he has fulfilled his obligation to have children. Not so the slave. The slave was freed at the whim and desire of his master. His new identity is imposed completely from outside him, which is why everyone agrees that there is no transfer of his past into his present. This is much like the above case of the silver bar.

The innovation in this case is intriguing. What we see here is a direct restructuring of the intangible essence of the person, in

---

168   Tsafnat Paneah Mahadura Tinyana page 66:

לא דהוא מצווה על פריה ורביה רק דמ"מ הא יש לו בנים ואף אם
אחר כך לאחר שנתגייר אם יוליד עוד בנים לא יקיים מצוה כלל דהרי
יש לו עכ"פ החיוב הוא שיהיו לו בנים ולא שיוליד בנים ולכך כיון
דיש לו נפטר ולא מהני כלל מה שיהיה לו עוד אבל גבי עבד אף אט
היו לו בנים בהיותו נכרי ואח"כ נעשה עבד ואח"כ נשתחרר מ"מ צריך
לקיים פו"ר דאף דגר שנתגייר כקטן שנולד ועבד שנשתחרר כקטן שנולד
וכן שנעשה עבד כקטן שנולד אך נ"מ דגבי גר השינוי הוי על ידו
בדעתו וברצונו ואף דהוי פנים חדשות מ"מ הצורה עדיין קיימת
עליו וכ"כ דמ"ש רבינו גבי כלי שרת שנשברו דאם התיכן הוה כחדשים
מ"מ קדשים חזינו דהצורה נשארה עליהם ושמן עליו חזה נקרא גדר
שינוי הדרגי אבל עבד הוא בא בגדר פתאומי דכל זמן שהוא עבד כמו
שאינו ולכך אין עליו שם מציאות כלל ונעשה בריה חדשה
ממש ולכך לא קיים פדר

this case, his identity as a Jew or non-Jew. In the case of the coins, their intangible or spiritual restructuring was a result of direct tinkering with their physical stratum. Here, however, the individual's intangible spiritual identity is being directly tinkered with and fundamentally transformed.

Another aspect of this is that the change from non-Jew to Jew is not incremental or one of degrees. It is an essential, non-linear jump from one spectrum of reality to another. As a result, there is no vestige or semblance of the convert or slave's former identity in his present status, because a non-linear transformation, by definition, is one that does not build gradually, but rather is a radical quantum leap. This, in turn, means that we do not associate the current, radically new status of being of the newly made Jew with the former, other being from which they came. In the words of the Rogatchover, "*kol davar ha-ba be-geder shinui pitomi, ein lo shem he'av*" (any item which undergoes a sudden [non-incremental] change does not retain its father's [its former] identity).

✳ ✳ ✳

The Talmud has an interesting law concerning childbirth. If a woman gives birth prematurely, in her seventh month, we consider the baby to be a viable, living being, provided it lives thirty days and escapes *nefel* status. A *nefel* is a child who, because of premature birth or any other defect, cannot survive, and it is not viewed in halakhah as constituting a living being. All laws regarding living children will not apply to it, such as redemption of the firstborn, circumcision, and the like. In addition, it is considered to be like a stone on Shabbat, so it is *muktsah* (one is forbidden to move it).[169]

However, a child born in the eighth month of pregnancy is considered to be absolutely non-viable, and is not given a thirty-day grace period to prove its viability. If it does indeed live past a certain point in time, then it has, against all odds, demonstrated its health and viability. But during the time before it proves its sustainability, the Talmud calls it a *met*, a dead child.

---

169   The Talmud states that the mother can bend over the baby and nurse it without moving it.

The question begs to be raised: How can we call this living, breathing being "dead"? Consider the passage in *Yebamot*,[170] which declares that a child born in the eighth month does not shake off his "dead," non-viable status until reaching twenty years old. This means that we can have a healthy, robust nine-teen-year-old breathing right before us, and still halakhah calls him a dead person, a *met*.

The Rogatchover, in explicating a two-tiered view of reality, clarifies this enigmatic statement of the Talmud. Indeed, from the perspective of the tangible spectrum, one cannot in good faith call this being a dead child, yet on the intangible spectrum—and ritual halakhah is enmeshed with the intangible—one can indeed proclaim this child to be devoid of any real status, or "dead".[171] This concept goes further, however. The child is not just considered to be dead on the intangible spectrum. Indeed, it has lost its very identity as a member of the species. Its intangible, essential character as human is non-existent, until it demonstrates otherwise by outliving this status, because its *tsurah pratit*, its identity, is gone. This is why a non-viable child does not even cause ritual impurity (*tumah*) as all dead humans do.[172] This is also true with animals; an animal born prematurely cannot be ritually slaughtered since it is considered not to be a member of its (otherwise kosher) species.[173] This total annihilation of its very category and identity can only come about from its lack of a spiritual, intangible identity.

---

170   80b

171   See Mahadura Tinyana page 49:

> ואף דבגמרא שבת דף קלו אמר שם דהוי בגדר
> מת ר"ל הצורה שיש בו דשייך בה שחיטה מתה ממנו
> ונתבטלה וכן גבי מילה שם ר"ל דתואר של זכר נתבטל
> ממנו דהרי גם בן שמונה כל זמן שהוא חי אינו מטמא
> ויש בו דין אבר מן חחי

and page 56:

> דלכך לא מהני שחיטה
> לולד בן ח' משום דעדיין אין עליו שם בקר וצאן
> ואף
> דבשבת דף קלו אמר הטעם משום דהוי כמת. ר"ל
> דהצורה הפרטית שיש עליו מתה דהרי אינו מטמא

172   Instead it is considered as a limb torn from the mothers body, *eiver min hachai*, which has its own set of ritual impurity laws.

173   See Hulin 72a.

This is also the reason for the opinion[174] that the blood of a baby born in the eighth month does not ritually prepare an item for impurity, as all other blood does.[175] The same dispute holds true regarding other areas of ritual purity and impurity, such as the impurity of *rekev*, the decomposition of the corpse.[176]

Thus it is possible for a being to exist solely on the tangible spectrum, though it lacks not just life, but even a basic category of being, in the eyes of halakhah.[177]

---

174   See Makhshirin Chapter Sixth Mishnah Seven.
175   Certain items must come into contact with liquid before being able to contract impurity.
176   See the Yerushalmi Nazir Chapter Seven halakhah Two.
177   See Sh"ut Warsaw Siman 261 page 202:

באמת זה מחלוקת התנאים בספרי פ׳ חוקת אם

דם בן ה׳ מטמא, ע״ש ר׳ ישמעאל ור״ע, ומרבה שם מן

לכל [וכל נפש אדם להביא בן ח׳], וע״י במכשירין סוף

פרק ו משנה ז ג״כ אם דמו מכשיר [בן שמונה ר״י אומר

חוץ מדמו], וזה כוונת הירושלמי נזיר פ״ז ה״ב גבי נפלים

אם יש להם רקב, ומבואר שם דתליא במחלוקת אם דם

מטמא, ור״ל הך מחלוקת דספרי. וע״י בחולין(דף עב ע״א

וע״ש ברש״י ע״ב, דלכך אין מטהר שחיטת בן ח׳ משום

דאין להם שם פרטי של בקרך וצאנך רק כללי

Chapter Five

Klal and *Prat*

What is a society? Is it merely a collection of individuals working together towards a shared interest? Or is it perhaps something greater than just the sum of its parts? Maybe it is a little bit of both. Or perhaps a society or collective is neither. Instead, it may be some sort of novel entity as yet unexplored.

The primary innovation of the Rogatchover is the idea that there are two types of collectives. The first he terms a *shutfut,* or "partnership." The second type he calls a *tsibur,* or "group entity."

The definition of those two terms is as follows. A *shutfut* is a specific type of collective in which individuals come together for a common goal or interest. In this type of collective, the individual components constitute the group, yet remain separate from it. Essentially, it is an aggregate.

A *tsibur*, however, represents a type of collective unit that, once formed, is divorced from its individual components. In other words, the group takes on new properties and characteristics that are entirely different from the individual's properties and rights.

Whenever we are dealing with a group, the halakhic challenge is to determine what sort of group it is. Is it a *shutfut*, in which the main ingredients are the individual components, and the primary halakhic concern is the separate parts of the group? Or is it a *tsibur*, in which case the primary halakhic concern is the singular whole? For such is the power of the *tsibur*, that a group of many is seen as one indivisible whole.

Where do we see this in the Talmud? Consider what the Mishnah says in *Berakhot* (49b):

"What is the formula for *zimun*? If there are three, he [the one saying grace] says, 'Let us bless [Him of whose bounty we have eaten]'…if there are ten, he says, 'Let us bless our G-d'…it is the same whether there are ten or ten myriads…If there are a hundred, he says, 'Let us bless the Lord our G-d'…if there are a thousand, he says 'Let us bless the Lord our G-d, the G-d of Israel'… if there are ten thousand, he says, 'Let us bless the Lord our G-d, the G-d of Israel, the G-d of hosts, who dwells among the cherubim, for the food which we have eaten.'"

The Talmud then asks (50a) whether there is an inconsistency here. First the Mishnah says that the liturgy (*nusah*) is the same whether there are ten people or tens of thousands. But immediately it goes on to say that there are differences in the *nusah* for groups of ten, a hundred, a thousand, and ten thousand.

The Talmud answers that the issue is a dispute. The prior statement, that there is no difference once there are ten people, belongs to Rabbi Akiva, while the second statement, that there are differences, is attributed to Rabbi Yosi the Galilean.

What could be the reasons underlying this difference of opinion? What motivates Rabbi Akiva to say that once we cross the "ten threshold," there is no more differentiation of the blessing, while Rabbi Yosi asserts that there is a distinction?

Presumably, Rabbi Yosi feels that a larger group warrants a more prestigious blessing, since the assembly is a greater one. Therefore, for a group of one hundred, we add "the Lord," and for a group of one thousand, we add "the Lord, G-d of Israel." This culminates with the group of ten thousand, where we add "the Lord, G-d of Israel, the G-d of hosts, who dwells among the cherubim."

Rabbi Akiva's position, then, is puzzling. Does he not acknowledge that the greater the group, the more prestigious the assembly, and thus the blessing should be more significant?

While there are other more conventional approaches of defending Rabbi Akiva, the Rogatchover has a unique view on this issue. He sees in this technical liturgical argument an ontological and philosophical backdrop against which the technical disputation springs forth.

Rabbi Akiva holds that the type of collective formed when ten Jews are together is a *tsibur*. Therefore, there is no difference in quality between a group of ten and a group of a hundred, since once there are ten, and the collective is formed, there is no further recognition of the individual components. After the *tsibur* is formed, a greater quantity does not add anything to its quality.

As such, the "ten threshold" concept is a radical departure from the incrementally increasing quantitative approach that characterizes the *shutfut* concept advanced by Rabbi Yosi. From Rabbi Yosi's point of view, a collective is of the *shutfut* variety. Thus, since the individual components that make up the collective are not negated and nullified therein, but rather are extant and discernible, the greater their number, the greater the collective becomes, and hence more prestigious blessings are required.

Another example of this conceptual divide is developed by the Rogatchover as follows. The Talmud in *Bava Batra* (8a), while discussing the Mishnah, brings Rabba, who states the following: "If a man vows that he will derive no benefit from the men of a certain town, he must derive no benefit from anyone who has resided there twelve months, but he may derive benefit from one who has resided there less than twelve months."

What about a man who comes to live in this town after the vow is taken? If this man lives in the town for twelve months, is he then included in the scope of the vow? This very issue is debated by the *Ran* [*Nedarim* 84a, s.v. *Rav Nahman amar*] and the Ritva [*Nedarim*, end of chapter 5]. The *Ran* holds that even if a man arrives after the vow, and then resides in the town for a year, he is included in the vow, but the Ritva disputes this.

What is the underlying conceptual background to this *mahloket*? Although there are other more conventional approaches that could be advanced,[178] the Rogatchover takes a unique path in explaining this issue.[179]

It hinges upon what one's primary barometer of reality is—the individual or the collective. If the collective is primary, then even if someone moves to this town after the vow has taken effect, he is still included in its scope, because all the inhabitants of the town constitute one single group or *tsibur*. Any individual who joins the *tsibur* is subsumed into the collective. Because there is no recognition of separate individual components in the *tsibur*, this person is now under the umbrella of the vow, even though he was not part of the original collective.

שאם אדם נודר מן הכלל, חלות הנדר חלה על מציאות כלל, שכן

---

178   Such as viewing the dispute as revolving around whether he was referring to a collective- "the town" or the individuals- "inhabitants". From this vantage point the dispute would simply be that one opinion holds that by referring to the people (*anshei ha'ir*), the vower was placing the vow on the individuals. Therefore anyone who came to live in the city afterwards is obviously not within the scope of the vow. The other opinion would be that by referring to the town as a whole and not specific people, the vower was placing the vow on the collective. The reason that someone who came into the collective afterward is included is because we assume that he is avowing himself from anyone who joins this collective at any point in time.

Put simply, if someone says "I disavow myself from having any association with all the people living in Manhattan", we might consider the structure of the vow to be that he is disavowing himself from people who live in Manhattan. Therefore anyone who afterwards becomes a resident automatically falls under the vow. Or we might say that it is the people who were Manhattaners when he took the vow that he wanted to disavow himself from. Therefore anyone who became a resident afterwards is not included.

179   *Sheelot u-Teshuvot Tsafnat Paneah Dvinsk, helek 2, siman 204:*

האַרכתי בזה הרבה

במה דפליגי הר"ן והריטב"א בהך דב"ב דף ח גבי מבני העיר אם באו לדור אח"כ עי' ר"ן נדרים דף פד ע"א,

ובריטב"א נדרים ספ"ה, וזה אם מהכלל נעשה פרטים,

וא"כ אין נ"מ אם בשעת נדרו לא הוה' ואם מהפרטים

נעשה הכלל אז רק אותם שהיו.

הכלל קיים ומשבא פרט נוסף לכלל אדם אחר שלא היה בשעת

הנדר - הכלל חופף גם עליו והוא בכלל הנדר לעומת זאת אם אין

בכלל אלא מה שבפרט, היינו אין הציבור בחינת יחידה, אלא אוסף

של פרטים, כיון שפרט זה נוסף לאחר הנדר, אינו בכלל הנדר

[*Bereshit, Pirke Mavo,* p. 54]

But if one considers the group as a *shutfut,* which does not negate the individual members, then this person is not under the umbrella of the vow, since he was not there at the time of the vow.

* * *

The question whether there can be any interaction between *shutfut* and *tsibur,* and the nature of that interaction, is interesting to explore. It appears that it is not a choice of one or the other. Both forms of community exist within halakhah. The question is simply which one applies in any specific case. We are not dealing with an ontological or epistemological query, but rather a question of application and predominance. The idea of interaction between these two types of groups would seem nonsensical, because a collective is seemingly either a *shutfut* or a *tsibur,* not both. But there are indeed situations where a single group will have aspects of *tsibur* and *shutfut* at once.

The Rogatchover explains that there are two distinct kinds of communal need. One is a need entirely communal in nature. The other is a need that is individualistic in nature, but one that every single group member has. While examples are not obvious from the text, it appears to me that this distinction might apply to a Torah scroll versus prayer books. A Torah scroll is solely a communal need, while a prayer book is an individual need on a mass scale, thus making it a communal need as well. In other words, a Torah scroll is a need of the *tsibur,* while prayer books are a need of the *shutfut.*

An interesting application of this is that the Rogatchover says, in the case of a *tsibur's* need, that the majority can coerce the minority to help pay for the item. In the case of a *shutfut*'s need, the minority cannot be forced to help fund it.[180]

This can be supported by the Talmud in *Bava Batra* (55a). The Talmud there states that a *pardakht* (loafer) can be compelled to pay the city tax. (In those times, a fixed sum was imposed on a city as a tax, and the city as a whole had to pay the fine.) The loafer discussed in the Talmud is someone who does not benefit from the city's economy or social services, who has nothing to do with the city other than living there. Yet the city can compel him to pay into the tax pool. This is because simply by dint of living in the city, he becomes responsible for its support. According to the Rogatchover, however, this loafer can only be compelled because the tax is structured in such a way that it is not imposed on individuals, but rather on the community as a whole.

In practice, matters would be different if the tax were structured to address both the city and the individual at once. For example, if there were a fixed sum to be paid by each person in the city, but the fine itself had to be paid by the municipality, not the individuals. There the Rogatchover would presumably hold that we cannot compel the loafer to pay, since this need is of the *shutfut*, not the *tsibur*.

A prime example of *tsibur* is the case of the idolatrous city (*ir ha-nidakhat*). This is a city where the majority of the residents worship idols. The ramifications of this are vastly different from a case of individual idol worship. The Bible states (*Devarim* 15:13):

---

180   Shut Dvinsk helek 2 siman 13:

והנה עיין בתוספתא סנהדרין ספ״ב

דהא דדי ברוב ציבור, זה רק בצרכי ציבור ע״ש, ור״ל

כך דכל דבר דהוה רק משום שותפות אז אין לרוב לכוף

המיעוט וצריך הסכם הכל, וכל מקום דהוה, גדר ציבור

שם יכולים הרוב לכוף המיעוט, דלא גרע מהף דב״ב דף

נד ע״א גבי פרדכ׳ מסייע ור״ל דנותנים להציבור

והציבור עושה צרכו של ציבור, והנה הוצאות בה״כ יש

בזה ב׳ גדרים הנצרכים דוקא להציבור, שם היחידים

בטלים להרוב ודברים הנצרכים לכל אחד זה רק גדר

שותפות ואינם בטלים

[בשו״ת צפ״ד ח״ב פי׳ יג]

יג כִּי-תִשְׁמַע בְּאַחַת עָרֶיךָ, אֲשֶׁר יְהוָה אֱלֹהֶיךָ נֹתֵן לְךָ לָשֶׁבֶת שָׁם—לֵאמֹר. יד יָצְאוּ
אֲנָשִׁים בְּנֵי-בְלִיַּעַל, מִקִּרְבֶּךָ, וַיַּדִּיחוּ אֶת-יֹשְׁבֵי עִירָם, לֵאמֹר: נֵלְכָה, וְנַעַבְדָה אֱלֹהִים אֲחֵ-
רִים—אֲשֶׁר לֹא-יְדַעְתֶּם. טו וְדָרַשְׁתָּ וְחָקַרְתָּ וְשָׁאַלְתָּ, הֵיטֵב; וְהִנֵּה אֱמֶת נָכוֹן הַדָּבָר, נֶעֶ-
שְׂתָה הַתּוֹעֵבָה הַזֹּאת בְּקִרְבֶּךָ. טז הַכֵּה תַכֶּה, אֶת-יֹשְׁבֵי הָעִיר הַהִוא—לְפִי-חָרֶב: הַחֲרֵם
אֹתָהּ וְאֶת-כָּל-אֲשֶׁר-בָּהּ וְאֶת-בְּהֶמְתָּהּ, לְפִי-חָרֶב. יז וְאֶת-כָּל-שְׁלָלָהּ, תִּקְבֹּץ אֶל-תּוֹךְ
רְחֹבָהּ, וְשָׂרַפְתָּ בָאֵשׁ אֶת-הָעִיר וְאֶת-כָּל-שְׁלָלָהּ כָּלִיל, לַיהוָה אֱלֹהֶיךָ; וְהָיְתָה תֵּל עוֹלָם,
לֹא תִבָּנֶה עוֹד.

"You shalt smite the inhabitants of that city with the sword, destroying it utterly, and all that is in it and the cattle, with the
sword. And you shalt gather all the spoil of it into the midst of
the city, and shall burn with fire the city, and all the spoil within,
for the LORD thy G-d; and it shall be a desolate heap for ever; it
shall not be built again."

As the concept develops in the Talmud and *Rishonim*,[181] several important distinctions become clear. First, a majority of the
city must turn to blasphemy for it to become an *ir ha-nidakhat*.
Second, the wives and children of idolaters are killed as well,
notwithstanding their lack of involvement in the sin. Third, the
idolatrous men of the city are put to death "by the sword," which
the rabbinic tradition interprets as beheading, instead of the
usual punishment for an idolater, stoning.

Several serious questions arise from this intriguing case of Jewish law. First, how can we kill innocent women and children?
This is an astonishing anomaly and, to my knowledge, the only
place in the vast corpus of Jewish law where we kill ostensibly
innocent Jews.

Second, there is a principle in halakhah that when a man is sen-
tenced to two separate capital punishments, we kill him with the
more stringent form of punishment. This is because the harsher
penalty is more inclusive and will effect atonement for the lighter penalty as well. If so, how can we kill this city of idolaters with
a lighter penalty (beheading), when an individual idol worship-
per is liable for a harsher penalty (stoning)? The people of this
city have committed two entirely different sins with the same
act. First, they have served idols as individuals, incurring all the
resultant penalties. Second, they have committed this sin as a
group, whether knowingly or not, and thus have incurred a sep-

---

181   Sanhedrin 111b; Rambam- Hilkhot Akum 4:6

arate set of penalties for a separate sin. Therefore, they should seemingly be given the harsher sentence of the two.

Third, this is a ludicrous situation. If there are one hundred men in this town, and fifty of them serve idols, they are punished as in a normative case of idol worship: stoning, no collective punishment of their families, and no burning of their property. But if one additional male, the fifty-first, serves idols, the consequences are drastically altered for all the previous fifty, though they have no connection to the fifty-first man.

Lastly, we must consider the more general implications of this. There is a case in the Talmud of a city besieged by a hostile foreign army. The army offers terms to the city under siege as follows. Send out one person to be killed, and they will depart immediately; otherwise, they will not leave until every last person is slaughtered.

What would one assume in this case based on the law regarding the *ir ha-nidakhat*? If an innocent woman can be killed merely because she associates with an idolater, then surely she can be killed to save an entire city of millions?

In fact, however, the law is that the besieged city is not allowed to send out any person to be killed. Come what may, we do not kill innocents. The implication of this is that, through the prism of Torah thought, the individual is seen as having infinite value, which is why one person is just as important as an entire city.

In the Talmud Yerushalmi, *Terumot*, chapter 8, halakhah 4, it says:

תני סיעות בני אדם שהיו מהלכין בדרך פגעו להן גוים ואמרו תנו לנו אחד מכם ונהרוג אותו ואם לאו הרי אנו הורגים את כולכם אפי׳ כולן נהרגים לא ימסרו נפש אחת מישראל

"If a group of people were walking along a road and gentiles surrounded them, saying 'Give us one of you to kill, or we will kill all of you,' even if all of them must be killed, so be it, since we do not surrender even one life to be killed."

What an abrupt turnaround. In the case of an idolatrous city, we attribute almost no value to a woman's life, but in the case of a besieged city, we say that one life is worth as much as a million lives! What's going on here? How can these two laws be part of the same system? Is there a coherent, consistent thread running through both, or can they only be understood in isolation?

The key to understanding all this is that halakhah relates to individuals in two fundamentally different ways: collectively and individually. In the collective modality, the individual is not seen as an independent, self-sustaining entity. In fact, if the collective is a *tsibur*, the individual is not seen at all. This perspective yields halakhot that operate from a worldview in which there is no absolute value to any one person. Instead, the collective is viewed as the dominant reality, and the individual only as an accessory.

But when the individual is seen and recognized, there is not only an absolute value allocated to the individual, but even infinite worth. This is because halakhah attributes limitless value to the individual—when the individual is recognized at all. The minute a *tsibur* is formed, there is no more recognition of the individual. This in no way contradicts the tremendous value given to a single person, but that value only exists from the individualist perspective of halakhah, not the collectivist.

Let us return to the idolatrous city and reassess the facts based on this analysis. This explains why we give the lesser punishment of beheading to the group. Once the majority serves idols,[182] a *tsibur* of idol worshippers is formed. The law deals with the idolaters as a single indivisible whole, not as separate individuals. There is no option of giving them the harsher penalty of stoning reserved for the individual, because the law sees no individuals here. Rather, we have a collective that has turned to idolatry. This is why their property is burned, because the law is concerned with utterly eradicating this collective and all traces of it. Not so with an individual. An individual who commits idol-

---

182   It is important to bear in mind that the *tsibur* is only being constructed via the prism of this particular sin of idol worship. As such regarding any sin that is not idol worship the person can still be related to in an individualized way and punished accordingly. This is why the *meisis* or the "persuaders" who seduced people into idol worship are indeed stoned. Insofar as the sin of seduction is concerned they are separate parts from the group-unit and are judged separately.

atry has only gone against the law personally. Therefore there is no concern with his family or property. But a group that serves idols has not just committed a sin; they have created an entire category and collective unit that serves idols. This represents a challenge to the law on an entirely different scale.

This explains the anomalous law that innocent women and children are to be killed. It is not that innocent individuals are killed. Instead it is the collective that is being eradicated. The women and children are viewed as being part of it. There is no more individual relationship to the law; the relation is now a collectivized one, in which there is only recognition of the group as one singular whole, divorced from its individual components. The law kills them because the law is simply wiping out the category of the *tsibur* of idolatry to which they belong.

The minute that individuals clearly remove themselves from the collective, they are immediately exempt from punishment. Once the law "sees" them again, and they are not subsumed in the collective, their innocence is recognized. They can demonstrate that they are separate from the group by fleeing the city. Once out of the city, they have removed themselves from the collective, are seen as individuals, and are therefore innocent.

Moreover, this is why even the property of the innocent is burned. It is because the city as a whole[183] has become a collective of idol worshippers. Therefore everything in the city is destroyed. The property of the city cannot be removed and hence cannot be divorced from the collective. But this is not true of innocent inhabitants of the city. They can flee, thus demonstrating their independence from the collective.

* * *

A central area of analysis in the development of individualism and collectivism in the Rogatchover's system concerns the Temple sacrifices. This is because the concept of a communal sacrifice is a rich area in which to explore the definitions and boundaries of a communal entity.

---

183   This is why halakhah requires a majority of the city to have served idols.

Sacrifices are financed via the *mahazit ha-shekel*. Every Jew contributes a small sum of money once a year to the Temple treasury. What is the relationship of an individual Jew to the sacrifice brought in the Temple, the *Bet ha-Mikdash*? Can we say that each person has a portion, or some type of ownership, in the daily offerings brought in the Temple? The first question we must consider is monetary or fiscal. In halakhah, the smallest sum of money that one can be said to own, or have an association with, is called a *shaveh perutah*. In modern currency, this is about fifty cents.

Say that one million Jewish people contribute a *shaveh perutah* in a given year. To calculate percent ownership, we would have to divide the value of one sacrifice into a million parts. However much a single animal might cost, it would not be a large enough sum to allot a *shaveh perutah*'s worth of ownership to each of one million Jews. That much is clear. What is not clear is if the principle of ownership requiring a *shaveh perutah* is indeed set in stone, as we assume above. Perhaps there are times when there is some sort of ownership of, or bond to, an object or part thereof worth less than a *shaveh perutah*. For example, it is forbidden to steal even less than a *shaveh perutah*'s worth of goods, notwithstanding that we usually do not consider such a miniscule amount to have an owner in the conventional sense of the word.[184]

But putting the monetary issue aside, we must deal with the implications of this for our analysis concerning the nature of the collective. If a collective for the purpose of communal sacrifice is a *tsibur*, or indivisible unit, then certainly no individual can have a personal, specific connection to the sacrifice in any way. The Rogatchover seeks to prove that the group in question is indeed a *tsibur*, not a *shutfut*.

He supports this claim from several places. The first is the Talmud in *Zevahim* (4a).

To understand the following passage of Talmud, we must make note of the concept of "change of owner" (*shinui baalim*). This

---

184   See Sukkah 27b and the commentators for a discussion on this. See also the Rambam beginning of *hilkhot gezeila*. See also Likkutei Sichot volume 34 page 54 and the footnotes.

term means that the priest (kohen) must have the proper intent and awareness of for whom a sacrifice is being offered, and of its legitimate owner. If a person brings the sacrifice, and the kohen gets confused and does the service with the understanding that it is being offered by a different person, that sacrifice is invalid and must be brought again.

The Talmud in Zevahim 4a explains that there is no possibility of the kohen making such a mistake with a communal offering. The reason for this, however, is unclear. If the kohen clearly has in mind that this sacrifice is only being offered by half the nation, for example, then is that not an incorrect intent regarding ownership? This question, however, does not seem to have enjoyed any serious discussion in the commentators.[185]

The way the Rogatchover articulates the problem is as follows. Since we know of a case where the twelve tribes bring twelve separate sacrifices, and each one is considered a communal sacrifice (as we see below in Horayot), is it not possible for the kohen to have the wrong tribe, i.e., the wrong community, in mind? This would seem to be a case where shinui baalim applies.

In this case, the Rogatchover sees more support for his viewpoint on sacrifices, namely, that communal sacrifices are communal in

---

185   I did find one conventional explanation in the Teshuvot Vehanhagot krach 5, siman 41. He writes that incorrect intent of ownership is only possible when the other person who is wrongfully being thought of by the Kohen, is outside the scope of this sacrifice. In other words the sacrifice does not have any connection or relevance to him at all. This is not the case by the community, since the entire nation is receiving benefit and is affected by the communal offering. Therefore since there is no one outside the scope of the communal sacrifice, there cannot be any incorrect intent of ownership. Three considerations that might be pointed out are that a) this would not answer the question the way the Rogatchover frames it b) this is a forced and strained restructuring of the principle of shinui balim and c) we still can ask the following question:

A rasha, wicked person, should not receive atonement from a communal sacrifice since he has willfully excluded himself as the verse states zevach reshaim toeva, the offering of the wicked are an abomination and therefore not received in the temple. If so, ca not there still be a case of incorrect intent regarding ownership, since there is an individual who is outside the scope of the sacrifice? To answer this, the Teshuvot Vehanhagot simply states that therefore we must say that we do not consider the individual status of any one person by a communal offering. Why this is though, is not explained. In the Rogatchover's analysis it will become abundantly clear the necessity and coherency of such an attitude.

a *tsibur* sense, not a *shutfut* sense. In other words, communal sacrifices are seen as belonging to an indivisible single unit, the community of Israel, not to an immense aggregate of individuals. Just as with a private offering, where if a *kohen* has in mind that only the head of the person is bringing the *korban* and not his feet, nonetheless it is a valid and legitimate sacrifice, since one cannot differentiate body parts within a single person in this case. The exact same idea applies in the case of a national sacrifice. Even if the *kohen* has in mind the wrong tribe, or explicitly and consciously excludes any portion of the nation from the sacrifice, it is of no consequence. This is because the entire nation is designated as one single unit for this offering, and within one single entity, there cannot be differentiation.[186] [187]

Once we have defined communal sacrifices as pertaining to an indivisible *tsibur*, we can properly appreciate the following pas-

---

186   This would also answer a problem raised by Reb Akiva Eiger (*shaalot utshuvot siman* 9) regarding women's participation in communal sacrifices. He writes that women were not included in communal sacrifices since they did not give the sacrificial monies, the *machtzit hashekel*. If this is the case then our question can be applied specifically to women as well. That is, why ca not the Kohen invalidate the communal sacrifice by having in mind that it belongs to women and not men? For that matter if a man did not give the sacrificial monies then the Kohen would invalidate the sacrifice simply by having in mind this man?

However once we understand that communal sacrifices are not brought from a community of individuals but from a community of one indivisible group-unit, all these serious halakhic issues are resolved. All women are included in the sacrifice automatically, as are all men who did not give money, since within one single entity there is no possibility of halakhic differentiation.

187   Although this would mean that no Jew had any individual connection to the sacrifices and that instead the relationship was utterly of a general communal one, there is a third way. This is a radical synthesis proposed by the Lubavitcher Rebbe in Likkutei Sichot volume 33 page 111. He suggests that notwithstanding the fact that the collective by sacrifices was a *tsibur*, nonetheless each person retained some sort of specific connection on a personal level to the money given and hence to the sacrifice itself. The mechanism he conceptualizes for fusing these two opposites is an abstract one. He asserts that two opposite realities can only be harmonized by a third transcendent platform that interfaces and serves as a medium between the two. This third element was the *nasi* or the spiritual leader of Jewry at that time. This man was someone who incorporated the entire community within himself (see Rashi on *bamidbar parshat chukat* 21, 21) but who was nonetheless a single individual who did not lose his independence by being fused with, and embodying the entire community. As such, the leader represented a middle point on the spectrum of personal identity and collectivization. He therefore affected a blend of *tsibur* and *yachid* thus allowing the sacrifices to have a personal bond to each individual Jew even though the collective was of a *tsibur* variety.

sage of Talmud in *Horayot* (6a): "Our Rabbis taught: If one of the congregation died, they are still liable; if one of the court, they are exempt."

A little background knowledge is in order. Tractate *Horayot* is concerned with the laws relating to erroneous decisions or rulings issued by a *bet din*, and acted upon by the people, who have relied on the court's authority. The law is that the *tsibur* must bring a communal sin offering to atone for their accidental transgression. Each tribe brings their own sin offering, resulting in twelve sin offerings being brought.

In the passage quoted above, the Talmud states that if one of the members of the Jewish nation dies before the mistake in the ruling is found, and they had a chance to bring the sin offering, then the community must still bring a sin offering. If, however, one of the seventy members of the *Bet Din Ha-Gadol*, the halakhic supreme court, dies before the sin offering is brought, then the community is exempt from the sin offering.

This is because the law regarding sin offerings is that if one of the owners of the animal dies, then the animal cannot be sacrificed (*hatat she-metu baaleah einan nikravin*). In other words, the Talmud is telling us that the real owners of the sin offerings are the sages of the court, because they are the ones who issued the incorrect ruling that the people relied upon. Therefore, the sin is essentially theirs. This is notwithstanding the fact that the tribes bring the actual sacrifices, not the court.[188]

The Talmud then brings a dispute on the above statement.

"Who is the author [of this statement]? R. Hisda, in the name of R. Zera, in the name of R. Yirmiyahu, in the name of Rav, said: It is R. Meir who maintains that the court, and not the congregation, brings the sin offering. Hence, when one of the congregation dies, they are still liable, since all the members of the court are alive. If, however, one of the court dies, they are exempt, be-

---

188   This in point of fact is disputed in Horiyot 2a. The Sages say that indeed the court is the one who must bring the sacrifices for it is their sin, while Rabbi Yehudah says it is the people who must in actuality bring the sacrifice, even though it is the court that sinned.

cause it is then a sin offering one of whose joint owners died, and for this reason they are exempt.

R. Yosef disagreed: Let this statement be established in accordance with the view of R. Shimon, who maintains that the court, together with the congregation, [brings the sin offering]. Nonetheless when one of the congregation dies, they are still liable, because **a congregation does not die** [emphasis mine]."

What is this concept that the congregation does not die? If all of the *tsibur* commits the inadvertent sin, then they are all joint owners in this sacrifice, and thus, if one dies, one of the owners has died, rendering the sacrifice invalid. Or so it would seem.

A *tsibur*, however, cannot die, because a *tsibur* is not contingent upon specific individuals. An individual may cease to exist, but a *tsibur* does not. Therefore, since in the *tsibur* there is no recognition of individual components, when one person dies, it does not mean that one of the owners of the sacrifice has died. This animal's owner is one indivisible unit—the community. The community exists in the exact same fashion after an individual's death as before.

This is not the case, however, if a group is understood as a *shutfut*. In *shutfut*, one person's death must be reckoned with, because that person's existence is recognized as part of the group. Therefore, from a *shutfut* perspective, if one person dies, then one of the owners of the sacrifice has died, in which case it is invalid.

So far does the *tsibur* approach extend that even if an entire generation dies and a new generation of youth becomes the new community, this "new" community is still obligated to bring a communal sin offering for the transgression of the earlier generation. This sacrifice is valid; we do not consider one (or all) of its owners to have died. To such an extreme goes the logical progression of the *tsibur* perspective. This can be supported from *Tosafot* in Tractate *Meilah* (9b), s.v. *korbanot*:

קרבנות ציבור לציבור, פירוש אף אם מתו אותו הדור של עולת

ציבור ציבור קיימא כי דור הולך ודור בא

* * *

Can the concept of *tsibur* coexist with a *yahid*, an individual beyond the radius of the *tsibur* who retains his own independent existence? Or is the *tsibur* so overwhelmingly collectively based that it cannot interact with an individual beyond its purview?

It appears that the *tsibur* can indeed interact with a *yahid*.

The Talmud in Yoma 50b discusses several things. First, the question is whether the bull sacrifice on Yom Kippur is the *kohen gadol's* (high priest's) personal offering, or if it is a communal offering. On one hand, the *kohen gadol* must consecrate the bull from his private property. On the other, the offering effects atonement for all the *kohanim* (priests). Does this imply that the offering is communal?

The question eventually evolves into asking whether the *kohanim* receive atonement as partners (*be-kviuta mitkapri*) in which case the offering is communal, or whether they receive atonement through a different process (*be-kufya*), in which case it is private. What does *be-kufya* mean? The commentators explain that it means that the *kohanim* are considered to be "hovering" over the sacrifice of the *kohen gadol*. This means that the community does not have any ownership or tangible participation in the offering; rather, they are included in the consequence of the offering (atonement), but not the offering itself. They receive atonement, but not partnership in the sacrifice.

This, then, is a case of the *tsibur* of the *kohanim* interacting and engaging with the *yahid* to such an extent that the atonement of the *kohanim* is dependent on this symbiotic relationship.[189]

---

189   Some contemporary political parallels may be drawn. As stated, the Rogatchover asserted that in halacha the individual always is supreme. However sometimes halacha is operating from a tzibbur-centric framework and thus the collective comes first since the individual is not recognized.

Our current society is in a state of upheaval concerning different social welfare and entitlement programs. I think that the nature of the discourse on these subjects is predicated to a large extent on how we conceive of society in general and specifically American society.

To give a concrete example it would be useful to examine Social Security. The nature of Social Security can be seen in two very different ways. One is what I will call a mass-scale individual need. By this I mean a program that caters to the individual, the only obvious caveat being that it caters to the individual on a mass scale. The other perspective would be that this program is at its core servicing the needs of society. As a society we don't want and can't have our elders becoming broke upon retirement as this would cause innumerous problems to the healthy functioning of society.

While this difference may be very theoretical, it can and often does alter the way one understands and advocates for social security. Take for example the fact, that people retiring today are part of the first generation of workers who have paid more in Social Security taxes during their careers than they will receive in benefits after they retire. It's a historic shift that will only get worse for future retirees, according to an analysis by The Associated Press.

A married couple retiring last year after both spouses earned average lifetime wages paid about $598,000 in Social Security taxes during their careers. They can expect to collect about $556,000 in benefits, if the man lives to 82 and the woman lives to 85.

Taking this information into account perhaps it is not possible anymore to conceive of Social Security as a mass-scale individual need if it will in fact detract from the individuals overall fiscal status instead of enhance it. The only alternative moral justification for Social Security would be that it is a societal program meant to better society and is not predicated on enhancing the status of the individual.

The same two-fold approach can be applied to Obamacare and indeed was quite clearly explicated by Justice Scalia in his dissent. Specifically, I think that the core dispute underlying the two sides are two very different conceptions of social welfare programs. Namely, whether they are societal in nature or individual in nature. The majority ruled that merely by dint of one day having to engage in the market, the individual is already considered within the market. This opinion essentially is asserting that the emphasis is placed on society. Since society will one day be forced to deal with this person's health, and it is more beneficial to society to mandate that this individual be within the market now instead of in twenty years, then this person is considered within the healthcare market. Whereas the dissent is suggesting that the emphasis is placed squarely on the individual. Does this individual need healthcare? If the answer is no, then what need is there for further discussion? At the end of the day, a society is merely a collective of many individuals and a social welfare program should then be servicing the needs of the individual, just on a mass-scale.

A stark divide on this issue was embodied by the difference between Soviet Russia and Communism on the one side and American Democracy on the other. The emphasis and conceptualization of the group and collective in communist countries was primarily understood as the group constituting the sole factor to be contended with. A extreme embodiment of the tzibbur construct.

While this is a drastic and dramatic expression of the shutfut and tzibbur divide, the truth is that even within the U.S. we have been experiencing on a smaller scale the expansion of the tzibbur approach to society. America has turned to increasing collectivization. From the federalist papers to establishing a Central Bank to implementing a mandated national health-care system (regardless of whether one is for or against it) is a long and winding road conceptually and practically.

While one is tempted to equate tzibbur and shutfut conceptualization of society as the Left and Right of the political spectrum, it would be an oversimplification and sometimes inaccurate portrayal. Consider that the same people who would strongly advocate for the right to personal freedom and less government intervention are also often the same ones who would advocate outlawing abortion and homosexuality. While the fact that these are religiously motivated concerns definitely complicates the point, I think it still has validity and impact. As well, the same ones who want to increase a central authority's power of intervention in a vast array of issues would also be the same people to assert that women should absolutely have the freedom to have an abortion, that other countries should not be interfered with and that illegal immigrants should not be bothered or otherwise harassed. Obviously these are simplifications (perhaps overly so) and I have articulated these positions without much nuance but the general point is, I think, a strong and valid one.

We can perhaps say the following without much qualification. In general the libertarian view seems to favor viewing society as a group of individuals- the shutfut approach. While the liberal view seems to favor viewing society as a single mass unit of identity and cohesion- the tzibbur approach.

Chapter Six

"Colorful Halakhah"

What is color? Does the appearance and color of an item have anything to do with its internal identity? Or is it of an external nature, merely a layer of appearance that interacts with the viewer, and not a statement of its intrinsic character?

The Rogatchover developed an intriguing and engaging theory for understanding how halakhah views color.

The Talmud in *Hulin* (136b)[190] records a dispute between Shammai and Hillel regarding figs of different colors. The law is that one cannot take *terumah*, one of five different tithes a Jew has to take from his produce in order to remove its sanctity and permit it for consumption, from one species of produce for another species of produce. For example, one cannot tithe oranges for

---

[190] דתניא היו לו שני מיני תאנים שחורות ולבנות וכן שני מיני חטין אין תורמים ומעשרים מזה על זה ר' יצחק
אומר משום ר' אלעאי ב"ש אומרים אין תורמין וב"ה אומרים תורמין

"If one had two different colored figs, one black and one white, Bet Shammai says we cannot tithe from one to the other and Bet Hillel says we can."

apples. Each plant, vegetable, and fruit has to have the tithe separated from its own species in order to make the rest of the produce permitted for consumption.

The Talmud asks whether one can take *terumah* from black figs in order to permit white figs. Is that permissible? Shammai says no and Hillel says yes.

In the world of the Rogatchover, this debate revolves around the nature of color. Is it merely an incidental part of an item, or is it integral to its existence?[191] Is it intrinsic or extrinsic? The Rogatchover[192] [193] [194] explains this as follows.

If color is an essential property of an entity, then white and black figs are considered separate species, and a person cannot tithe from one to the other. If, however, color and appearance are merely incidental, then the hue of the fig is not a determining factor, and it is permissible to tithe from one to the other.

The issue of color, and the conceptual position one takes on it, gains new gravity when we come to the laws of Shabbat. We know that there are thirty-nine forbidden forms of labor on

---

191   The Rambam in Moreh Nevukhim (part 1, chapter 73) discusses the nature of color. He brings the opinions of the Mutakallemim that color is intrinsic to physical matter. They say that if one takes snow, for example, the white color is there in every piece of snow and is part of its very existence. The Rambam however rejects their opinion and says that one sees that when things are ground down into tiny flecks and turn into powder the color is gone. Therefore color is only part of the whole and not existent in the individual parts.

192   See Michtevei Torah#283:

בגדר

צורח בלא חומר מחלוקת בית שמאי ובית הלל חולין דף

קלו ע״ב אם מראה הוה מציאות אף דזה גדר צורר בלא

חומר, דאם יטחן החומר לדק נתבטל המראה כמ״ש בספר

המורה בהקדמות של המדברים

193   See also Shut Warsaw Siman 50:

ועיין בחולין דף קלו

ע״ב דב״ש וב״ה פליגי אם שינוי מראת הוי מין אחד

או ב׳ מינים

194   Michtevei Torah #55:

ותליא אם מראה הוה עצם איכות, או רק

מכמות,

In other words, this question can be formulated in a way that lends itself to a discussion of quality versus quantity. See Chapter ? for more on this.

Shabbat. One of them is coloring, or *tsoveah*. But a dye that can be removed is not considered coloring insofar as the laws of Shabbat are concerned. The Rambam states this clearly:[195]

"A person is not liable unless the dye he uses will make **a permanent change** in the article's color [emphasis mine]. When the application of color will not have a permanent effect, e.g., one who applies red clay or vermilion to iron or brass and colors it, is not liable, for it can be removed immediately without dyeing it at all. Whenever a person performs a labor that does not have a permanent effect on the Sabbath, he is not liable."

The Rambam in *Hilkhot Shabbat* (chapter 9, halakhah 14) states:[196]

"A person who creates a color is liable [for performing] a derivative of the labor of dyeing. What is implied? One mixed gallnut juice into vitriol until the entire mixture turned black, or mixed isatis into saffron water until the entire mixture turned green, and the like."

So, in mixing different hues in water and creating colors, one infringes upon the prohibition of coloring. The *Raavad* objects to the Rambam's ruling,[197] noting that in the Talmudic discussion of mixing dyes and colors, there is no mention of the prohibition of coloring. Instead, a different category of forbidden work is given as the source for the prohibition of mixing colors into water. The dispute is whether one who mixes color into water has infringed upon the Biblical injunction not to color on Shabbat. The Rambam says they have, but the *Raavad* objects.

On the surface, it is a simple dispute, with not much nuance. But the Rogatchover[198] injects into it a conceptual battleground

---

195   Hilkhot Shabbat Chapter 9 halakhah 13.

196

העושה עין הצבע—הרי זה תולדת צובע, וחייב. כיצד: כגון שנתן קלקנתוס לתוך מי עפצא, שנעשה הכול שחור; או שנתן איסטיס לתוך מי כרכום, שנעשה הכול ירוק; וכן כל כיוצא בזה

197

ואני לא הייתי סבור שיתחייב משום צובע עד שיצבע דבר שנגמרה בו מלאכת הצבע אבל צביעת מים שאינה לצורך עצמן לא, ושריית דיו וסמנין משום לש באו לה ולא משום צבע המים, כמו שרית הכרשינין וכעין מים וקמח או מים ועפר.

198   In Michtevei Torah #37:

הארכתי בזה, במים,

between the Rambam and the *Raavad* about the very nature of color and appearance.

The Rambam essentially is arguing the following. Water that was colored has been completely altered and given a new identity. The color, he says, has penetrated the essence of the water. One is therefore liable for coloring on Shabbat because he has created a permanent hue in the water. The *Raavad* disputes this, asserting that when one colors water, there is no real effect on the water. One has merely added a layer of tint and hue to the water, but the water remains essentially the same, colorless. In actuality, no real change has been made in the water, and thus there is no infringement of the law, since halakhically an act is not coloring if there is no permanence.

Why is this, though? Why must we have permanence in order to call this halakhic "coloring" instead of a superficial overlay?

It is because, according to the Rogatchover, to color something is not just to give it a new layer of appearance, but to fundamentally alter its identity. From the halakhic perspective, coloring and painting is an irrevocable creative act of redefinition. As such, it must obviously be permanent; once an entity has been redefined, it now has a new identity, which cannot be taken from it. Anything less is not redefinition, but instead just adding an external layer that can later be removed.

To justify this incredible statement, let us look at several building blocks of the Rogatchover's theory.

According to Jewish law,[199] a thief can acquire a stolen item if he effects a permanent change in it. For example, if a thief steals raw wool, then smooths and dyes it, it becomes his property. This is because, in essence, the original item no longer exists, and so it is impossible to return it.[200] If, however, the change effected by the thief can be undone, then he has not acquired the item and

---

אם עצם הדבר נשתנה, או רק שיש בהם הצבע, ועיין
במת דפליגי הרמב״ם והראב״ד בתל׳ שבת פ״ט הי״ז,
וסבירא ליה דחז, רק עירב ולא מציאות שינוי

199   Bava Kama 79a
200   According to rabbinic law, even a change that can be reversed transfers ownership to the thief in order to encourage robbers to repent. See Bava Kama 95a

must return it, since it is able to revert to its original form and thus is still extant. This, in turn, creates an obligation to return the stolen object.

The Talmud in *Bava Kama* (101a) asks[201] an intriguing question. When one steals dye and uses it to color a piece of wool, what is the thief's obligation regarding returning the stolen dye? The Talmud says that it depends on how we understand the idea of color. As Rashi asks,[202] "Is appearance an existence or not?"

If color has a substantive existence of its own, then halakhically the dye is considered to be extant (and located on the surface of the wool). If color is not accorded a substantive existence, then we view the dye as having been absorbed into the wool and subsumed by it. It no longer exists as an independent entity.

The question then becomes[203] the following. One possibility is that the dye is not on the wool, i.e., it is gone by means of absorption, and hence the thief must pay the owner. The other is that the dye still exists independently on the surface of the wool, and therefore the thief need not pay the owner, because he can say to him, "Here is the dye before you."

This passage of Gemara is a core building block of the Rogatchover's theory of color. We have here a practical halakhic query based on a philosophical question of the nature of color.

201

איבעיא להו

יש שבח סמנין על הצמר או אין שבח

סמנין על הצמר

"They asked- is there substance to the color on the wool or is there no substance to the color on the wool".

202

כלומר חזומא מילחא היא או לאו

מילחא

203

אין שבח סמנין

על גבי הצמר ובעי שלומי ליה או דלמא

יש שבח סמנין על גבי צמר וא״ל מנחי

קמך שקלינהו שקלינהו

"Is the dye not on the wool [i.e. it is gone by means of absorption], and hence the thief must pay or is the dye on the wool and therefore the thief need not pay since he can tell the owner 'here is the dye before you.'"

The Rogatchover contends[204] that in our case, the color permeates the very essence of the wool and irrevocably alters its identity. This means that the thief need not make restitution to the owner, because the dye indeed still exists, and he can say, "Here is the dye before you."

This is true even if one bleaches the wool and removes the dye. Since the color has permeated its core, it has changed it forever, even if the new color departs from it.[205] Thus we see that to paint is to fundamentally create a new entity. Once that new entity is formed, it makes no difference if it sheds the outer layer of appearance that was introduced to it, since the new appearance has drilled into its metaphysical core.

This explains the Talmud's ruling that if one dyes wool with a liquid that is absolutely prohibited (i.e., it is forbidden to have

---

204   In Michtevei Torah #37:

ורק גבי צמר אמרינן יש

שבח סמנים ע"ג. ר"ל דגוף הצמר נעשה כמו עיקר

האיסור, ולא מהני אם העבירו ע"י צפון, זה דיוק הגמ'

ב"ק דף קא, דאל"כ למה לו להדליק, יעבור עליו צפון,

וע"כ דנעשה עצם, וכמו חתיכה נעשית נבלה גבי בשר

בחלב,

205   In this respect, color can be linked to the halakhic concept of *chatikha nasa neveila* or 'a piece that becomes a carcass'. This is the halakhah that a piece of meat that absorbs some milk is fundamentally changed into a new entity.

"Rav said (Hulin 108a), once the milk has imparted taste to the piece of meat, the meat itself becomes *neveila* (meat which was not properly slaughtered), and causes all of the other pieces of meat to be prohibited."

The Rishonim explain that Rav does not relate to the piece of meat as a mixture of meat and milk, but rather views the meat as if it were inherently prohibited. Therefore, when this meat is mixed with other pieces of meat, we do not attempt to contrast the drop of milk with the rest of the mixture, but we must rather neutralize the impact of the entire piece of meat on the mixture. The Talmud describes this phenomenon as "*Chaticha Na'aseit Neveila*,". How can we understand this phenomenon?

The permitted meat is transformed into a prohibited substance and is viewed as the prohibition itself instead of just something that was impacted by the forbidden item. In our case, the piece of meat itself is viewed as a prohibited substance and we no longer focus on the milk that prohibited the meat in the first place.

This is true even if one squeezes all the milk out of the piece of meat. It is of no consequence since the meat underwent a metamorphosis and its identity transformed into a prohibited item and is not anymore contingent on the original forbidden agent, the milk.

any sort of pleasure from it at all), we must burn the wool. The question is, why can we not bleach the wool and extract all the color and dye that was inserted into it?

According to our analysis, it is crystal clear. Even once we extract all the dye, this wool remains something that has, as part of its identity, the forbidden liquid. Hence, it is prohibited entirely and forever, since the dye has irrevocably altered its core identity.

A similar parallel to this can be found in the Tosefta of *Avodah Zarah* (chapter 7, halakhah 1).[206] The Tosefta records a dispute about the wood of an *asherah* tree. An *asherah* tree is one planted with the intent to serve it as an idol. The law is that it is prohibited entirely (*assur be-hanaah*). One cannot receive any form of benefit from it, and it must be burned. What about something dyed by soaking it with branches from an *asherah* tree? The Sages say it must be burned, but the dissenting opinion says that we soak the item in plain water until the color it has received from the *asherah* tree is gone.

The underlying conceptual bases for these legislative positions are rooted in different understandings of color. The Sages say that the color has permeated the core of the item, and even if one succeeds in removing the color by soaking, this item must still be burned, since it has been redefined by the *asherah* tree. The other opinion says otherwise. Color is, at the end of the day, only what we can see on the surface. If the color from the tree is gone, then there is no problem.

Let us now turn to a slightly different application of this theme.

The Talmud in *Sotah* (16b) brings a dispute about color. The law is that a *metsorah* (a sort of spiritual leper) must undergo a purification process that involves slaughtering a bird and letting the blood drip into an earthenware vessel containing fresh spring water. The Biblical source for this is *Vayikra* 14:5:

וְצִוָּה, הַכֹּהֵן, וְשָׁחַט, אֶת-הַצִּפּוֹר הָאֶחָת—אֶל-כְּלִי-חֶרֶשׂ, עַל-מַיִם חַיִּים

206

קלא אילן שרשם בעצי אשרה ישרף אחרים אומרים מטילין אותה לחומר עד שיחזרו מראיו לכמות שהיה

"And the priest shall command to kill one of the birds in an earthen vessel over running water."

And then again in 14:51:

וְלָקַח אֶת-עֵץ-הָאֶרֶז וְאֶת-הָאֵזֹב וְאֵת שְׁנִי הַתּוֹלַעַת, וְאֵת הַצִּפֹּר הַחַיָּה, וְטָבַל אֹתָם בְּדַם הַצִּפֹּר הַשְּׁחוּטָה, וּבַמַּיִם הַחַיִּים

"And he shall kill one of the birds in an earthen vessel over running water. And he shall take the cedar-wood, and the hyssop, and the scarlet, and the living bird, and dip them **in the blood** of the slain bird, and **in the running water**" (emphasis mine).

Disregarding the complex array of items to be dipped, what is clear is that the Torah requires the *kohen* to dip the bundle of items into blood and water. This is easily enough accomplished, because the blood of the slaughtered bird has to be allowed to drip into a vessel of water.

The dispute in *Sotah* concerns how much water there can be in the vessel, and what proportion of blood must be in the concoction.

Rabbi Yehudah says[207] that no more than a *reviit* (a couple of ounces) of water can be in the mixture, because if there is any more water, the blood will be completely absorbed into the water, and will not be seen.

The Sages dispute this, asserting that there is no maximum amount of water. Even if the water looks clean and not at all like blood, this is of no consequence.

Tosafot remarks that we know from several places in Torah that even with an amount of water much bigger than a *reviit*, if one mixes even a small amount of wine into it, the wine will be visible and recognizable. If this is the case with wine, then it must be all the more true for blood, which is a more vibrant hue of red. *Tosafot* answers that Rabbi Yehudah is saying that the color and appearance of blood is not enough. Rather, the blood must

---

207

מביא מים שדם ציפור ניכר בהן וכמה
רביעית

have a distinctive consistency and solidity. If not, one has merely dipped the bundle of items into blood-colored water, and not blood itself.

The Rogatchover[208] sees in this text a source for his theory of color in halakhah. Rabbi Yehudah essentially is saying that color does not permeate the essence of an item; it is merely incidental and external to its real identity. If this is true, then even if the water is bright red, it is not really like blood. To be like blood, it must also have the consistency and texture of blood. Only if the blood can be felt and seen to be independent of the water can we say that this mixture is halakhically considered to be blood. Dipping the mixture of items into it satisfies the obligation to dip into blood. This is because he holds that appearance does not define a thing's identity. When Torah commands us to dip something in blood, it must be real blood. The Sages, however, say that appearance does speak to a thing's true identity. Therefore, a blood-water mixture falls into the category of blood, and we can use this mixture for dipping even if there is no substance to the elements of blood in the water.

With this in mind, we can understand a puzzling passage of Gemara in *Makot*.

There are certain requirements a mikvah (ritual bath) must meet to be kosher for use. A mikvah must contain forty *seah* of water, the amount considered necessary to allow the complete immersion of a person of average size. (A *seah* is about thirteen liters.) There are thirty-four *lug* in a single *seah*. After multiplying, we see that a mikvah needs 960 lug of water.

Another one of the rules of a mikvah is that the water must not have been contained in a vessel or filled by means of a vessel, but rather must have been gathered naturally, i.e., through rainfall. Once the mikvah has naturally attained the standard quantity of

---

208   In Michtevei Torah #37:

ועיין בתום׳

סוטה דף טז ע״ב׳ וברמב״ם בחל׳ ביאת מקדש פ״ה, הי״ב

משמע קצת דכשר, ובחילוק תוס׳ סוטה דף טז הנ״ל,

ובאמת בנטילת ידים פסול, וזה ד״ל חזותא בחולין דף

קז, ור״ל אף כת״ג׳ ואתי שפיר מ״ש התוס׳

forty *seah* of water, nothing, except reduction or discoloration, can then affect its efficacy.

When it has not yet filled to the required volume of forty *seah*, however, the mikvah is not yet fit for use. The addition of only three *lug* of drawn water, that is, water carried in a vessel, invalidates the mikvah in its entirety. The addition, however, of milk, wine, or fruit juice neither disqualifies the mikvah nor contributes to the required forty *seah*. It simply has no effect.

The Talmud in *Makot* (3b) explains[209] that three *lug* of water mixed with paint invalidates a mikvah, while three *lug* of water that a tiny amount of wine (a *kortov*) has fallen into and colored red does not. What is the difference between the two? In both cases, three *lug* of water has discolored the mikvah. Seemingly it should be invalid in either case. Why does the paint and water mixture invalidate the mikvah, while the wine and water mixture does not?

The Talmud answers that this is because a mixture of water and wine is called diluted <u>wine</u>, i.e., we do not perceive it as colored water. Rather, it is seen as diluted wine. A paint and water mixture, however, is still essentially perceived as water that has been colored, instead of paint that has become runny and more liquid. Therefore, since we know that wine has no effect on a mikvah for good or ill, the wine and water mixture does not invalidate it. The paint and water mixture, however, is still perceived as water, and water that discolors a mikvah does indeed disqualify it.

But why is the mixture of wine in water perceived entirely different then paint in water?

The difference lies in the nature of the coloring or dyeing that these waters undergo. In one case, actual wine is mixed with water, coloring it red. Hence, the water becomes a fundamentally different entity and is now diluted wine. But the paint and water mixture, in this particular case, is just water that has sat

---

209 ואמר רב יהודה אמר רב שלשת לוגין מים שנפל לתוכן קורטוב של יין ומראיהן כמראה יין ונפלו למקוה לא פסלוהו מתקיף לה רב כהנא וכי מה בין זה למי צבע דתנן ר' יוסי אומר מי צבע פוסלין את המקוה בשלשת לוגין א"ל רבא התם מיא דצבעא מקרי הכא חמרא מזיגא מקרי"

in a bowl with paintbrushes and leaves,[210] without having actual paint mixed in. As such, it does not take on an entirely new identity.

This makes such a fundamental difference because, as we learned from the case of purification of a *metsorah*, the issue of solidity depends on one's position on color. The wine and water mixture contains actual wine. This means that even though we say that color has no relevance to the internal identity of water, as in Rabbi Yehudah's position above, nevertheless, in our case, actual wine has been added. Hence there is solidity and substance to the wine in the water.

That being the case, there is only pure color and appearance, without solidity to the color. Therefore we still perceive it as water, and hence it invalidates the mikvah, as per the law that discolored water invalidates a mikvah, while wine does not.

Since forming color and appearance is seen as an irrevocable creative act, as we saw in the case of the thief and the wool, it is no surprise that the Talmud employs this imagery for G-d's act of creation. The Talmud in *Nidah* (31)[211] compares the forming of man to one who paints with different colors. The Talmud in *Berakhot* (10a), using a clever etymological twist, interprets the verse "there is no rock like G-d" as saying "there is no artist like G-d."

This fascination and fixation with portraying G-d as an artist is because the act of forming color and appearance is seen halakhically as an existential and fundamentally creative act.

---

210   See Bet Yosef Yoreh De'ah Siman 201

211

על כי נוראות נפליתי נפלאים מעשיך ונפשי יודעת מאד בא וראה שלא כמדת הקב"ה מדת בשר ודם
מדת בשר ודם נותן זרעונים בערוגה כל אחת ואחת עולה במינו ואילו הקב"ה צר העובר במעי אשה
וכולם עולין למין אחד דבר אחר צבע נותן סמנין ליורה כולן עולין לצבע אחד ואילו הקב"ה צר העובר
במעי אשה כל אחת ואחת עולה למינו

"R. Yose the Galilean gave the following exposition: What is the meaning of the Scriptural text, 'I will give thanks unto Thee, for I am fearfully and wonderfully made; wonderful are Thy works; and that my soul knows well'? Come and see the contrast between the potency of the Holy One, blessed be He, and that of mortal man.

If a dyer puts different ingredients into a boiler they all unite into one color, whereas the Holy One, blessed be He, fashions the embryo in a woman's stomach in a manner that each element develops in its own natural way."

The Talmud in Berakhot (10a)[212] also indulges in this fascination with G-d as an artist.

212

מאי דכתיב (תהילים קג) ברכי נפשי את ה' וכל קרבי את שם קדשו אמר ליה בא וראה שלא כמדת הקדוש ברוך הוא מדת בשר ודם מדת בשר ודם צר צורה על גבי הכותל ואינו יכול להטיל בה רוח ונשמה קרבים ובני מעים והקב"ה אינו כן צר צורה בתוך צורה ומטיל בה רוח ונשמה קרבים ובני מעים והיינו דאמרה חנה (שמואל א ב) אין קדוש כה' כי אין בלתך ואין צור כאלהינו. מאי אין צור כאלהינו אין צייר כאלהינו

"What does it mean " Let my soul bless the Lord and all my innards his holy name"? He replied, come see how the ways of the Lord are entirely different then the ways of flesh and blood [i.e. man]. Flesh and blood paints a picture on the wall and is not able to insert into it life or a soul, stomach and intestines. Whereas G-d is not so. He can paint a picture within a picture and inserts into it life and a soul, stomach and intestines. This is what Hannah said "there is none as holy as the Lord for there is nothing besides you and there is no rock as our G-d". What does it mean no rock? It means there is no artist like our G-d."

Chapter Seven

Hillel and Shammai

The schools of Shammai and Hillel were intellectual and scholarly rivals for hundreds of years and were major influencers of the development of Torah. Between Hillel and Shammai themselves there were only three (possibly five) disputes. But 316 arguments between the schools they founded are recorded in the Talmud. Of these arguments, 221 revolve around various *halakhot*, 66 are *gezeirot* (preventative laws), and 29 are discrepancies over Biblical and legislative interpretations. Despite Shammai having a tendency to be strict and Hillel leaning towards the lenient, in 55 of these disputes (fully one-sixth), Shammai ruled on the side of leniency.

Many theories have been proposed as to the central (or at least one of the central) differences between the schools. Before offering the Rogatchover's thesis I will briefly cover (in order of ascending credibility and substantiveness) some of the theories bandied about in the world of Talmudic scholarship.

The Psychological Theory

One theory is that the core difference was a psychological one. Namely that Hillel scholars were kinder, and peace loving men, whereas Shammai scholars were stern, uncompromising and harsh.

The typical proof brought in support of this theory is the following Gemara in Shabbat 31a:

"A gentile once came to convert to Judaism, on the condition that he could learn the whole Torah while standing on one foot. He approached Shammai, who rejected him, so he went to Hillel, who taught him: "That which you dislike do not do to your fellow: That's the basis of Torah. The rest is commentary; go learn!"

Another gentile who wanted to accept only the written Torah came to convert. Shammai chased him away, so he went to Hillel. The first day, Hillel taught him the Hebrew alphabet. The next day he reversed the letters. The convert was confused: "But yesterday you said the opposite!?" Said Hillel: "Now you see that the written word alone is insufficient. We need the Oral Tradition to understand the Written".

A third gentile was very impressed by the Priestly garments and came to convert. Again, Shammai dismissed him, but Hillel encouraged him to study more. After learning, he came to realize that even David, King of Israel did not qualify to serve as a priest in the Temple, because he was not born a Cohen."

More support for this approach is brought from the following (Pirkei Avot 1:12):

"Hillel said: Love people and bring them closer to Torah".

Another quote (Pirkei Avot 2:4): "Hillel taught; do not judge your friend until you reach his place."

While the simplistic and contemporary applications of this theory are appealing, a more thorough analysis reveals that this almost certainly cannot be the core difference between the schools.

Consider the following quotes. Shammai said (in Pirkei Avot 1:15): "Welcome everyone with a pleasant demeanor".

As well as the following (Pirkei Avot 3:4): "Hillel condemned a skull he saw floating by on the river saying, "Because you drowned others you yourself were drowned".

Not exactly the typical statements one would expect from these two schools if they were indeed split by kindness and sternness.

More sources at odds with this theory:

Gitin 90a: "Hillel said one has grounds for divorce even if his wife committed the most minor of mistakes such as burning his dinner. Shammai on the other hand said one can only divorce his wife if she was promiscuous."

Yebamot 14a : "Even though Bet Shammai and Bet Hillel argued about the issue of sisters, rivals (*tzarot*), an old bill of divorce (*get yashan*), a doubtfully married woman (*safek eishet ish*), a woman whom her husband had divorced and who stayed with him over-night in an inn (*lan imo bepundak*), money (*kessef*), valuables (*shava kessef*), a *prutah* (small coin) and the value of a *prutah*, Bet Shammai nevertheless did not abstain from marrying wom-en from the families of Bet Hillel, nor did Bet Hillel refrain from marrying women from the families of Bet Shammai.

[In other words, notwithstanding that all these are serious mar-ital issues that they disputed, they both still waived their legis-lative misgivings and married each other even though many of these disputed legal issues were bound to come up.]

This teaches that they showed love and friendship towards each other, thus putting into practice the Biblical text: Love truth and peace."

Mishnah Yebamot 15:2: A woman arrives from a distant land (and therefore cannot reasonably be expected to produce wit-nesses) and relates that her husband has died, asks to be rec-ognized as a widow and thus be eligible to receive her *ketubah* (marriage settlement) and remarry.

Bet Shammai accepts her request while Bet Hillel declares, "She may marry, but not claim her marriage contract." According to Bet Hillel, she is released according to the laws of matrimony but not as far as monetary laws are concerned since these may be judged only in a Bet Din with two witnesses. In other words, since her release was not carried out in a normative legal manner, she is not entitled to receive her marriage settlement.

So, while Bet Shammai draws the full legal conclusion and frees the woman from all vestiges of her former marriage, Bet Hillel separates the financial contract from the discussion of her personal matrimonial status.

Again, hardly the practices one would posit of the harsh and stern Shammai postulated by this theory. The disproofs to this theory are manifold, but I will suffice with these. As we will see, this theory has some elements of truth to it though the proponents of this theory have misappropriated these elements and sought to build upon these points in seclusion to all else, which is a crucial mistake.

In general it is a critical mistake to assume that Shammai and Hillel, two of the biggest schools of scholars in Torah, developed legislative positions in accordance with their own personal emotional preferences and not from an objective standpoint and a careful measured analysis of the subject matter.

The Socioeconomic Theory

Another theory proffered is that there were socioeconomic differences between the schools; that is, that Bet Shammai expressed the attitudes of the upper classes and Bet Hillel, those of the lower.[213] For example, when Bet Shammai maintained that on the eve of the Sabbath or a festival one should first recite the blessing over the day and then that over the wine, and Bet Hillel contended that the wine should be blessed first (Berakhot Chapter 8 Mishnah 8), each school's position can be seen to reflect its socioeconomic background. The wealthy commonly used wine at their meals, and so its use in no way indicated the festive nature of the Sabbath or festival. For the poor, however, the pres-

---

213   There are those who combine the psychological and socioeconomical theories.

ence of wine at the table suggested the specialness of the day, so Bet Hillel decided that the blessing over it had to be recited first.

Again this theory is laid bare to criticism when one considers the lack of supporting evidence and the scarce amount of debates it explains between the schools. As well, it possesses the same critical mistake as before in assuming that the Shammai and Hillel scholars let emotional and social factors be the primary determinants of their analysis and subsequent legal rulings.

The Hermeneutical Theory

Some scholars have maintained that the two schools had distinct analytical approaches. For example, Bet Shammai tended to be more literal in its exegesis, explaining the verse "when thou liest down and when thou risest up" (Deut. 6:7) to mean that the *shema* should be recited in the evening while reclining and in the morning while standing. Bet Hillel understood the intention to be that the *shema* is said at the time when people are accustomed to lie down and when they arise (Berakhot Chapter 1 Mishnah 3), thus lending themselves to a more abstract approach in their understanding of the Torah.

The Intent Theory

Some have proposed that Bet Hillel insisted that a halakhic act had to be accompanied by intention, whereas Bet Shammai emphasized the deed itself. A common example pertains to the law that foods consumed on a festival must be prepared the day before. The question arose as to whether an egg laid on the festival day could be eaten (Betsah Chapter 1 Mishnah 1). Bet Shammai permitted its consumption because it viewed the egg as having been readied, albet by the hen, the day before. Bet Hillel however, regarded this preparation as inadequate, since no one could have anticipated that the egg would actually be laid on the festival day and therefore no one had intention for the egg, thus rendering it *muktzah*.

The Analytical Theory

A fifth theory postulated is that Shammai held that one should view things as they are with a cursory glance and from an immediate and summary analysis. On the other hand, Hillel held that one should gaze deeply into something and observe all its particulars and inner details before pronouncing judgment.

An expression of this conceptual divide can be seen in the following three *gemarot*:

1. Ketubot (16b-17a):

The Rabbis taught: How does one dance before the bride?

Bet Shammai say: [One describes] the bride as she actually is.

Bet Hillel say: "[Call her] a beautiful and graceful bride."

Bet Shammai said to Bet Hillel: What if she is lame or blind? Shall we say to her, "A beautiful and graceful bride"? But the Torah said, "You shall distance yourself from matters of falsehood"!

What does this debate hinge upon? Proponents of this theory want to say it is a reflection of the intellectual divide between the schools. Shammai says if she is ugly then how can one lie and say she is beautiful? This is because Shammai advances a simplistic view of reality. If she does not appear beautiful then one cannot invent her beauty.

Hillel says no. We must look closer and peer into the bride's character. If the *chattan* is marrying her, surely she appears beautiful in his eyes! Perhaps she has sterling brilliant emotional and intellectual faculties? Perhaps the groom likes her form and unique composition? Indeed if she is a cripple, do not praise her feet but there are other ways to be attractive and desirable then feet.[214]

---

214   The same pattern can be said to apply to the stories of the converts above. Shammai related to the potential converts according to the general impression they initially projected, while Hillel patiently considered the full picture into which the person could blossom.

2. Berakhot Chapter 8 Mishnah 5:

There is an argument between Bet Shammai and Bet Hillel about what the *beracha* on seeing the fire by *havdalah* is. Bet Shammai say that the *beracha* is

ברוך אתה ה' אלו ק ינו מלך העולם שברא מאור האש

– Blessed You Hashem, our G-d, King of the world, Who created the light (single) of fire.

Bet Hillel says, that the *beracha* ends on the words

בורא מאורי האש

– Who creates the lights of fire (plural).

This is because the philosophy of Hillel is, that one must inquire closely after the nature of an item before deciding *halakhah*, therefore since if one gazes into the fire they will see various different colors one must make a blessing that incorporates the different parts of the item being blessed. Hence: "Who creates the lights of the fire".

Whereas Shammai rejects this and says that since from a superficial quick glance the flame of a fire appears to be just one color, no further inquiry is necessary and one makes a blessing "Who created the light of the fire", thanking G-d for the one (color of) flame.

3. Keilim Chapter28 Mishnah 4:

A third example of this pattern can be seen in the interpretation of the difference of opinion between the School of Shammai and the School of Hillel in regard to whether or not the covers of sacred scrolls are susceptible to the contraction of ritual impurity. The School of Shammai maintains that regardless of whether the cover of a scroll is embroidered with ornamental patterns or not, the cover is susceptible to ritual impurity. Bet Hillel rejects this.

The ruling of the School of Hillel is based on the principle that it is functional articles, not ornaments, which are susceptible to ritual impurity. As such, an ordinary cover is considered as an article which serves a purpose, and therefore is susceptible to ritual impurity. The primary purpose of an embroidered cover, however, is considered its aesthetic dimension, and not the function it serves. Hence, such a cover is not susceptible to ritual impurity.

The advocators of this theory explain why the School of Shammai does not make a distinction between one type of cover and the other. Since at first glance, both types of covers appear the same, no differentiation is made between the rulings that apply to them. The School of Hillel, by contrast, accentuates the particular characteristics of each type of cover, and accordingly, places them in different categories. In this instance as well, the School of Hillel's approach is characterized by a patient process of distinction that focuses on the particulars, while the approach of the School of Shammai focuses on the general impression that immediately arises.[215]

The Futuristic Theory

Another thesis developed to explain the different approaches of the schools of Hillel and Shammai is that the core difference is based on a concept called *"kol ha'omed le'hai'asos ke'asui dami"*; anything which is about to happen is considered as if it already happened.[216]

According to this concept, a plaintiff possessing a I.O.U. document that has been validated and is going to be used to collect payment is considered to already have the money that he is about to collect.

According to Shammai, we consider something that will happen to have the same validity as if it already transpired.

---

215   The intent is not that the School of Shammai does not have the ability to discern particulars. On the contrary, our Sages (Yebamot 14a; Tosafot, Eruvin 6b) describe them as being "sharper and more astute," than the School of Hillel. Nevertheless, according to this theory, their powers of discernment were focused on abstracting a general impression from the particulars, and not on appreciating the particulars per se.

216   See Bet Haotzer Maarechet 1 Klal 27 at some length

Hillel says on the other hand that until the event transpires we cannot view it as having occurred. (See Yebamot 38b and Sotah 25b for complex situations where this would make a difference in certain rulings of the court.)

The Potential Theory

The most convincing and compelling theory postulated until the time of the Rogatchover was the theory of *koach* and *poel*, or potential versus actual. What this means is that there are two basic ways in which one might view something: in light of its potential, or by its actual, manifest state. We might say of a certain person: He has tremendous potential, but his actual performance is poor. The same can be said of a corporation, a relationship, an experience, or anything else. Or we might say: There's potential for disaster here, but it can be contained and prevented from actualizing.

Some of us are potential-oriented, which means that we would admire the person, invest in the company, stick it out with the relationship and treasure the experience—depending upon its potential. Others among us are more actual-oriented, viewing things in terms of their bottom line—their actual, tangible impact upon reality.[217]

This then is the central issue over which Shammai and Hillel divide. For example, the sages of Shammai consider the moment of the Exodus to be the eve of the fifteenth of Nissan, when the people of Israel were free to leave Egypt, while the sages of Hillel place the moment at midday of the following day, when the Jews actually exited Egypt's physical borders. (The question of the precise moment of the Exodus has certain *halakhic* repercussions, such as the procedure for reciting *hallel* on the Seder night.)

In another debate, the sages of Shammai consider a fish susceptible to *tumah* (ritual impurity) from the moment the fisherman pulls his catch out of the water, since at this point the fish has been removed from the environment which is its source of life and is therefore *halakhically* considered to be dead, bringing

---

217   The difference between the seventh theory and the sixth above is subtle but existent.

with it the *tumah* that descends upon a creature when it dies. Hillel disagrees, contending that as long as the fish is actually alive (though its potential for continued life has been destroyed since its death is inevitable), it is immune to *tumah*, as are all other living plants and animals.

This is also the basis of their differing perspectives on Chanukah. The House of Shammai, which views things in terms of their potential, sees the first day of Chanukah, with its potential for eight days of light, as the point in which all eight days are there. As a result, according to Shammai one should light all eight lights on the first night.

But after one day has gone by and passed from potential into actuality, there are left only seven days in their most meaningful form—the potential form. The sages of Hillel, on the other hand, see the actual state as the more significant; to them, the eighth day of Chanukah, when all eight dimensions of the festival have been actualized, is when the festival is at its fullest and most real.

Rabbi Shlomo Yosef Zevin in "Le'or Halakhah" (pages 174 to 180) brings 14 examples of debates that can be seen to reflect this core difference.[218]

"The Spiritual and the Tangible"

The schools of Shammai and Hillel were intellectual and scholarly rivals for hundreds of years and were major influencers of the development of Torah. Between Hillel and Shammai themselves

---

218   The Lubavitcher Rebbe in a profound essay (Hadranim Al Harambam Vehashas Volume 1, "Siyum Al Shisha Sidrei Mishnah") takes the Koach and Poel theory to new heights. He says that if Shammai and Hillel already argued once over Koach and Poel as to what takes precedence then what need is there to repeat this debate numerous times in the Talmud. Rather each case recorded contains a novel and unprecedented application of their theory or a "Tzrichuta". So if the fish case was recorded after the Chanukah case that means that the Koach (potential reality) in the fish case is more extreme and even further from the current reality then the Chanukah situation. The same would apply for Hillel, namely there must be some element of Poel that is weaker and less concrete by the fish case that necessitated the Talmud to inform us that even in a situation where the current reality is weak and less grounded, Hillel would still assert that the present outweighs the potential state. The Lubavitcher Rebbe then proceeds to find a Tzrichuta within this theory for numerous debates of the Shammai-Hillel schools.

there were only three (possibly five) disputes. But 316[219] arguments between the schools they founded are recorded in the Talmud. Of these arguments, 221 revolve around various *halakhot*,
66 are *gezeirot* (preventative laws), and 29 are discrepancies over
Biblical and legislative interpretations.[220] Despite Shammai having a tendency to be strict and Hillel leaning towards the lenient,
in 55 of these disputes (fully one-sixth), Shammai ruled on the
side of leniency.

Many theories have been proposed as to the central (or at least
one of the central) differences between the schools. The theories
as to the core conceptual difference between the schools range
from psychological and hermeneutical, to socio-economic and
analytical preferences.

The Rogatchover Gaon's key insight into the core difference between Hillel and Shammai is related to their differing perspectives on the degree to which spiritual versus tangible elements of
reality should be referenced in determining halakhah.

The Talmud in Chagiga 12a states: "The school of Shammai says,
the heavens were created first and then the earth. The school of
Hillel says, the earth was created first and then the heavens."

What does this argument revolve around? Is there an underlying
theme?

Indeed there is.[221] [222] Shammai says the heavens were created
first. By heavens Shammai means spirituality and the intangible. In Shammai's view spirituality is the primary determinant in

---

219   Jewish Encyclopedia, House of Hillel and House of Shammai.

220   Jewish Encyclopedia, Bet Hillel and Bet Shammai.

221   In Michtevei Torah letter #289:

וזה שיטת ב״ה בחגיגה דף יב
דחומר נברא תחלה ואח״כ הצורה היולית, אך ב״ש ס״ל
להיפך, דצורה היולית נבראת תחלה ואח״כ חומר, זה
באמת בכל התורה דעיקר צורת הדבה.

222   In Mahadura Tinyana page 180:

וזה הגדר דפליגי בחגיגה
רף יב, דשמים נבראו תחלה לדעת ב״ש, ור״ל דהצורה
הוא העיקרית, ע״כ. ובשו״ת צ״פ (וּוארשא) סי׳ נ
במחלוקת ב״ש וב״ה בחגיגה יב, שמים נבראו כוי, ר״ל
אם המציאות הוא הצורה או החומר,

halakhah and is the main barometer of reality. Therefore it was created first since it is the dominant reality.

[Spirituality in this context does not have any sort of other-worldly implication. It simply means something that exists in our universe yet is immaterial and lacks concrete substance].

Whereas Hillel says that in our physical world, material considerations are of primary importance, and one must use the physical spectrum as the dominant deciding factor in *halakhah*. Therefore the earth, meaning physicality, was created first.

The Rogatchover[223] proceeds to pinpoint this dispute as the epicenter of two *gemarot* that seemingly have no possible connection to this.

The Talmud in Tractate Shabbas 62b says the following:

A woman may not go out on Shabbat carrying a spice bundle (an ornament worn around the neck in which women would place spices so as to create a fragrance) or a flask of balsam oil. If she did go out she has transgressed the Shabbat and is required to bring a *korban hatat* (an atoning sacrifice in the Temple). This is Rabbi Meir's opinion.

Rabbi Eliezer disagrees and says she has not transgressed the Sabbath and is exempt from a *korban*. The reason she is exempt is because a pendant containing spice or a small flask containing oil are considered to be in the category of *takhshit*, (ornaments). Items that are categorized as a *takhshit* are Biblically permitted to be worn on Shabbat since it is not considered carrying when going out with them. Just as wearing a shirt on one's back is not considered "carrying", so too items that while not being essential have aesthetic or secondary uses and benefits are allowed to be worn on one's person.

Rabbi Eliezer then qualifies his ruling and states that she is only exempt when the spice bundle contained spices inside and the

---

223   In Tsafnat Paneah Sh"ut Dvinsk siman 50:

דזה רק צורה ולא חומר, עי׳ ברכות מג, נשמה

נהנה כו׳ דאין בו ממש, ופליגי בזה שבת סב, אם יש

עליו גדר פחות משיעור,

flask contained oil inside. But if they did not have spice or oil inside them then she is obligated to bring a *korban* (meaning she has transgressed the Sabbath). Since it is not the norm to wear a pendant or a flask when they are empty, they are not considered ornaments when worn empty. Therefore, since they are not able to be classified as ornaments, they revert to *masa* (carrying) status.

[To facilitate a fluid, smooth understanding of the next part of the *gemara* it is necessary to preface the following principle about carrying on Shabbat. In order to transgress the Shabbat it is not enough to simply carry something outside in the public domain. One must carry a certain minimum quantity in order to be Biblically culpable. Each item has its own minimum requirement or *shiur*. For example one carrying food must take out (generally) enough food equal to the size of a dried fig.

The minimum amount for other objects may be less or more, depending upon the specific item in question. For example, one taking out a vessel such as a jar would be Biblically liable even for carrying out a tiny jar, since one has carried a whole, complete vessel. However with food it is not dependent on whether one has carried a complete item, but rather depends on the amount of food being transferred into the public domain.]

The Talmud later in Shabbat on page 93b, discusses an intriguing case concerning one who takes out a jar containing food, where the food does not satisfy the minimum requirement yet the jar does satisfy the *shiur* (since it is a complete vessel). What is the *din* (law)?

Seemingly there should be no question as to their culpability. For the jar (which satisfies the *shiur*) they are liable, and for the food (which does not) they should not be liable.

Yet it is more complex than that. Since the jar is being used as a receptacle for the food, it is viewed as not having its own independent existence and is merely an accessory of the food. Thus one cannot be liable for carrying the jar, since it is not its own *halakhic* entity. Rather, it is an extension of the food. Yet for the food one also cannot be liable since the amount of the food is less than the *shiur*. Thus, counter-intuitively, for carrying out more (the food as well as the jar) one ends up not being liable. (As opposed to if one would have just carried out the jar without the food, in which case they would indeed have been liable).

The Gemara attempts to deduce something from Rabbi Eliezer's opinion. Rabbi Eliezer said that when the flask is empty one is liable since then it is not a *takhshit* (because it is not the normal custom to wear an empty flask).

But what about the scent of the balsam oil that still emanates from the flask? Is not that comparable to the case brought before where one took out food less than the *shiur* in a vessel?

Here too one is taking out two things. The scent that is wafting from the flask (which is less than the *shiur*, since there is no substance to scent that we would then be able to pin a minimum *shiur* on) and the flask itself (which satisfies the *shiur* since it is a complete vessel). Yet still Rabbi Eliezer holds that one is liable in this case! Is he not arguing on the Mishnah on 93b and forming his own opinion? Because according to the Mishnah on 93b one would be exempt since for the scent they cannot be liable because it lacks a minimum *shiur*, and for the flask they also cannot be culpable since the flask is carrying the scent, so the flask is merely an accessory and extension to the smell.

The Talmud answers that these two cases are not conceptually parallel. For smell has no tangibility *(leit bei mamasha)*. Since there is no substance to the scent the flask is considered to be empty and cannot be said to be an accessory to the scent.

What essentially is the discussion here in the Gemara? The Rogatchover sees it as being predicated upon the tension between the tangible and the intangible realms.

Scent here is classified as belonging to the spiritual realm. It is not tangible or concrete at all, and *halakhically* it is viewed as being the only sense that is a sensory tool of the soul, as opposed to being a sensory faculty of the body. (This is why on Saturday night at the closing of *shabbat* we smell spices to comfort the soul as we head into the lesser holiness of the week).

This then is the point. Is smell part of our reality? Are nontangible items viewed as determinants in our decisions and perspectives? If they are, then the smell of the oil in the flask should be viewed as being "something" just that it is less than the *shiur*. If that's the case then the two cases are conceptually parallel and we can build a corollary from one case to the other case. That would dictate that just as when one carries out food in a jar one is *patur* (exempt), since the jar is considered to be an accessory to the food and the food itself lacks the minimum requirement, so too when one carries out a scented flask without actually having scented oil inside, one should be *patur*, since again, one cannot be liable for the jar being that it is an accessory of the scent.

If scent is not viewed as part of our considerations, and *halakhah* only deals with tangible factors, then fragrance is not considered an entity and the flask is properly defined as being empty, thus ending any hopes of building a comparison from the two cases.

Peppery Potential

Another expression[224] of this battle of perspectives is in a Mishnah in Tractate Uktzin (Chapter 3, Mishnah 6). The Mishnah records a dispute between Bet Shammai and Bet Hillel regarding black cumin (*katzach*). Shammai says it is *tahor* (ritually pure) and not susceptible to *tumah* (ritual impurity) since it is not considered a food, as it is too harsh and bitter to eat. [Only food, vessels and structures are able to become ritually impure]. Hillel says it is susceptible to *tumah* since it able to be eaten. On the surface they seem to be arguing about the physical existence of cumin and disputing a factual truth, which is not considered to be an optimal way of understanding *halakhah* and Talmud *(ein makhloket be'metziyut)*.

However our analysis will shed light on this strange, seemingly factual dispute. In order to do so we must first avail ourselves of another statement from the Talmud.

---

224   In Mahadura Tinyana page 180:

ועי' במאי דפליגי בסוף עוקצין

פ"ג מ' ו ב"ש ובי"ה דלב"ש קצח פטור מן המעשרות

והטעם דס"ל דהעיקר הוא הריח, וזה ריחו קשה (ברכות

דף מ). ובשו"ת שם: דס"ל (לבייש) דהעיקר הוא הצורה

והיינו הריח

The Talmud in tractate Berakhot 40a states:

What is *katzach*? Rabbi Chama the son of Chanina said, one who eats a lot of cumin (*katzach*) will not experience illness or heart pains. Rabbi Shimon Ben Gamliel then asked, but *katzach* is recorded as being one of 60 plants that hasten death?

The resolution in the Talmud is that one of the teachings (that *katzach* averts pain and illness) was stated regarding its taste, and the other (that *katzach* hastens death) was concerning its smell. The smell is harsh and hastens death, whereas the taste is healthy and wholesome.

That being the case, Bet Shammai holds that black cumin is not susceptible to *tumah* since its smell is harsh and unhealthy and not fit for consumption. Whereas Bet Hillel holds that we only consider tangible factors and since smell is intangible it is not a factor. Thus we only consider the taste, and the taste is healthy and fit for consumption. Therefore it is susceptible to *tumah* since it is *halakhically* considered a food.

Alcoholic Abstraction

This essential argument between these two schools is also reflected in the following Gemara in Berakhot 43b:

If one has wine (which he intends to drink) and scented oil (which he intends to smell) in front of him, he should take the oil in his right hand and the wine in his left hand. He should then make a blessing on the oil, smell it and then make a blessing on the wine and drink it. This is the opinion of Bet Shammai.

Bet Hillel says the exact opposite: "One should take the wine in his right hand and the oil in his left, make a blessing on the wine and then proceed to the oil.

The explanation given by the commentaries is that Bet Shammai holds that the blessing on the oil takes precedence (and thus is held in the right hand) since the pleasure gained from it is immediate and does not require an action on one's part, whereas the wine's pleasure is only once one drinks it and digests it.

Bet Hillel however reasons that wine, which is consumed by the body, is more significant than oil, which is merely smelled, therefore the blessing on the wine takes precedence.

Yet it has not been explained why Hillel holds that tangible intake of pleasure (consumption of the wine) is more significant than intangible intake of pleasure (smelling)?

Additionally what does Shammai say to Hillel's point about consumption of pleasure versus merely smelling pleasure?

According to our analysis it is clear. Hillel holds that tangible pleasure is more significant than intangible pleasure in accordance with his world view that tangible factors are the primary determinants, as opposed to intangible factors.

And Shammai retorts that quite the contrary, intangible and abstract factors are the primary determinants. Thus the oil (merely smelling) takes precedence.

Solid Sotah

There is a debate in the Talmud about how much of G-d's name needs to be erased before we force the *sotah*[225] to drink the *sotah* waters. Bet Hillel says at least two letters (the first *yud* and the first *hei*) need to be erased. Bet Shammai says even just one letter being erased is enough to compel the drinking of the water. (Yerushalmi Sotah, Chapter 2, halakhah 4).

Elsewhere in the Gemara there is an inquiry concerning how many letters a Sefer Torah must possess in order to retain its status of sanctity. We know from the oral tradition that it needs 85 letters, but the Rabbis were not sure if the 85 letters needed to be together, or even if they could be scattered over the whole Torah scroll (Shabbat115b).

---

225   The *sotah* was a woman suspected of adultery that was brought to the Temple and given a special concoction to drink, which had divine powers to ascertain the veracity of her claims of innocence. She had the option of demanding a divorce instead of drinking the potion. But if the potion had already been prepared, she was forced to drink it, because part of creating the drink involved erasing the Divine name. The sages debated how much of the Divine name needs to be erased before she would be compelled to drink.

In addition, there is an argument about how many extra letters invalidate a *mezuzah* whether even just one or at least two extra letters are required to make it *passul* (Menachot 32b).

What is the thread running through these questions? The commonality they all share is that[226] [227] they all revolve around the identity and character of a single letter. In Hebrew, there are no one-letter words. A word can be composed of even two letters, but a single letter can only ever remain a letter, and will never be a word. That being so perhaps a letter does not have its own inherent identity? Maybe it can never be seen as its own idea, and is always a building block of a word, without ever embodying meaning and content on its own.

Or perhaps there is some intrinsic meaning to a letter on its own and it is considered to be its own *halakhic* entity, notwithstanding its deep seated need to pair with another letter in order to form a word.

Although seemingly disconnected, this is actually the same debate that we saw regarding the *sotah* waters. Shammai says that even if only one letter of G-d's name was erased, that is sufficient to activate the full status of *sotah*. Shammai says this because in his view a single letter is its own entity, and thus by erasing even one letter from G-d's name, one has fragmented the name of G-d and the sanctity of the document has been destroyed.

---

226   In Mahadura Tinyana page 180:

וכן ס״ל לב״ש בירושלמי סוטה

פ״ב (ה״ד) דאף אם כתב אות א׳ מן שם יש בו קדושה,

 וב״ה לא סבירא להו. עי׳ במה דפליגי בזה בשבת קטו,

אם גם להציל מן הדליקה אם גם אותיות מפחורין הוי כן

לצרף לפ״ה אותיות, ע״ש

227   And in Mahadura Tinyana page 52:

והנה מבואר במנחות רף לב, גבי כתבו אגרת, ע״ש בדברי

דבינו דאם הוסיף אפילו אות א׳ בפנים במזוזה אפילו

בפ״ע פסולה המזוזה, ובאמת זה תליא בהך מחלוקת דב״ש

וב״ה דהירושלמי פוטר, פ״ב ופ״ג אם אות א׳ יש עליו גדר

מציאות, או לא חל עליו שם גדר בפ״ע רק חלק, כיון

דכל תיבה באות אי, ע״ש דמבואר דאם כתב בפרשה

פוטר לבייש אות אחת יתירה בפני עצמה שלא בתיבה

שוב נפסלה כל הפרשה סוטה, ואז אם מחקה חייב מלקות

משום השמות שבה, וב״ה ס״ל דוקא עד שיכתוב שתי

אותיות יתירות

Hillel disagrees. One letter on its own is nothing,[228] and is merely a part of the whole. Therefore, by erasing only one letter from G-d's name you have not erased a significant entity and therefore the sanctity of G-d's name is still there. Consequently the Sotah waters were not activated and the woman is not forced to drink and can still recant.

Obviously this is also the debate regarding a mezuzah. If one letter has intrinsic identity, then even one extra letter is adding to the mezuzah scroll and thus it invalidates the entire scroll.

As well as the 85 letters argument. If a single letter stands on its own conceptually and *halakhically* then the 85 letter requirement can be satisfied from 85 single letters. If a letter is not its own entity, then the 85 must be comprised of paired letters.

What does all this have to do with the differing weltanschauungs of Shammai and Hillel? Well if tangibility is the primary determinant of *halakhah* and reality, then a single letter would not stand on its own. This is because in concrete terms and from an empirical viewpoint, a single letter can never contain content or meaning, because there are no single letter words. Thus, a single letter on its own is not considered to be its own entity.

If however, as Shammai asserts, intangibility and spiritual elements are factors to be reckoned with, then a single letter does stand on its own. This is because spiritually each letter of the Hebrew alphabet contains intrinsic and individualized holiness and metaphorical and symbolical meaning.

---

228   In Mefaneach Tzfunot page 55 footnote 1 Rabbi Kasher adds the following:

ומבואר דס"ל שאות אחת לבייש הו' עליה גדר צורה, וחייב

ולב"ה פטור משום שאין עליה גדר מציאות של תיבה. וע" צפנת פענח

השלמה צד 93 . ויש להוסיף עפמ"ש בתניא להגרש"ז באגרת הקדש

סה : "אך האותיות הן בבחינה חומר וצורה, הנקרא פנימית.

וחיצונית וכו. עיי"ש, ולפ"ז ב"ש לשיטתם דעיקר הצורה גם אות

אחת יש לה פנימיות, משא"כ לב"ה דהעיקר החומר ופחות מהשיעור

שתי אותיות אין על זה שם מציאות של תיבה. וראה צ"פ תרומות

סג ע"א

This whole subject is further amplified in light of how the Rogatchover understands[229] the infusion of holiness into G-d's name. The Yerushalmi in Tractate Berakhot (Chapter 5, halakhah 1) states:

"If a scribe was writing a Sefer Torah and was in middle of writing the name of G-d, then even if the king himself asks him a question, he is not allowed to respond".

The Rambam codifies this in Hilkhot Teffilin (Perek 1, halakhah 15):

"If one was writing a Torah and did not have full intent when writing G-ds name, (*kasav shelo lishma*) the entire Torah is invalid. Therefore if a scribe is in middle of writing G-ds name he should not even respond to the king".

Simply speaking, the reason is that by responding to the king the scribe is partially distracted and not able to have full concentration on writing G-d's name. Yet, why ca not the scribe stop writing, respond and then continue writing G-d's name? This way he could have full concentration while writing G-d's name, with only a short intermission between starting to write and finishing the name?

The reason the Rogatchover offers, is that G-dliness is not able to be compartmentalized. What this means is that the name of G-d in a Torah is expressing and constitutes an actual embodiment of G-dliness. G-dliness is not an existence given to fragmentation and separate disparate parts. Thus, since it is absolute and not able to be partitioned, the physical letters of the name of G-d (which is the vehicle in which this G-dliness will be revealed and communicated to the world) must also be one and absolute.

---

229   In Mahadura Tinyana page 140

באמת הטעם דהוה מציאות אחת ואי אפשר
לחלק
לפיכך הכל מודים בכותב את השם (בשבת אינו חייב) עד שעה
שישלים אף־על־פי שענין שיעור הכתיבה בשבת (שתי אותיות משם
גדול) יש חילוקי דיעות, מכל מקום ביחס לכתיבת שם השם הכל מודים,
שאינו חייב עד שישלים
זה אינו דבר מצטרף ח״ו רק עצם פשוט ואינו מתחלק

However we can ask, why ca not the tangible expression be dissimilar in its character from the idea and truth it carries and embodies?

This is because from the perspective of Torah and halakhah the physical must resonate and be a transparent conduit through which G-dliness will flow into the world. There can be no friction between the physical and the G-dly. Therefore the physical letters (that are the expressers of the divine truth inherent in the name of G-d) must reflect in their physical character the G-dly characteristics of divine truth. They therefore cannot be written in a way that is fragmented.

Thus do we find that the authentic way of writing G-d's name was by holding four quills in between the five fingers and writing all four letters of G-d's name at the same time. The secret knowledge of how to perform this maneuver was known by one man who refused to share it with others bringing down the condemnation of the Sages upon him.[230]

This explains an intriguing halakhic discrepancy. The *din* (law) is that one is not allowed to write on Shabbat. How much does one need to write in order to have transgressed this Biblical prohibition? The halakhah is that two letters is what is required to have negated the Biblical directive not to write. Yet the Yerushalmi (Shabbat, *perek* 13, *halakhah* 1) states that "all agree that regarding writing G-d's name, one has not transgressed until he writes the complete name of G-d (more than two letters)."

What is the reason for this legislative inconsistency concerning writing G-ds name? After writing a Yud and Hei (the first two letters of G-d's name) one should be liable to the full strength of the law!

However our analysis on the nature of the relationship between G-dliness and the letters of G-d's name sheds light on this enigma. Since the letters of G-d's name are not given to fragmentation and disparateness therefore by only writing two letters of G-d's name one has not written anything. The letters existentially do not stand on their own and only are viewed as an entity, in their complete state of all four letters of G-d's name together.

---

230   See Yoma 38a.

Domestic Dualities

This distinction holds good[231] in another important controversy, regarding the relationship between two women who both were married to a man who died childless. Generally, the deceased's brother would have a *mitzvah* to marry one of his brother's widows however there are situations where a brother may be exempt from *yivum* (marrying his brother's widow) or *chalitza* (performing the ritual that releases his brother's widow). One such case is if the brother is related to the widow in a way such that *yivum* would constitute a Biblically forbidden relationship an "*issur ervah*" (see Yebamot 3b). The first Mishnah in Yebamot lists those cases where the widow would be forbidden to the brother but was not forbidden to the deceased.

But what about the other wives? If only one of the deceased's wives is forbidden to the brother does that automatically exempt all the other wives? Concerning this situation there is an argument about the other widows, who are theoretically permitted to the deceased's brother.

Shammai permits the non-related widows to marry the brother, and Bet Hillel forbids it (Mishnah Yebamot 1:4).

According to Bet Shammai, from a legal point of view there is no point in linking the fate of the widows together. The widow who is his wife's sister cannot enter into a Levirate marriage with him because it is a prohibited marriage, while the other widows are autonomous unto themselves and can marry the brother of the deceased.

Bet Hillel holds the opposite opinion: the two women are not autonomous, their status is conditional on their being the ex-

---

231   In Mefaneach Tzfunot page 55:

במהד"ת ע' 081 וכן זה הגרר ביבמות רף יג ע"ב

גבי צרת ערוה, ערוה אבראי קיימא, ע"ש דף מד ע"א.

ובסגנון אחר בס' השלמה דף ב ע"א: וכבר כתבתי בזה

אם איסורים הם רק תואר בהדבר או עצם, ובזה פליגי

ב"ש וב"ה, ביבמות רף יג גבי צרת ערוה, דב"ש ס"ל

דאיסור הוא עצם. וכמו איילונית שם רף יב, וע"ש בתוס'

דף ח ואבראי קיימא ע"ש רף מד ע"א.

wives of the same deceased man and their destinies continue to be interconnected.

What is the core matter being debated? Bet Shammai holds that even though one of the wives is forbidden to the brother this does not affect the other wife. Why is this though? The Talmud in Yebamot 3b states that the other widows are released from any obligation to the brother if only one of them is forbidden to the brother?

Shammai however does not view the prohibited wife as even existent (*ervah abrai kayma*), that we would then be able to say that due to her unavailability she exempts the other wives. Since she is *assur* (forbidden) she is not even considered to be in front of the court. This is because the *issur* is not peripheral or secondary, but rather, an *issur* is laid onto the very essence of the forbidden item or person. This is of course a more abstract and intangible "take" on the nature of an *issur*.

Hillel on the other hand views the related and forbidden widow as being here and existent in the case, just that the *issur* prevents her from marrying the deceased's brother. This is in keeping with Hillel's tangible and grounded world-view.[232]

Categorical Colors

The Gemara in Hulin 136b brings a *makhloket* (dispute) between Shammai and Hillel regarding different colored figs.[233] The *din*

---

232   This touches upon another well-known debate concerning the definition of a Torah prohibition: Whether the *issur* affects the very essence of the item *(issur cheftza)* or is instead merely a rule forbidding a person *(issur gavra)* to engage in the *assur* item. While one might make the argument that Shammai, in keeping in tune with his intangible dominant theme, would gravitate more towards an *issur cheftza* opinion, and Hillel would relate to an *issur gavra,* I have not seen this correlation made anywhere. While the Rogatchover makes a very similar correlation in the above case, it is clear (to me at any rate) that he means it in a way that is very localized and specific to levirate marriage.

233   See Michtevei Torah#283:

בגדר

צורה בלא חומר מחלוקת בית שמאי ובית הלל חולין דף

קלו ע״ב אם מראה הוה מציאות אף דזה גדר צורה בלא

חומר, דאם יטחן החומר לדק נתבטל המראה כמ״ש בספר

המורה בהקדמות של המדברים.

See also Michtevei Torah #55:

is that one cannot take *terumah* (one of five different types of tithes a Jew had to take from his produce) from one species of produce for another type of produce.

So, for example, one could not take a tithe of oranges to permit apples etc. Each plant, vegetable or fruit had to have the tithe separated from it to make the rest of that species of produce permitted for consumption.

Here the Gemara asks, what about taking *terumah* from black figs in order to exempt and de-sanctify white figs? Is that permissible? Bet Shammai says no and Bet Hillel says yes.

This is a dispute revolving around the tangible versus intangible question. What is color? Is it merely an accessory part of an item, or is it an absolute existence? The Rambam in *Moreh Nevukhim* (part 1, chapter 73) discusses the nature of color. He brings the opinions of the Mutakallemim that color is intrinsic to physical matter. They say that if one takes snow, for example, the white color is there in every piece of snow and is part of its very existence.

The Rambam however rejects their opinion and says that one sees that when things are ground down into tiny flecks and turn into powder the color is gone. Therefore color is only part of the whole and not existent in the individual parts.

At any rate, we see that there are differing perspectives on the nature of color. According to some it is merely a superficial layer of existence while others view it as being firmly part of the item that it is coloring.

This then is the debate about black and white figs. According to Hillel, we permit the taking of *terumah* from black to white, because the different colors are not important and significant enough to make us consider the black and white figs as different

---

ותליא אם מראה הוה עצם איכות, או רק
מכמות

And Tsafnat Paneah Sh"ut Warsaw Siman 50:

ועיין בחולין דף קלו
ע"ב דב"ש וב"ה פליגי אם שינוי מראת הוי מין אחד
או ב' מינים

species of produce. This in turn is because the colors are only skin deep and not reflective of the essence of the figs. This in turn is because Hillel is grounded in concrete reality. This allows Hillel to see that different colors are simply just that, and not existential divides.

Whereas Shammai considers the differently colored figs to be different types of fruit. Therefore one cannot take *terumah* from one to the other. This is the result of Shammai's abstract perspective that different colors actually create a different category.

Slippery Sukkah

The Gemara in Sukkah 3a brings a *makhloket* between Shammai and Hillel regarding one who is sitting in a sukkah, but his table is outside the sukkah. Hillel says this is acceptable and one has fulfilled their obligation, while Shammai says it is *passul* (invalid).

This is yet another reflection of our theme. Hillel says it is kosher since the man is sitting in the sukkah. The fact that his table is outside the sukkah is inconsequential compared to the fact that he is actually sitting in the sukkah.

Shammai however views the situation differently. Yes, the man is in the sukkah, but his table, which is where the food is, is outside. This means that symbolically, and even practically, we cannot just look at the concrete facts in front of us and we must consider the overarching implications of the fact that his table, which is the primary vessel of the Sukkah, is outside the Sukkah. Again we have a more abstract and intangible "take" on the situation.[234]

---

234   This is further amplified when one considers the fact that one of the reasons brought for Shammai is that since the table is outside he might gravitate towards the food and slowly shift forward away from the Sukkah eventually winding up eating slightly outside the Sukkah. This means that Shammai predicates his opinion on an eventual gradual possibility. In basing his halakhic decision on a possibility instead of the actual reality in front of us (namely that the man is in the Sukkah), Shammai is again asserting the intangible perspective of reality since a possibility is insubstantial compared to an actual present reality.

Attractive Ambiguity

The following is a possible application of the Rogatchover's theory and not one made explicitly by him.]

Ketubot (16b-17a):

The Rabbis taught: How does one dance before the bride (i.e. how does one praise the bride and make her happy)?

Bet Shammai say: [One describes] the bride as she actually is.

Bet Hillel says: "A beautiful and graceful bride."

Bet Shammai said to Bet Hillel: Say she is lame or blind; shall we call her, "a beautiful and graceful bride"? But the Torah said, "You shall distance yourself from matters of falsehood"!

Presumably, Bet Shammai adopts two assumptions:

1. That truth and falsehood are measured by objective standards and it is therefore *sheker* (falsehood) to praise an unattractive *kallah,* even though the groom clearly finds her beautiful in some way.

2. That there can be no extenuating circumstances in which lying may be permitted. Conversely, to defend his position, Bet Hillel has the option of rejecting either assumption.

The approaches taken to explain this dispute are numerous. But from our standpoint the difference is very clear. Hillel is grounded in a concrete tangible worldview. As such, more preference is given to physicality and one might say that Hillel is more "patient" with tangibility. That being the case, Hillel holds that the *kallah* can be praised for her beauty, since there certainly is something the *chattan* finds beautiful and attractive in his *kallah.* If it is not immediately discernible, all that means, is that one must look more closely at the *kallah* to find her beauty. This is an approach that requires one to subscribe to tangibility as the primary determinant in order to have the patience and belief that there are physical elements extant in the *kallah* that one will be able to praise.

Shammai rejects this since if there are no tangibly evident qualities to praise in the *kallah*, then one cannot make up things out of thin air to praise. Because Shammai allocates less value and less significance to the physical spectrum, his worldview does not lend itself to analyzing in depth the particulars of the *kallah* in order to find something tangible to praise.

(Alternatively, Shammai holds that if there are no readily discernible physical qualities to praise, then instinctively one must revert to the main barometer of reality, namely spiritual considerations. This is why one must praise the *kallah* by referring to the refined character traits that she possesses. This is according to those who explain Shammai's statement of *kallah kemot sh'hee* (praise her as she is) to mean that one must praise her other qualities.)

Subtle Separation

[The following is a possible application of the Rogatchover's theory and not one made explicitly by him.]

The Talmud in Gitin 90a brings an argument between Shammai and Hillel regarding what constitutes proper grounds for divorce. Shammai said that only if one's wife is promiscuous can one legitimately divorce her. Hillel said that a husband can divorce his wife even if she committed the smallest of offenses, such as burning his dinner.

Perhaps we might also explain this dispute based upon our analysis. Hillel, who considers physical factors of supreme importance, would grant greater substance to even minor offenses, since he is closer to the tangible spectrum of things.

Shammai being further from physical considerations would only consider major physical offenses as being substantial. This is because only a physical act of massive proportions, such as adultery, would have the necessary strength and magnitude to reverberate across the multiple levels of reality to reach the intangible view of things and create grounds for divorce.

Student vs. Master

[The following is a possible application of the Rogatchover's theory and not one made explicitly by him.]

The Gemara (Bava Basra 133b) tells a story about a man who had sons who were not behaving correctly. He therefore gave all of his property to Yonatan ben Uziel. When the man died, Yonatan ben Uziel sold one third of the property for his use, consecrated one third, and returned the last third to the man's children. When Shammai heard about this, he challenged Yonatan, telling him that he should not have given the third back to the children, since the man gave him the property in the first place to avoid their receiving it. Yonatan ben Uziel rejected Shammai's argument claiming that since the man had given the property to him, it was fully in his hands to do whatever he pleased with it.

Here too we might say that Shammai felt that Yonatan had not acted properly since the intent and purpose of the man giving him the property, which is intangible considerations, were being negated.

Yonatan ben Uziel, who was the prize pupil of Hillel, responded that, simply put, the property now belonged to him and he could legally do with it whatever he wanted. He was in effect rejecting any spiritual considerations, such as the giver's intentions.[235]

Sinai and Harim/Quixotic Quality

Another instance[236] of the Talmud's preference can be seen in Horiyot 14a:

---

235   The Talmud says that Hillel had eighty students. Thirty of them reached the level of Moshe, fitting to receive the Heavenly presence. Thirty of them reached the level of Yehoshua, fitting for Hashem to stop the sun in their merit. Twenty reached the level of outstanding students. The greatest of them was Yonatan ben Uziel, while the lowest was Rabban Yohanan ben Zakkai.

Rabbi Yohanan ben Zakkai was fully versed in all aspects of Torah—Tanach, Mishnayot, Gemara, Halachot, derivations of *halakhot* from verses, close inspection of the text of the Torah, enactments of the Sages, logical arguments, comparisons of *halakhot* by similar language, astronomy, mathematical meanings of verses, parables, dialogues of *sheidim* (demons), trees, and angels, and large and small things (Bava Basra 134a).

236   In Mahadura Tinyana page 180:

עיי יבמות דף יד דלכך

Rabbi Shimon Ben Gamliel and the Rabbis debated. One said that *sinai* is a superior quality in learning, while the other side said *oker harim* is a finer trait.[237]

Who is a man embodying *sinai* qualities? Rav Yosef.

Who is a man embodying *oker harim* abilities? Rabbah.

They sent the debate to the east (*eretz Yisrael*) for a resolution and the answer sent back was: *sinai* (vast knowledge) is superior.

Sinai verus *oker harim* is essentially a debate on quality versus quantity. *Sinai*, which is broad global knowledge, equates to quantity of knowledge. *Oker harim*, which is localized sharp thinking, equates to quality of thought.

With this in mind, we can uncover a further layer of depth here, which is that quantity versus quality itself, is at its core, a debate about tangibility versus intangibility.

Quantity is a tangible and quantifiable (the very word implies concrete objective data) factor. It is a physical reality of having more. For example, the concept that majority rules, since there are more people who hold a certain view, is a concept predicated upon tangible, readily observed phenomena.

Quality on the other hand is a whole different beast. It is non-concrete and intangible. Although the majority wants a certain approach, if the minority are smarter and more experienced, follow them, says quality.

ס״ל דעשו ב״ש כדבריהם משום דמחדדי טפי אף דב״ה
רובא, וא״כ חזינן דאזלינ בתר הצורה אף דבהעצם הוי
מיעוטא.

237   *Sinai* literally means Mount. Sinai. Here the Talmud uses *sinai* as a metaphor for the quality of vast knowledge and scholarship. As if to say, one who has the entire Torah at his fingertips as it was given at Mount Sinai.

Oker harim literally means the "uprooter of mountains". The Talmud uses it as a metaphor for one who has sharp and incisive analytical skills. Although this individual may not know all of Torah by heart, and is not as knowledgeable as the other, he is possessed of superior and deeper intellectual abilities.

Thus the Rabbis and Rabbi Shimon are debating what the more desirable and admirable trait in Torah study is.

We now come back to *sinai* versus *harim*. This is yet another place where the Talmud makes clear its position that tangible factors must outweigh (for the time being, see later) intangible elements. Hence *sinai* is superior, hence quantity is superior, (as seen in that majority rules is a Jewish and Torah concept used in the *halakhic* decision-making process), and hence tangible and physical phenomena must be of primary consideration to us, while spiritual factors are of secondary importance.

What does this have to do with Shammai and Hillel? The Talmud in Yebamot 14a records that Bet Shammai held the high ground in terms of superior thinkers and scholars, while Bet Hillel had a larger number of scholars and Torah legislators.

However, Bet Hillel followed their own opinion *le'halakhah* (practically). This was an astonishing phenomenon, when one considers that Bet Hillel knew and acknowledged Bet Shammai's superior caliber of scholars and legislators!

Yet according to our analysis, it was a phenomenon that makes perfect sense. Since Hillel held the view that tangible factors must always trump intangible ones, they concluded that their quantity of scholars outweighed the quality of Shammai's.

Shammain Sin

The Talmud in Berakhot 58b relates the following:

Rav Pappa and Rav Huna were walking along a road and they met Rabbi Chanina. Rabbi Chanina proceeded to make the blessing of *chacham harazim*,[238] telling them that they are as wise as and equal to 600,000 people in his eyes.

They then rebuked him, saying "Are you indeed this smart and knowledgeable [to make such a character judgment]?!" A short time later, Rabbi Chanina died.

What is the inner layer of meaning to this enigmatic story?

---

238   The blessing of *chacham harazim* is a blessing made upon seeing 600,000 people gathered together acknowledging G-d's omnipotent ability to create infinite variations of wisdom within people.

Rabbi Chanina was a follower of Shammai.[239] He subscribed to their world-view. He therefore felt that since they were indeed as wise as 600,000 people, he could make a blessing. This is because even though in concrete terms there was not the required number of people gathered together to make the blessing, yet qualitatively there was the required amount of wisdom in spiritual terms.

He was punished so severely because the *halakhah* is that anyone who follows the opinion of Bet Shammai is liable to the death penalty (Berakhot 11a).

Tangible Torah

Who do does *halakhah* follow? Who has the final say?

It turns out that it's not so simple. Although intangible and spiritual factors are considered to be a stronger reality, as we will see in a discussion about the era of Moshiach, tangibility is closer to the human experience, and as such is the primary determinant in the decision-making processes of Torah.

Since Torah is a system for dealing with our physical world and since physicality is a stronger reality to us, therefore it is the main factor in *halakhah*.

In light of this, consider the following *halakhah* (Yerushalmi Yoma, *perek* 6, *halakhah* 1):[240]

---

239   In Mahadura Tinyana page 180:

ובזה יש לבאר הך

דברכות דף נח ע"ב גבי עוברא דר"פ ור"י

ורב אחא בריה דדב איקא דבריך עלייהו ויהבו ביה עינא

ומת, ועי"ש ברמב"ן במלחמות (ולא מברכינן חכם הרזים

אלא על אוכלסיא ואע"ג דחשיבי טובא), ור"ל כך, משום

חז, רק בגדר תואר (אוכלסא) והנה וכוי, עכ"פ כאן נמי

חזינן דר"א בריה דרב איקא דאחשבינהו כמו אוכלסא

ובריך עלייהו ברוך חכם הרזים ס"ל ג"כ כך, א"כ ס"ל

כב"ש (דצורה הוא העיקר) ולכך נענש כמבואר בברכות

דף יא (כל העושה כדברי בייש חייב מיתה), ובמ"א אבאר

בזה

240   Pirkei Mavoi Bereshit page 21.

If one has two animals he can use for a *korban*, but one is stronger and of superior stock while the other simply looks better aesthetically, which one is he to bring? The one that is stronger physically is the preferred animal and is used as the *korban*.

The requirement by *korbanot* is to bring the best animal. Here we are faced with a decision in which one animal is superior physically while the other is superior in matters that are not as concrete. Take the tangibly superior one, says the Torah, thus informing us that when we need to make a decision, we should use tangibility as our main measuring stick of reality.

Summary

We see that in all of the above examples, the Rogatchover's thesis can be utilized as an umbrella for many of the other theories that have been proposed.

Even more, these other theories can be collapsed into our analysis and can be seen as resultant and subsequent (in their logic) to the Rogatchover's analysis. The Rogatchover in his brilliance not only developed a new thesis for the Shammai-Hillel debates, but one that is the most comprehensive, has many more applications, and hence has greater credibility.

The analytical theory in particular (that Bet Hillel is more patient with examining physicality) is predicated upon the Rogatchover's. Why indeed does Bet Hillel take a more penetrating and in-depth look at the physical reality? It is because it is more important to them and they allocate greater value to the physical than does Bet Shammai. This in turn is because Hillel views the material as the primary determinant.

The seventh theory of *koach* and *poel* (potential versus actual) can also be seen as a derivative of the Rogatchover's thesis. Consider:

The whole concept of allocating value and significance to something that does not exist currently, but rather exists potentially is predicated upon an intangible view of reality. Empirically it is not here in front of us, we cannot see it or measure it yet Shammai says it is a legitimate factor to contend with. Not just is it also given credence, it outweighs an actual reality in front of us! The fish is still flapping around on the deck of the ship so how can Shammai assert that it is *tamei*?! Yet so strongly is the world view of Shammai pervaded with a spiritual abstract lining that the potential certainty of the fish's death outweighs the concrete scene in front of us and *halakhah* asserts that the fish is dead with all the legal ramifications that ensue.

Messianic Mania

The Rogatchover's pinpointing of the fundamentally different approaches related to spirituality verus tangibility can be applied to the well-known and fascinating assertion that in the times of the Moshiach the *halakhah* will switch to be in accordance with Bet Shammai (Mikdash Melech to Zohar, Vol. I, 17b).

To understand this phenomenon we must first analyze the difference between the schools in how they view man's purpose and place in this world.

The Talmud (Eiruvin 13b) relates the following:

For two and a half years, there was a difference of opinion between the School of Shammai and the School of Hillel. These (the School of Shammai) would say: "It is better for a person not to have been born than to have been born."

And these (the School of Hillel) would say: "It is better for a person to have been born than not to have been born."

The School of Shammai, who highlights the intangible and hence allocates greater substance to potential then the actual, says that it is better for a person not to have been born, because the potential for personal fulfillment already exists in the spiritual realms. A person's existence in this world is, at its best, merely an expression of his spiritual potential. This is essential to fulfill G-d's purpose in creation, but "for a person," i.e., from his own individual standpoint, it is preferable that he had not been created.

The School of Hillel, who focuses on the tangible and hence actual expression, maintains that it is through the descent into this world that a soul reaches the heights of fulfillment. For the observance of the Torah and its *mitzvot* on this material plane lifts a person to a level above where they previously were in the spiritual realms. Therefore, it is preferable for the person to have been born.

Who is the *halakhah* in accordance with? Practically, we can only follow one school. When considering who it should be, we must consider the implications of each school's conceptual base. Hillel's perspective translates into the following:

We are creatures of the actual. We cannot live on potential nourishment, or be emotionally satisfied by potential relationships; on the whole, we judge people by their actual conduct, as opposed to their potential to behave a certain way. Reality, to us, is what is, not what might be.

This is largely due to the fact that we are physical beings. It is a most telling idiosyncrasy of our language that immaterial means insignificant. If we cannot touch it or see it, it's not real to us. The existence of a potential or possibility for something is not enough, for how do we know that it will amount to anything? In addition, even if we have assurances as to the eventual actualization, the fact remains that an entity that exists merely in a potential intangible state simply does not resonate within us as being a reality.

This is the reason that the halakhah follows Bet Hillel.

In day to day life we grant supremacy to the tangible and material and intangible factors are only accorded secondary status. However, when Moshiach comes it will be a time of, as the Rambam says, (Mishnah Torah, Hilkhot Melachim 12:5):

"The Jews will be great sages, and know the hidden matters".

Also, (Mishnah Torah, loc. cit. 11:4):

"Moshiach will perfect the entire world".

As well, (Isaiah 11:9):

'They will neither harm nor destroy on all my holy mountain, for the earth will be full of the knowledge of the Lord as the waters cover the sea [bed]".

We see that when Moshiach comes, our spectrum of reality will be elevated to a more refined and subtler level. Spiritual and intangible truths will resonate even within our physical spectrum.

So the *halakhic* switch to Shammai will be an instinctive natural gravitation, instead of a conscious legislative effort. Automatically the fragrance of the small vessel being carried on *Shabbat* will seem real and practical, the intrinsic independent identity of a single letter will be clear, and the validity of subscribing to a spiritual-based worldview will seem compelling and precise.

Chapter Eight

Rambam, Letters and Biblical Interpretive Style

The Rambam,[241] in *Hilkhot Avodah Zarah* (chapter 2, halakhah 2), writes, and the Rogatchover comments:

צונו הקב״ה שלא לקרות באותן

הספרים וכו׳ ואפילו להסתכל בדמות הצורה אסור וכ׳

זה רק בשעה שהם נעבדים אבל בשעה שהם נעזבים מותר כמבואר

בירושלמי פרק ג׳ דע״ז וכן בספריהם ג״כ ולכך רבינו ז״ל קרא

בספרי הבלים שלהם כמבואר במ״נ ח״ג

This is only in the time when they are served as idols. But in the time when they are forsaken it is permissible to study their doctrines and theology. As is explained in the Yerushalmi, chapter 3 of Avodah Zarah. The Talmud explains that the law forbidding a Jew to look at certain images of idols is only when they are be-

---

241

איקוניות למה הן אסורות מפני שמקטירין לפניהן בשעה שהן עולות א״ר יוחנן מותר לראותן בשעה שהן יורדות מה טעמא בהכרת רשעים תראה

ing built. But when they are deserted and no longer worshipped, then one is allowed to look at them. The Rogatchover applies the same principle to studying forbidden doctrines of thought. And the same applies to their books; **therefore our Teacher,** the Rambam, studied their books of vanities, **as is explained in Moreh Nevukhim, Part 3,** chapter 39. The Rambam writes: "Many of the commandments I did not understand. Neither their content nor the rationale behind them. Only when I studied their doctrine of the Sabians and their perspectives did I understand."

* * *

The Rambam, in *Hilkhot Yesode ha-Torah* (chapter 5, halakhah 6), writes:

כענין שאמרו באונסין כך אמרו בחלאים כיצד מי שחלה ונטה למות ואמרו הרופאים שרפואתו בדבר פלוני מאיסורין שבתורה עושין ומתרפאין בכל איסורין שבתורה במ־
קום סכנה חוץ מעבודת כוכבים וגילוי עריות ושפיכת דמים שאפילו במקום סכנה אין מתרפאין בהן ואם עבר ונתרפא עונשין אותו בית דין עונש הראוי לו:

When a person becomes sick and is in danger of dying, if the physicians say that his cure involves transgressing a given Torah prohibition, [the physicians' advice] should be followed. When there is a danger [to life], one may use any of the Torah prohibitions as a remedy, with the exception of the worship of false gods, forbidden sexual relations, and murder. Even when there is a danger [to life], one may not use them as a remedy. If one transgresses and uses them as a remedy, the court may impose the appropriate punishment upon him.

The Rogatchover comments as follows:

יש לומר הטעם כמו דאמרינן בסנהדרין דף ע"ב עב משמיא קא
רדפי לה. ועיין בתוס ב"ק דף מ"א גבי כגון שקפץ עליה השור דזה
לא מיקרי תתלתו באונס כיון דתחלת הדבר עשה מעצמו ע"ש

To understand this piece, an introduction is necessary. In general, for all mitzvot, if one is ordered to transgress on penalty of death, one should transgress rather than die, except for three *isurim*: murder, idolatry, and *arayot* (prohibited sexual relations, mainly incest and adultery). These three prohibitions follow the rule of *"yehareg ve-al yaavor"* (one must die rather than transgress).

In halakhah four of this very chapter, the Rambam rules:

> When anyone about whom it is said: "Sacrifice your life and do not transgress," transgresses instead of sacrificing his life, he desecrates [G-d's] name. If he does so in the presence of ten Jews, he desecrates [G-d's] name in public, nullifies [the fulfillment of] the positive commandment of the sanctification of [G-d's] name, and violates the negative commandment against the desecration of G-d's name.
>
> Nevertheless, since he was forced to transgress, he is not [punished by] lashing, and, needless to say, is not executed by the court even if he was forced to slay [a person]. The [punishments of] lashes and execution are administered only to one who transgresses voluntarily...

That being the case, why does the Rambam rule in halakhah Six that if a person is deathly ill and infringes on the prohibition of idolatry to heal himself (such as using material from a tree that was deified), he is liable for the death penalty in court? Does not this fall under the principle stated in halakhah four that "Nevertheless, since he was forced to transgress, he is not punished... execution is administered only to one who transgresses voluntarily..."? Is not this case, where the person's life is threatened, one of involuntary infringement? The Rogatchover explains as follows:

We can say that the reason for this difference is as it says in Sanhedrin (72b): "From heaven they are pursuing her." The Talmud there is discussing the case of a fetus that is endangering the life of the mother, yet has stuck its head out of the womb. The law is that we cannot do anything to the fetus to save the life of the mother, because "we do not push aside one life to save another." The Talmud then states that this case is one where "heaven is pursing the life of the mother," i.e., the mother's life is endangered by the natural phenomenon of childbirth.

The Rogatchover is making a distinction from the case in halakhah Four where a Jew is being forced at gunpoint to kill someone. Since it is the very prohibition itself which is not letting him kill, thus endangering his life, if he infringes on the prohibition and kills the person, the courts cannot punish him, since the prohibition itself was threatening him. In our case in halakhah Six however, the sickness, which is a natural phenomenon, is the force threatening this man's life. Therefore if he infringes on the prohibition of idolatry to save himself, he is not considered to be one forced involuntarily to negate the Torah's directive, since the directive itself is not the force threatening him.

And see Tosafot in Bava Kama (41) concerning the case where the ox jumped on her that this is not called a case in which **the beginning was involuntary, since the beginning of the matter** is performed by her, **see there.** The Talmud is discussing a case of bestiality where an ox is in heat and tries to have relations with a woman. The woman, seeing this, acquiesces and has relations with the animal. In general, there is a dispute regarding the culpability of someone forced to begin a forbidden act who then acquiesces and does the forbidden act willingly. *Tosafot* explains that, in our case, all agree that the woman is liable, since the ox only expresses interest, but the actual act is done willingly by the woman.[242]

* * *

The Rambam, in *Hilkhot Avodah Zarah*, halakhah seven rules as follows:

---

242   In a similar vein the Rogatchover explains (in Hilkhot Shvisas Esor Chapter Two Halacha Eight) that the law, that we can only feed someone whose life is in danger on Yom Kippur an amount less than a kezayit, was only stated regarding a person who needs to eat certain foods to survive. An example of this is a pregnant woman who smells a certain food and desires it to the point where not having it threatens her life. But a person who does not need a certain food, rather they just ca not be fasting (such as the Talmud's case of *bulmot*, a condition where a ravenous hunger overtook a person and threatened their life), can have as much food as they like at once without the need to give them less then a kezayit. The reason for this is that in the latter case, the Torah's directive, to fast on Yom Kippur is directly threatening their life. Therefore they can disregard it. But in the former case, of the pregnant woman, the Torah's directive is not directly threatening her since it is not the fast which endangers her but rather the absence of certain foods. See there and Mahadura Tinyana page 2 for more on this.

ואלו הן דיני המגדף אין המגדף חייב סקילה עד שיפרש את השם המיוחד
של ארבע אותיות שהוא אל"ף דל"ת נו"ן יו"ד ויברך אותו בשם מן השמות
שאינם נמחקים שנאמר ונוקב שם ה' על השם המיוחד חייב סקילה ועל
שאר הכינוים באזהרה

These are the laws which govern a blasphemer: A blasphemer is not liable to be stoned to death until he states
G-d's unique name, which possesses four letters,

י-נ-ד-א

and curses that name with one of the names of G-d
which are forbidden to be erased, as [Leviticus 24:16]
states: "One who blasphemes G-d's name…"

One is obligated to be stoned to death for blasphem-
ing G-d's unique name. [Should he blaspheme] the other
names for G-d, he [transgresses] a prohibition.

Then, in halakhah eight:

אזהרה של מגדף מנין שנאמר אלהים לא תקלל בכל יום ויום בודקין את
העדים בכינוים יכה יוסי את יוסי נגמר הדין מוציאין את כל אדם לחוץ
ושואלים את הגדול שבעדים ואומרים לו אמור מה ששמעת בפירוש והוא
אומר והדיינים עומדים על רגליהם וקורעין ולא מאחין והעד השני אומר
אף אני כמותו שמעתי ואם היו עדים רבים צריך כל אחד ואחד מהן לומר
כזה שמעתי

Which verse serves as the warning prohibiting blasphemy? [Exodus 22:27]: "Do not curse G-d."

[The procedure for the trial of a blasphemer is as follows.] Each day, [when] the witnesses are questioned,
[they use] other terms for G-d's name, [stating,] "May
Yosi strike Yosi." At the conclusion of the judgment, all
bystanders are removed [from the courtroom]. The
judges question the witness of greatest stature and tell
him, "Tell us what you heard explicitly." He relates [the
curse]. The judges stand upright and rend their garments. They may not mend them [afterwards].

The second witness states: "I also heard as he did." If there are many witnesses, they must all say, "I heard the same."

The Rogatchover comments:

ר"ל כך דהגה גבי עדם

צריך שיעיד כל אחד ולא שיסכים לתבירו וא"כ צ"ל

דאף אגי כמוהו זהו כמו שאמר מה שאמר חבירו וכמו דאמר בשבועות

ד' כ"ע מ"ב גט אומר אמן ועי' שם ד' ל"ו ע"א ועי' הוריוח דף ג,

מ"ב גבי הירכין ובירוש' פ"ג דר"ה גבי עדות החדש ומי, מה שכתב

סרי"ף זיל בסנהדרין על הך רדף ס"ה מה לעדים זוממין שכן ישנן

כו, עיש ועי' בנזיר ה, כ"א אך כל זה אם הוא תוליד אבל לאחר

כדי דיבור של הראשון אף דחד בחבריה מתפס לא הוי רק כעין יד

ועי, בב"מ ה, צ"ח ע"ב גבי שאילה בבעלים ושבת ה, עיא ע"א. אך

כ"ז לדידן דסבירא לן בהך דמכות דף ו' וסנהדרין דף ט' דלאימיקרי

כת אתת רק תוכ"ד אך ר"ע לא ס"ל כן עי' בתוס' סנהדרין הנ"ל,

והנה במשנה נקט והשלישי אומר אף אני כמוהו א"כ הוי לאחר כ"ד

מן הראשון ובכך אמר בגמ' כאן סתמא כר"ע אך אנן דלא ס"ל כר"ע

לכך נקט רטנו ואם היו עדים רבים דהייגו סתם רבים ג' צ"ל רק

כזה שמעתי דהיינו ה' בתוכ"ד של הראשון ולא כתב אפילו מאה

כמו"ש בהל' סגהדרין פי"ב הלכה ג' עיש

The intent of the Rambam is as follows. **Regarding witnesses,** the law requires that each one testify himself, and not just confirm what their fellow stated. If so, we must say this law that allows the other witnesses to say "I also heard as he did," and does not require each witness to state the testimony himself, is based on the idea that this statement of "I also heard as he did' is halakhically considered to be as if the person literally **said the** actual **testimony that his fellow,** the first witness, **said.**

As it says in Shevuot (29b) concerning one who says Amen. Shmuel said "Whoever says amen after hearing an oath, it is as if he himself uttered the oath." The same principle applies here, namely that the witness who says an affirmation, a non-ritualistic amen, is considered to have said the original testimony himself.

And see there page 36a. The Talmud states that "One who says Amen after an oath is as one who says the oath from his own mouth".

And see Horayot page 3b regarding bowing the head. The Talmud explains that even though each judge must individually rule on a case, a judge can nod his head to approve of an opinion that a different judge said. Here too we see the idea that an affirmation can be halakhically considered as if the person affirming actually stated his approval and opinion.

And the Yerushalmi Chapter Three of Rosh Hashanah halakhah One **concerning the testimony of the** new moon and **month.** The Talmud is discussing a story in which the witnesses that the court in Jerusalem sent to the Diaspora became mutes along the way and could not testify in court. Instead the court in the Diaspora asked them if the new month was established and accepted them nodding their heads as testimony.

And see what the Rif wrote in Sanhedrin…

And see Nazir page 21b where the Talmud states that "One who says 'I am a Nazir' and his friend heard and said 'and me too' they are all Nezirim".

But all this is only where the second witness said 'I heard as he did' within *toch kdei dibbur* a span of three seconds **from when the first witness** who gave the testimony **stopped talking. But after a** *toch kdei dibbur* amount of time **passed from the first witnesses testimony, even though one affirmed after the other, it is only** considered as **a form of approval** and agreement to what was said—not as if the second person stated it himself. This would disqualify the testimony in all the cases mentioned above.

And see Bava Metzia page 98b concerning lending with owners and see Shabbat page 71a.

But all this is only according to us since as we hold in Makkot page 6a and Sanhedrin page 9a. The Talmud is discussing the situation where more than two witnesses come as a group and testify and then one of the witnesses is disqualified. The argument is whether one disqualified witness imvalidates the entire group or not. Rava states that the group is only considered as one if the testimonies were all stated within *toch kdei dibbur*. Statements made within this brief interval are legally considered to be as one continuos statement. Therefore all the witnesses who give testimony within this time frame are halakhically considered to be one single set. Those who testify after this time span are considered a new set of witnesses. But Rabbi Akiva does not agree with this see Tosafot in Sanhedrin quoted previously. Now the Mishnah stated that the third witness said 'I heard as he did'. This means that the third witnesses statement was after the toch kdei dibbur time span from the first witness. This is because the short time span only allows enough time for the second witness to say 'I heard as he did'. This is also why the Gemara says here in Makkot that the unidentified statement here belongs to Rabbi Akiva. But since we who do not hold like Rabbi Akiva, our teacher the Rambam chose to simply state in halakhah Eight "If there are many witnesses, they must all say, 'I heard the same.'" Because many without specification implies three. And there is time for the second and third witness to state simply 'I heard the same' within *toch kdei dibbur* of the first. He did not write the language of the Mishnah 'even one hundred witnesses' as he did indeed write elsewhere in Hilkhot Sanhedrin Chapter Twelve halakhah Three see there.

To sum up, the Rogatchover explains why the Rambam deviates from the wording of the Mishnah even though elsewhere he is loyal to it. He explains why the Rambam switches from writing that "the second witness states: "I also heard as he did." To writing that "If there are many witnesses, they must all say, "I heard the same."

* * *

This letter is taken from "Teshuvot HaGaon MiRogatchov" by Moshe Grossberg (page 11) and the deconstruction of the letter was taken from the "Hamek Teshuva". The letter is a good example of the style of abstraction that the Rogatchover used in his responsa. The core concept is explained in Chapter Five in this book. The question asked was whether a minority group within a congregation can start their own congregation and build a separate Shul.

I have just now received your letter—I seem to remember having sent you a letter a couple years ago regarding the status of a bet haknesset. The matter is like this: there are many contradictory statements about whether an item that belongs to the community is owned and connected to the essence i.e. the general communal group of the inhabitants of the city or whether it is owned and connected to the individuals of the city. See Nedarim page 47b regarding a bet haknesset and see also the Ritva there. And also the same question would apply to the Books. Does the Mishnah mean the specific Sefer Torah for reading publicly in Shul which is only connected to the general community? Or does Books mean general books needed for the public to learn from which is connected to each individual?

The Mishnah in Nedarim is discussing two people who forbid each other to have any benefit from each other. The question is whether they can use public communal property since perhaps each individual owns in some sense the public property and thus if they use or benefit from it they are infringing on their prohibitory vow. The background is that according to halakhah the municipal property of a town is not ownerless and equally owned by all people in the world but rather is owned by the individual inhabitants of the town. This is why the townspeople can decide to sell any communal property such as a Shul, study hall etc. (see Megillah 26a). Therefore everyone in town is considered partners in these properties and one who uses any of them is benefitting from the property that belongs partly to the fellow from whom he is forbidden benefit. The Mishnah then clarifies what is considered communal property of the town: "the town square, the bathhouse, the synagogue, the Ark and the Books".

The Rishonim argue what the meaning of the Books is. Rashi explains it to mean the Sefer Torah (the Torah Scrolls) while Tosafot asserts that it means the general books used in a synagogue. The Rogatchover is positing a philosophical backdrop to this Rishonic dispute. Rashi who says that Books means a Sefer Torah is asserting that communal items are only items which are owned generally and have no individual bond to any one person. This is because the Rogatchover has a theory that a Sefer

Torah, being an item of extreme holiness cannot fully descend into the human realm and be owned entirely by a human being. It can only be owned in its external layer what he calls its *tziyur* or intangible form.[243] With this perspective the Rogatchover explained numerous puzzling Gemarot, among them the Yerushalmi[244] that rules that one cannot marry a woman by giving her a Torah. According to the Rogatchover's theory it is because even a Torah that belongs to one person is not fully owned by them.[245]

Tosafot disputes this and understands communal items to indeed have a specific connection to individuals which is why says that Books means the general books needed in a Shul which can and do have connections to individuals.

The item-specific dispute between these two Rishonim on the meaning of a term in a Mishnah transforms into a philosophical-concepts based argument with each item (Sefer Torah or general prayer and study books) representing and being symbolic of a different understanding on the nature of communal property and indeed two different conceptions of the status of communal groups. The Rogatchover continues:

See Bava Basra page 43a concerning a Sefer Torah that was stolen from a city and the thief was then caught. The law is that the thief cannot be judged by judges from that city nor may any of the townspeople give testimony. The reason is that since all the twonspoeple are partners in ownership of the Sefer Torah (it was the custom for all the people to pool their money together to purchase the Sefer Torah) they are biased (*noge'ah bidavar*) and are disqualified from giving testimony. The Talmud then asks why none of the townspeople cannot just give up their share in ownership and then testify against the thief. The answer given is that a Sefer Torah's function is **to be heard**. The commentaries explain this to mean that since this person will need to hear the Torah being read in the future and will benefit from it by ful-

---

243   See the appendix on interchangeable terms. This is another instance where the Rogatchover conflates what are usually disparate paradigms—Klal-Prat and Homer-Tsurah- into one general perspective.
244   Nedarim Chapter Five
245   This is also the reasoning behind the fact that one who says "all my porperty I will sell to you" has not included a Torah that they own. See Bava Basra 151a. See also the Chasam Sofer Choshen Mishpat Siman 143.

filling his obligation of hearing the Torah he cannot give up his ownership and interest in the Torah.[246]

The Talmud subsequently states that *hakol etzel sefer torah aniyim hen* which means "in regards to a Torah all are considered poor". The conventional meaning that the commentaries proposed was that the Talmud is saying that anyone who does not possess a share in a Sefer Torah is considered poor since one has an obligation to hear it being read and thus it is a tremendous deficiency if a town does not own one. The Rogatchover interprets this Talmudic statement in a novel way. In his conception since only the external layer of the Torah can be owned all humans are forever as a poor person with respect to a Torah since they cannot be said to really own it. Therefore, none of the townspeople can give up their share in ownership since the ownership is not theirs in the first place and does not really belong to them that they would be able to do with it as they wish.

And see the Rashbam there who writes that he should go to a different city see there. His intent was not that his connection is severed but that he should not be there in the city. The reasoning is that since the townspeople's connection to the Torah is by dint of them being part of the community of the city, if they leave they are automatically removed from a connection to the Torah.

For the fact that the Torah belongs to the townspeople is only because it is connected to the inhabitants of the city and he this person who is removing his ownership to be able to testify is among them and therefore cannot relinquish ownership. The only way to do this is by leaving the city.

I have already explained this at length specifically concerning the dispute between the Ran and the Ritva on the case in Bava Basra page 8a regarding someone who settles in the city who came afterwards if he has forbidden himself from them i.e. the newcomers.

---

246   If there was two Torah's in the city then a person would indeed be able to give up his share in ownership of the Torah that had been stolen since he need not hear the Torah reading from it in the future. See Shulhan Arukh Choshen Mishpat Siman 7 Se'if Katan 12.

The Talmud in Bava Basra 8a, while discussing the Mishnah brings Rabba who states the following: "If a man vows that he will derive no benefit from the men of a certain town (me'asnhei ha'or) , he must derive no benefit from anyone who has resided there twelve months, but he may derive benefit from one who has resided there less than twelve months".

What about a man who came to live in this town after the vow was taken? If this man now lives in the town for twelve months is he then included in the scope of the vow and forbidden to the vowed? This issue is debated by the Ran [Nedarim 84a s.v. "Rav Nachman Amar"] and the Ritva [Nedarim, end of chapter five]. The Ran holds that even if a man came after the vow and then resided in the town for a year he is included in the vow while the Ritva disputes this.

According to the Ran the term "anshei ha'ir" the inhabitants of the city is a term that refers to the general communal nature of the city. And since anyone who came afterwards is now included in that communal term they fall within the scope of the vow. The Ritva however, asserts that it is a term which applies to the specific individuals of the city and therefore someone who came afterwards would not be included in the vow.[247]

See the Ran in Nedarim 84a and the Ritva in Chapter Three.

And see also Bava Basra page 23b that it is explained there concerining the seven leaders of a city (it was the custom to appoint seven people to be in charge of a municipality) that they are part of the pulic domain. And see this idea in Meggilah page 26b that it does not help i.e. the seven communal leaders have no power over something that belongs to the public. The Talmud in Meggilah explains that a Shul in a city cannot be sold since ev-

---

247   A similar line of inquiry is developed in Shu"t Warsaw #231. The issue there was whether newcomers to a city can demote someone who was appointed to a position of communal importance such as a Rav, teacher or chazzan. In fact, the Halacha is that a person who is being appointed to a communal position needs the approval of each individual. Therefore if one conceives of the community as a composite of individuals then each new individual who becomes a resident needs to give his stamp of approval to any communal leader whereas if the conception of a community is more general and non-individual based then we do not need each newcomer's approval.

eryone uses it when they come to the city and therefore it is public property to the extent that the city municipality cannot sell it.

And see also Rashi in Hulin page 136a regarding a fence that one is required to build on the roof of their house. The Talmud explains that since the verse says "You shall make a fence for your roofs" this excludes synagogues and study halls since they are not anyone's property because everyone uses them.

However the main point is this: insofar as the law of a synagogue is concerned it is said to belong to the whole world. But concerning the status of its acquisition it is the exclusive property of the specific town.

And see Yebamot page 79a regarding a sword whether the portin of the mizbeach remains and the same idea applies in Zevahim 4a with respect to *shinui bailim* (the principle of a change of ownership. This term means that the Kohen must have the proper intent and awareness of who this sacrifice is being offered for and who its legitimate owner is. If one person is bringing the sacrifice and the Kohen gets mixed up and does the service with the intent that it is being offered by a different person, that sacrifice is invalid and must be brought again) of a matter of the community i.e. a communal sacrifice. The Talmud states that there is no possibility of *shinui bailim* with a communal sacrifice. Why can there be no *shinui bailim* according to the opinion in Horayot page 5b and the same thing with a bull and goat sacrifice that each tribe had to offer—just say that if it was offered for one tribe in the name and intent for a different tribe then it would be invalid? Why then does Zevahim 4a state that there is no possibility of *shinui bailim* with a communal sacrifice? If the Kohen clearly has in mind that this sacrifice is only being offered by half the nation then should not that constitute an incorrect intent regarding ownership?

However this is because the acquisition of a group in a communal item is only in the external appearance i.e. the *tziyur* of each tribe and not to the essential specifics and individuals. This is not the place to elaborate on this.

See the Tosefta in Sanhedrin the end of Chapter Two that the idea that a communal initaitve or funding project only needs a majority of society to approve it is regarding the needs of the general group—the tsibur. The intent is this: every item that falls into the category of *shutfut* (i.e. the conception of a group as a composite of individuals) then the majority cannot force the minority and it needs the approval of all. But any item that is in the status of tsibur (i.e. the group entity in which there is no recognition of individuals)—there the group can coerce the minority in its agenda and financial project. For it is not worse than the case in Bava Basra 55a concerning the loafer who must assist the city in paying taxes. The Talmud there states that a *pardacht* or "loafer" can be compelled to pay the city-tax. In those times a fixed sum was imposed on a city as a tax and the city as a whole had to pay the fine. This loafer discussed in the Talmud was someone who did not benefit from the city's economy or social services. One who had nothing to do with the city other than the fact that he lived there. Yet the city could compel him to pay into the money pool. Practically speaking this is because simply by dint of living in the city one is responsible to participate in supporting the city. According to the Rogatchover however this loafer can only be compelled since the fine was structured in such a way that it was not contingent upon individuals but rather on the community as a single whole. The intent is that he must give to the community and the community does with it what the community needs.

Now, regarding the needs of the community there are two types. Things that are needed by the group—here the individuals are nullified to the majority. The second type is things that are needed for each person—here the need is of the status of shutfut and they the minority are not nullified.

The Rambam in Hilkhot Shichenim Chapter Five halakhah Fifteen explains the Talmud in Bava Basra page 11b concerning a person who is part of an alleyway who wishes to reverse. In the times of the Mishnah the layout of a town generally consisted of a network of houses courtyards and alleyways that led to the public and main street. Houses usually opened into courtyards which opened into alleys. In this case, a residents house was situated between two alleys. This person now wished to seal his entrance into one alley and open his wall to create a entrance to the other alley. The Rambam explains that the other residents of the first alley can prevent him from sealing his entrance since if a tax is levied on the alley they will have to pay more of the sum then if an additional person was paying into the money pool. The intent is that through him reversing his entrance to a different alleythe others will have to pay more of the tax—in his place. Therefore they are able to prevent him. Because there the tax was levied on each alley as a whole in the status of a general group irrespective of specific individuals i.e. tsibur and not in the status of specifics. The same principle would apply for any expenditure of a city that fall into the status of the general group and through them leaving the financial burden of the other citizens would increase—then the majority can compel the few individuals not to leave. The other consideration, besides the financial one, that would support this ruling—that individuals cannot leave a congregation without the approval of the majority is since the holiness of the Ark and the Torah would also be lessened. See Megillah page 27b regarding a big and small city. The Talmud there states that the bigger the congregation the holier the Torah becomes. This is based on the principle of *berov am hadrat melech* "the bigger the group the more glory to the king".

Therefore my ruling is that certainly by the strict letter of the law the majority of the synagogue have the right to protest and coerce the minority not to leave.

* * *

This letter is from Hamek Teshuva as well #3:

What Rashi writes in Berakhot page 53a why we say amen after a blessing there are two cateogries and understandings of the signicificance of saying amen. The first is where answering amen is as if he himself the one saying amen is saying the blessing. The second category is where a person says amen and still is only considered as one who heard the blessing and fulfilled his obligation to say that blessing. In other words, sometimes we fulfill our obligation by having a representative say the blessing and we say amen. Other times, where halakhah mandates that a blessing must be said and cannot be fulfilled through an agent, one can still say amen at times since there is a category of saying amen in which halakhah considers that person to have said the blessing personally and individually.

See Shavuot page 29b "one who says amen is as if he fulfilled". The Talmud states in the name of Shmuel that "whoever says amen after an oath it is as if he himself said the oath". We see from here proof for the concept that merely saying amen can be considered as if one said the blessing himself. This is also the intent in Berakhot page 53b where it states that the one who says amen is greater than the one who actually says the blessing. And see the end of Nazir where it repeats the teaching of Berakhot 53b. And Rashi in Hulin page 87a see also Tosafot there.

Now regarding Zimmun where one blesses and everyone listens and says amen—it is not that they all fulfill their obligation of *birchat hamazon* through the one reading but rather it is as though all of them are blessing, therefore there is a special blessing of Zimmun. This is the intent in Berakhot page 45b that there is no blessing of Zimmun according to one opinion when two people eat together. Because there when only two eat together the other one is fulfilling his obligation of *birchat hamazon* through the status of listening i.e. the one blessing is his agent in this obligation and not the status of blessing where it is as if the listener himself said the blessings. This is not included within the principle of *berov am hadrat melech* since that only applies in a time where all are fulfilling the obligation. In other words the Rogatchover is asserting that the principle that it is better for one person to say a blessing and have everyone say amen rather than have everyone say the blessing by themselves, only applies where the listeners will be halakhically considered as the ones who said the blessing. If however they are only regarded as listeners and the one who blesses is considered the agent then the principle does not apply and is not a consideration. See Berakhot page 45 concerning this statement of *mar bar rav ashi and rav acha*. The Talmud describes the following story: Mar son of Rav Ashi and Reb Acha from Difti had a meal with one another. No one of them was superior to the other that he should have the privilege of saying the Zimmun. They said: the Mishnah which taught -'if three persons have eaten together it is their duty to invite [one another to say grace]'- this is only where one of them is superior [to the others], but where they are all on the same level, perhaps it is better that the blessings should be separate. They therefore said [the grace] each one for himself.

Since then there was no great man that they could nullify themselves to him, their participation would have been in the status of fulfilling their obligation through an agent i.e. as listeners not as speakers saying the blessing and this is not Zimmun since Zimmun is where one says the blessings and the others are considered as speakers themselves.

And see Rosh Hashanah page 34b regarding blessings and *tekiyot* (shofer blasts) see there. The Talmud records a debate whther the shliach tsibur (the one appointed as the agent of the congregation) fulfills the obliagtions of only people who can't bless themselves or whether he even fulfills the obligation of those who can bless themselves. The Rogatchover is suggesting that the argument is regarding the status of fulfillment where all the members of the congregation are considered as speakers themselves and not just listeners on the blessing.

I explored this at length the idea that the shliach tsibur does not merely fulfill the obligation of the community in the sense that he is their agent and they are listening but rather that it is as if everyone prayed themselves. This is why a congregation is called tsibur which implies one single unified entity i.e. they are unified and all are considered as praying together. Just as with a communal sacrifice which comes from the treasury and is of and belongs to the entire tsibur and requires *mamad*.

* * *

Biblical Interpretive Style

To give you a taste of the Rogatchover's biblical interpretive style, I have translated all his comments on Parshat Bereishit.

Bereshit 1:21

Overview:

The Rogatchover explains why there is an extra word kanaf 'winged' in the verse.

וַיִּבְרָא אֱלֹהִים, אֶת-הַתַּנִּינִם הַגְּדֹלִים; וְאֵת כָּל-נֶפֶשׁ הַחַיָּה הָרֹמֶשֶׂת אֲשֶׁר שָׁרְצוּ הַמַּיִם לְמִינֵהֶם, וְאֵת כָּל-עוֹף כָּנָף לְמִינֵהוּ, וַיַּרְא אֱלֹהִים, כִּי-טוֹב

"G-d created the large sea fish, all the creeping living creatures that the waters produced in swarms, according to their species, and all **the winged birds** according to their species".

The Rogatchover:

"Look in Hulin page 139. And there will also be a difference if the main part of a bird is the wings. Study the dispute in Hulin 141b."

The Background:

The Rogatchover zeroes in on the words "winged birds" (oif kanaf), and asks why there is the extra word "winged"? Obviously birds are winged; why is there a reiteration of the obvious?

The Talmud in Hulin 139b[248] explains that the word oif is used in Scripture to connote all types of birds, kosher and non-kosher. Whereas the word tzippur is used exclusively to connote kosher birds.

The Talmud then challenges this assumption[249] and attempts to say that the word tzippur, in fact, includes all birds (both kosher and otherwise) and that the word kanaf, being an extra and secondary clause, adds grasshoppers into the prohibition. The Talmud answers that in fact the word tzippur only connotes kosher birds while the word kanaf includes all non-kosher birds as well as grasshoppers.

248

עוֹף משמע לן - בין טהור בין טמא, צפור טהור אשכחן דאיקרי צפור, טמא לא אשכחן דאיקרי צפור

"*Oif* implies kosher and non-kosher. We find that kosher birds are called *tzippor*, but non-kosher birds we do not find being called *tzippor*."

249

תא שמע (דברים ד) תבנית כל צפור כנף מאי לאו צפור בין טהור בין טמא כנף חגבים לא צפור טהור כנף טמא וחגבים ת"ש (תהילים קמח) החיה וכל בהמה רמש וצפור כנף מאי לאו צפור בין טהור בין טמא וכנף חגבים לא צפור טהור כנף טמא וחגבים

"Come and hear: It is written: The likeness of any winged *tzippur*.

Surely '*tzippur*' includes both clean and unclean birds, and 'winged' includes locusts—No, '*tzippur*' refers only to clean birds, and 'winged' includes both unclean birds and locusts."

The Rogatchover brings this down and applies it here to explain the seemingly superfluous[250] word kanaf in our verse.

Consequently when the Torah says "winged birds" (oif kanaf), it is referring to all birds and the extra word kanaf is including grasshoppers which are winged yet not classified as "birds".

* * *

Bereshit 1:21

Overview:

The Rogatchover explains the extra word kanaf 'winged' by explaining that the verse is coming to define the dominant characteristic of the bird. In the process a Talmudic dispute is resolved.

וַיִּבְרָא אֱלֹהִים, אֶת-הַתַּנִּינִם הַגְּדֹלִים; וְאֵת כָּל-נֶפֶשׁ הַחַיָּה הָרֹמֶשֶׂת אֲשֶׁר שָׁרְצוּ הַמַּיִם לְמִינֵהֶם, וְאֵת כָּל-עוֹף כָּנָף לְמִינֵהוּ, וַיַּרְא אֱלֹהִים, כִּי-טוֹב

"G-d created the large sea fish, all the creeping living creatures that the waters produced in swarms, according to their species, and all **the winged birds** according to their species".

The Rogatchover:

"Look in Hulin page 139. And there will also be a difference if the main part of a bird is the wings. Study the dispute in Hulin 141b."

The Background:

The Rogatchover zeroes in on the words "winged birds" (oif kanaf), and asks why there is the extra word "winged"? Obviously birds are winged; why is there a reiteration of the obvious?

The Talmud in Hulin 139b explains that the word oif is used in Scripture to connote all types of birds, kosher and non-kosher. Whereas the word tzippur is used exclusively to connote kosher birds.

---

250   It appears that not one Biblical commentator has ever pointed out this redundancy.

In the previous piece the Rogatchover explained that there is no reiteration and that each word is innovating something new. In this piece he offers a bit of a different themed answer.

Let us begin by asking ourselves what is the primary limb of a bird? What is its essential characteristic? Many people would instinctively respond that the wings of a bird are its primary tools for survival. However one can make a solid argument that the feet are its most essential tools for living. Without its feet it cannot maneuver on the ground and is at the mercy of its predators. While in the air it would be out of danger, but upon landing, and land it eventually must, it would be hard pressed to survive. The fact is that most of a bird's life is spent on the ground.

This issue is a factor in a Talmudic dispute. There is a mitzvah called "the sending away of the mother bird" (*shiluach hakan*), which mandates one to send away a mother bird before taking her eggs.

Regarding the *mitzvah* of sending away the mother bird (*shiluach hakan*), there is a dispute about what part of the mother bird to grasp while sending it away.

במה משלחה רב הונא אמר ברגליה רב יהודה אמר באגפיה רב הונא אמר ברגליה דכ־
תיב (ישעיהו לב) משלחי רגל השור והחמור רב יהודה אמר באגפיה דהא כנפיה נינהו

"How should he let it go? R. Huna said: With its feet. Rav Yehudah said: With its wings. R. Huna said: With its feet, for it is written:[251] "Send forth the feet of the ox and the donkey."

Rav Yehudah said: With its wings, for its wings are also [regarded as feet].

One opinion says you send it away with its feet while the other opinion says you send it by grasping its wings. Because "the feet of a bird are its wings". In other words the feet are its main characteristic.

---

251   The verse says (Isaiah 32:20):

מְשַׁלְּחֵי רֶגֶל-הַשּׁוֹר, וְהַחֲמוֹר

"Send forth the feet of the ox and the donkey"

The term "send forth the feet" implies that the phrase "send forth" *shiluach* refers to dispatching an animal with its feet.

The Rambam[252] holds that the halakhah is in accordance with the second opinion that the wings are the primary limbs of a bird.

This is reflected in the Torah's depiction of birds as *oif kanaf* (winged birds) since the primary part of a bird is its wings.

(It is interesting to note that the birds were created from the waters just like fish and share a central characteristic with them. Namely, the ability to fly. Birds and fish both fly, one through air and the other through water. Fish flutter their fins and scales just as birds flutter their wings and tails to navigate. They are a kind of 'earthly fish' adapted to swim in the air instead of water.

This coincides nicely with the Talmud's assertion[253] that the birds were created from a mixture of water and earth. I.e. they are a composite of both and live in both worlds.)

✷ ✷ ✷

Bereshit 1:22

Overview:

The Rogatchover addresses the singular terminology of "bird" instead of the plural, "birds", by explaining that birds are the only types of animals that do not have substantive divisions of class within the species.

וַיְבָרֶךְ אֹתָם אֱלֹהִים, לֵאמֹר: פְּרוּ וּרְבוּ, וּמִלְאוּ אֶת-הַמַּיִם בַּיַּמִּים, וְהָעוֹף, יִרֶב בָּאָרֶץ

"And G-d blessed them, saying: Be fruitful, and multiply, and fill the waters in the seas, **and let the bird multiply upon the earth.**"

The Rogatchover:

---

252   *Hilkhot shehitah* 13:5:

וכיצד משלח האם אוחז בכנפיה ומפריחה

"How does one send away the mother bird? You grab her by her wings and make her fly away".

253   See Bereshit 1:20 above with the Rogatchover's commentary.

"The intent here is grammatically singular [and not plural], because by birds there is no differentiation of different species [*gasa* and *daka*] and it is all considered one. And study Zevahim page 70b and study Tosafot in Hulin page 63b that there is only one species but many different types, look there."

The Background:

In verse 22 it states "G-d blessed them saying be fruitful and multiply and fill the waters of the seas and let the bird multiply upon the earth".

The obvious question being, why does the Torah say **bird** and not **birds?**

The Talmud in Zevahim 70b amidst a discussion of sacrificial laws states the following:

אווזין ותרנגולים טעמא מאי, דמינא דעופות נינהו, אבל

עז לאו מינא דעגלה גיגהו,

"Why ducks and chickens [i.e. why are they interchangeable]? Because they are both one species of bird. Goats and cattle are not the same species."

The Talmud here is discussing what the law is when one brings the wrong animal for a sacrifice.

Ducks and fowl are considered to be one category which is why regarding certain temple laws, if one brought the wrong bird it is acceptable after the fact since all birds are essentially the same species.

Tosafot asks[254] the obvious question that we see so many different **species** of birds, so why are all considered to be one and the

---

254   S.v. "aval":

אע"פ דאווזין ומרנגולין לאו מינא

דמוריס ובני יונה ומטהרין לא דמי

דהכא עגלה בהמה גסה ועז בהמה

"Even though ducks and chickens are not the same type, it is not the same as goats and cattle because a cow is a *behema gasa* while a goat is a *behema daka*. Whereas by birds there are no divisions of *dakah* and *gasah*."

same? He answers that even though there are so many different **types** of birds they are all considered to be just different sub-classes of the same species.

By land animals there are two general species according to Torah. Domesticated and wild or *behema* and *chaya*. Even within the category of domesticated there are further sub divisions of class, namely, large and small or *beheima gasa* and *beheima dakah*.

By water creatures too, as was explained in Bereshit 1:22, there are divisions of fish and sea creatures or *dagim* and *chayot hayam*.

Only by birds do we not find any speciation or divisions of class. Thus the Torah calls all birds by the singular "bird", since they are all in the same category.

* * *

Bereshit 1:20

Overview—The Rogatchover raises an inconsistency that the Talmud asks, about whether birds were created from water or from land. He then proposes a novel answer, based on the Rambam's assertion that there are creatures that are both water and air based animals.

וַיֹּאמֶר אֱלֹהִים—יִשְׁרְצוּ הַמַּיִם, שֶׁרֶץ נֶפֶשׁ חַיָּה; וְעוֹף יְעוֹפֵף עַל-הָאָרֶץ, עַל-פְּנֵי רְקִיעַ הַשָּׁמָיִם

"Let the waters produce swarms of living creatures and **birds that fly**. And let fowl fly above the earth in the open firmament of heaven."

The Rogatchover:

"Look in Hulin page 27b. And according to the Rambam's opinion that there is a species that is a fish as well as a bird, as is explained in Sefer Hamitzvot and Hilkhot Maachalot Issurim chapter two, we can say that that is the intent here. And this is not the place to elaborate."

The Background:

In verse 20 it says "Let the waters produce swarms of living creatures and birds that fly."

The Talmud in Hulin 27b asks,[255] in verse 20 it states that birds were created from water, yet in chapter 2 verse 19 the Torah says:

וַיִּצֶר יְהוָה אֱלֹהִים מִן-הָאֲדָמָה, כָּל-חַיַּת הַשָּׂדֶה וְאֵת כָּל-עוֹף הַשָּׁמַיִם, וַיָּבֵא אֶל-הָאָדָם, לִרְאוֹת מַה-יִּקְרָא-לוֹ; וְכֹל אֲשֶׁר יִקְרָא-לוֹ הָאָדָם נֶפֶשׁ חַיָּה, הוּא שְׁמוֹ.

"G-d had formed out of the ground every beast of the field and every bird of the sky"

The implication here is that birds were formed from the earth. Which was it, were birds formed from the waters or from the earth? The Talmud answers[256] that in fact birds were created from mud which is a mixture of earth and water. Thus, the Torah attributes birds as being land-formed creatures as well as being sea-formed creatures. With this in dispute in mind we must turn our attention to one more place of judicial argumentation to resolve the Biblical inconsistency regarding the origin of birds. There is a dispute amongst the Rishonim whether one can receive numerous sets of lashes (*malkot*) for the same act. For example, the prohibition of wearing wool and linen together (*shaatnez*) is stated twice. If one transgresses this injunction do they receive two sets of lashes or only one set for the one act?

255

ועוד שאלו כתוב אחד אומר ויאמר אלהים ישרצו המים שרץ נפש חיה ועוף יעופף אלמא ממיא איברו וכתיב (בראשית ב) ויצר ה' אלהים מן האדמה כל חית השדה ואת כל עוף השמים אלמא מארעא איברו

"He put to him further this question: One verse says. And G-d said: Let the waters bring forth abundantly the moving creature that hath life, and let birds fly above the earth, from which it would appear that birds were created out of the water; but another verse says. And the Lord G-d formed out of the ground every beast of the field and every bird of the air, from which it would appear that they were created out of the earth?"

256

אמר לו מן הרקק

"He replied: They were created out of the mud."

The Rambam holds that one can never receive numerous sets of lashes for a doubled prohibitory clause. He states this with some force in Sefer Hamitzvot:[257]

וכבר נתבאר ביטול דבר זה, ושאין לוקין שתי מלקיות על לאו אחד בשום פנים, כמו שביארו בגמרא חולין.

"This idea has no merit, as our Sages have explained in tractate Hulin that one can never receive two sets of lashes for a single prohibition."

Several other Rishonim argue with the Rambam, most vocal among them the Ramban (in Sefer Hamitzvot loc. cit.). They argue that one can receive numerous sets of lashes for the same act.

This argument is brought to fore in the Talmud. In Makkot 16b the Talmud discusses one who eats a creature called the *putisa*. The *putisa* is a *sheretz*. A *sheretz* is a type of creature that we would, in conventional terms, call, an insect. The *sheretz* has special laws concerning one who touches it and the resultant ritual impurity (*tumah*) that they receive. As well, the Torah forbids eating any *sheretz*. The Torah first states the general prohibition twice, and then enumerates a specific injunction against eating a land, sea, and air *sheretz*, respectively.

The law as stated in Makkot is that this person receives four sets of lashes for eating this crawling creature. Rashi and the other Rishonim learn that the reason one receives four sets of lashes is because the Torah twice says, a general prohibition regarding eating a creature (*sheretz*), and twice states a prohibition to eat a land based creature (which according to them is what the *putisa* is classified as). Thus for each clause, one receives lashes ending in four measures of punishment for the four infractions.

The Rambam however is forced to learn this law in a very different style since he holds that one does not receive multiple sets of lashes for a doubled prohibitory injunction.

---

257   *Mitzvah lo saaseh* (negative prohibition) #179.

Instead, he holds (in Sefer Hamitzvot[258] and in Mishneh To-rah[259]) that the reason one receives four measures is because this creature called the *putisa* is a land, sea and air creature all at once since it lives in all three environments. It swims, flies and crawls. Therefore one receives three sets of lashes for the three different prohibitions of eating a land, sea and air creature[260]. (The fourth

---

258   *Mitzvah lo saaseh* (negative prohibition) #179:

"כי הנה יתכן שיהיה דג ושיהיה שרץ המים, וכמו כן יהיה עוף

ויהיה שרץ המים, וכמו כן יהיה עוף ושרץ העוף. מהו פוטיתא, שהוא עוף שרץ

העוף ושרץ הארץ ושרץ המים, ולפיכך' חייבין עליה ארבע מלקיות."

"This is the *putisa,* which is a bird, a *sheretz ha'of* (an air creature), a *sheretz ha'aretz* (an earthbound creature), and a *sheretz hamayim* (a water creature), and one therefore receives four sets of lashes for eating it."

259   Hilkhot Maachalot Assurot Chapter 2 halakhah 23:

הרי שהיתה הבריה משרץ העוף ומשרץ המים ומשרץ הארץ כגון שהיו לה כנפים והיא מהלכת על הארץ

כשאר שרצים והיתה רבה במים ואכל לוקה שלש מלקיות

"The following laws apply if a particular creature is [included in the categories of] a flying crawling animal, an aquatic crawling animal, and a crawling animal of the earth, e.g., it has wings, it walks on the earth like other earthbound crawling animals, and it reproduces in the water. If one eats it, he is liable for three sets of lashes."

It should be noted that the Raaved argues with this most emphatically:

כתב הראב"ד ז"ל המאסף הזה אסף דברים שאינם בעולם שלא שמענו מימינו נמלה גדלה במים ולא

שרץ העוף גדל במים

"The compiler gathered ideas here that simply do not exist in this world and that we have never heard of- that there should be a land creature living in the sea or an air creature living in the sea!?"

260

מחמת שלאו זה כולל שרץ הארץ לא ילקה על שרץ הארץ שתים, לפי שאפילו באו לנו אלף לאווין

מפרשים כולם ב"שרץ הארץ" - אינו לוקה עליהן אלא מלקות אחת, לפי שכולם נכפלו בעניין אחד

בעצמו, ואפילו אמר: שרץ הארץ לא תאכלו, שרץ הארץ לא תאכל, אלף פעמים - לא יתחייב עליו אלא

מלקות אחת

האם ראית שאלה שקבעו את הכלל המשובש הזה סוברים שהלובש שעטנז לוקה שתים כיון שבאו בו

שני לאווין מפרשים? לא

ראיתי שהם סוברים כן, אלא זה היה מוזר בעיניהם אילו אמרו מי שהוא, ואין דבריהם מוזרים בעיניהם

באומרם ששרץ הארץ או שרץ העוף שרץ העוף לוקין עליו שתים: אחת מחמת הלאו המפרש בו ואחת משום 'אל

תשקצו את נפשתיכם בכל השרץ'. וזה ברור בתכלית עד שלא יעלם אפילו מן החרשים והאלמים.

"But just because this prohibition includes a *sheretz ha'aretz,* one cannot be lashed twice for eating one. The reason is that even if there were a thousand prohibitions—each one specifically prohibiting *sheretz ha'aretz*—one would still only be lashed once, since they are merely repeating the same prohibition. Even if was repeated, "Do not eat *(lo soch'lu)* a *sheretz ha'aretz,*" "Do not eat *(lo yei'o'cheil)* a *sheretz ha'aretz*" one thousand times, only one set of lashes would be given.

Have you seen those who propose this erroneous principle dictating two sets of lashes for a person who wears *shatnez,* since there are two prohibitions? I have not seen them say such a thing, and they would consider it strange if anyone else did. But they somehow do not find it strange when they rule that one set is for the infraction of eating a non-kosher fish since it also is classified as a non-kosher fish.)

The Rogatchover threads all this together and resolves the apparent Biblical contradiction.

According to the Rambam that there is a creature that is both a sea and air animal we can say that our verse (1:20) is only talking about air creatures that are also sea creatures. Therefore the verse states:

וַיֹּאמֶר אֱלֹהִים—יִשְׁרְצוּ הַמַּיִם, שֶׁרֶץ נֶפֶשׁ חַיָּה; וְעוֹף יְעוֹפֵף עַל-הָאָרֶץ, עַל-פְּנֵי רְקִיעַ הַשָּׁמָיִם

"Let **the waters produce** swarms of living creatures and **birds that fly.** And let fowl fly above the earth in the open firmament of heaven."

The waters are producing the birds here because the verse is speaking about the amphibious birds that also dwell in the water. Interestingly this would explain the anomalous terminology used in this verse for life, namely,

שֶׁרֶץ נֶפֶשׁ חַיָּה.

The term *sheretz* is one that throughout scriptures and the Talmud has a negative connotation. Its usage here as a descriptive term for life is strange and an unsual choice of words. It is not employed elsewhere as an adjective for life. According to the Rogatchover, it is in fact, a most precise choice of linguistic style. This is because the verse is speaking about a *sheretz* that lives in the water as well as the air, namely the *putisa* or some similar creature.

Whereas the verse in 2:19,

וַיִּצֶר יְהוָה אֱלֹהִים מִן-הָאֲדָמָה, כָּל-חַיַּת הַשָּׂדֶה וְאֵת כָּל-עוֹף הַשָּׁמַיִם, וַיָּבֵא אֶל-הָאָדָם, לִרְאוֹת מַה-יִּקְרָא-לוֹ; וְכֹל אֲשֶׁר יִקְרָא-לוֹ הָאָדָם נֶפֶשׁ חַיָּה, הוּא שְׁמוֹ.

---

who eats a *sheretz ha'aretz* or *sheretz ha'of* receive two sets of lashes—once for the specific prohibition and once for the prohibition, "Do not make yourselves disgusting [by eating] any small creature that breeds." This is totally clear even to the deaf and dumb."

"G-d had formed **out of the ground** every beast of the field and **every bird of the sky**"

which attributes birds as being formed from the earth and having nothing to do with water, is referring to all regular birds that were formed from the earth.

* * *

Bereshit 1:21

Overview:

The Rogatchover clarifies the ambiguous Talmudic dispute regarding the identity of the *teninim gedolim*. One opinion says that they were enormous fish called the Leviathan. The other opinion is that the *teninim* were not fish at all. They were what halakhah calls "*chayot hayam*", animals of the sea. This is a term that describes the creatures in the sea that are not fish-like, but rather somewhat resemble land-creatures. With this clarification he resolves several Talmudic conflicts.

וַיִּבְרָא אֱלֹהִים אֶת-הַתַּנִּינִם הַגְּדֹלִים

"And G-d created the great *teninim*"

The Rogatchover:

"Rashi comments that the *teninim* are great fish in the sea. In truth they are animals of the sea not fish. And this is the *arzil-ei*. It then follows that the Rashbam is correct instead of Tosafot. And they were included in the decree. Look in the Rambam Hilkhot *maachalot assurot* who writes that animals of the sea are forbidden to eat. And look at Tosafot in Avodah Zara page 39 regarding the sea-bulls. As well as the Rashbam in Bava Basra page 74 and Bava Kama page 45 regarding cross breeding. And this is not the place to elaborate."

The Background:

What were the *teninim* exactly? We know they were some sort of creature that lives in the sea. But what species are they? What are their characteristics?

The Talmud in Bava Basra 74b records a dispute regarding the identity of the *teninim*.

ויברא אלהים את התנינים הגדולים הכא תרגימו ארזילי דימא ר׳ יוחנן אמר זה לויתן

"And G-d created the great teninim". Here [in Israel], they explained: The *arzilei* of the sea. Rabbi Yohanan said, this refers to the Leviathan."

We have here two very different opinions what the *teninim* were. Let's start with Rabbi Yohanan who is the simpler of the two. He says quite simply the *teninim* are gigantic fish. Most probably some sort of sea serpent when we consider that the Talmud's descriptive terms of the Leviathan is

נחש עקלתון

"the twisted serpent". In fact they were so big that G-d killed the female lest they propagate and flood the world.[261] But the bottom line is that the *teninim* are placed in the category of fish (*dagim*) according to this opinion. Rashi brings this opinion from the Talmud when commenting on this verse.

The other opinion says that the *teninim* were not a species of fish but rather sea-animals (*chayot hayam*). In other words, some sort of mammal. Additionally the term sea-animal (*chayot hayam*) means animals in the sea that have land animals' characteristics such as legs and the like. The Rambam frames it as follows:

261

אמר רב יהודה אמר רב כל מה שברא הקב"ה בעולמו זכר ונקבה בראם אף לויתן נחש בריח ולויתן נחש עקלתון זכר ונקבה בראם ואלמלי נזקקין זה לזה מחריבין כל העולם כולו מה עשה הקב"ה סירס את הזכר והרג הנקבה ומלחה לצדיקים לעתיד לבא

"Rab Yehudah said in the name of Rav: All that the Holy One, blessed be He, created in his world he created male and female. Likewise, Leviathan the slant serpent and Leviathan the tortuous serpent he created male and female; and had they mated with one another they would have destroyed the whole world [due to their size]. What did the Holy One, blessed be He, do? He castrated the male and killed the female preserving it in salt for the righteous in the world to come."

"Any aquatic creature that does not have the characteristics of a fish, neither a non-kosher fish or a kosher fish, e.g., a seal, a dolphin, a frog, or the like."

The Rogatchover proves that in fact, these are not subtle differences but that according to halakhah, fish (*dagim*), and sea-animals (*chayot hayam*), are two entirely different species. We see this from the Talmud in Bava Kama 55a:

א«ר ירמיה אמר ריש לקיש המרביע שני מינים שבים לוקה

"R. Yirmiyahu reported that Resh Lakish said: He who couples two species of sea creatures becomes liable to be lashed... [for the prohibition of cross breeding (klayim)]

Tosafot[262] brings an opinion that since it is physically impossible to crossbreed different species of sea creatures, the Talmud's statement from Resh Lakish should be read "He who works with two species of sea creatures becomes liable to be lashed" instead of "he who couples". They infringe against the prohibition of working with two different species, instead of the prohibition for mixing two species.

Tosafot continues that in his opinion there is no need to change the text since sea-animals "*chayot hayam*" can in fact be cross bred. It is only species of fish that ca not be coupled but different species of sea-animals can be cross bred. This shows that physiologically fish and sea-animals are two entirely different species.

שם ד"ה המרביע: "ר"י בר יהודה היה מגיה, המנהיג ב' מינים שבים לוקה, משום דבבראשית רבה פ"ז ובירושלמי דכלאים (פ"א) משמע, דאי אפשר להרביע דגים. ומיהו אין צריך להגיה, דדגים דוקא הוא דמשמע דאין להרביעם, אבל מין חיות הים שייך ביה איסור הרבעה, והכא איכא לאוקמי במין חיה שיכול אדם להרביע".

262   "Rabbi Yehudah bar Yehudah emended the text to read "one who leads" because from Bereshit Rabba chapter seven and from the Yerushalmi in Klayim (chapter one) we see, that it is impossible to cross breed two different species of fish. However there is no need to change the text, because it is precisely species of fish that ca not be coupled. However species of sea-animals (chayot hayam) can indeed be coupled."

The Rambam as well[263] states that there is a categorical divide

between the two species:

אי זהו שרץ המים אלו הבריות הקטנות כמו התולעים והעלוקה שבמים והבריות הג־
דולות ביתר שהן חיות הים כללו של דבר כל שאינו בצורת הדגים לא דג טמא ולא דג
טהור כגון כלב המים והדלפון והצפרדע וכיוצא בהן

"What is meant by an aquatic teeming animal? Both small creatures like worms and leeches that inhabit the water and larger
creatures **that are beasts of the sea** (*chayot hayam*). To state a
general principle: Any aquatic creature **that does not have the**
characteristics of a fish, neither a non-kosher fish or a kosher
fish, e.g., a seal, a dolphin, a frog, or the like."

The Rogatchover deduces that if we take this idea to its logical
conclusion, it follows that the *teninim* were wiped out in the
great flood of Noah (*mabbul*). This is because according to the
Talmud[264] fish were not included in the decree of destruction.
The Rogatchover asserts that this is because since we just learnt
(from Tosafot in footnote 2) that it is impossible to cross breed
fish, the fish were not included in the decree of "all flesh [i.e.
man and animals] have perverted their ways [and inter-bred
with other species]".

However the *teninim* being sea-animals and not fish were able to
couple with other species and hence were included in the decree
of destruction. Whereas fish did not cross breed since they are
physically unable and escaped destruction.

We can also say that this dispute is a source of contention between the Talmud Bavli and the Talmud Yerushalmi. The Roga-

---

263   In Hilkhot *maachalot assurot* chapter 2 halakhah 12.
264   Kidushin 13a:
בדור המבול לא נגזרה גזירה על דגים שבים שנאמר (בראשית ז) מכל אשר בחרבה מתו ולא דגים שבים
"In the generation of the flood, there was no decree of destruction against the
fish in the sea as it states "everything that was on **dry land** perished" and not
fish in the sea."

tchover[265] in the Mishnah Torah (*maachalot assurot*) cited above makes this connection. The Talmud in Hulin 67b says that the Leviathan was a kosher fish.

ר) יוסי בן דורמסקית אומר לויתן דג טהור הוא

"Rabbi Yosi ben Dormaskis said the Leviathan is a kosher fish"

The Yerushalmi however, in Shabbat (chapter nine) states that it was a non-kosher fish. This debate is not over facts, as it seems, but rather conceptual.

Both Talmuds' agree that the Leviathan has fins and scales, the kosher signs, as well as other non-fish like characteristics. The debate then revolves around[266] whether the Leviathan should be classified as fish due to its fish-like properties or whether it should fall into the sea-animal category due to its non-fish like properties. The Yerushalmi in stating that it is not kosher, is saying effectively that its non-fish like properties are the dominant ones and the deciding factor in determining what species it is. The Bavli disputes this and holds that its kosher signs are sufficient to place it firmly in the fish camp and out of the sea-animal camp.

* * *

Bereshit 2:7

Overview:

The Rogatchover addresses the geographical significance of the earth that was used in the creation of Man.

וַיִּיצֶר יְהוָה אֱלֹהִים אֶת-הָאָדָם, עָפָר מִן-הָאֲדָמָה, וַיִּפַּח בְּאַפָּיו, נִשְׁמַת חַיִּים וַיְהִי הָאָדָם, לְנֶפֶשׁ חַיָּה.

גדר חיה, עיין ב"ב עד, ב: אורזילא דימא, ויש לומר שבזה חולקים הירושלמי והבבלי; שהגמ' דילי ס"ל בחולין סז, ב שלויתן דג טהור הוא, שיש לו סנפיר וקשקשת, ובירושלמי · זון · פ"ט דשבת מבואר דטמא הוא. והטעם, משום דס"ל דהוה בגדר חיה והיינו תנינים, כמבואר בגמ'."

265
266   See Rashi in Hulin 126b as well as Nidah 22b that discusses this issue as well.

"Then the Lord G-d formed man of the **dust of the ground**, and breathed into his nostrils the breath of life and man became a living soul."

The Rogatchover:

"Dust from the Earth—In the Yerushalmi chapter 7 of Nazir (halakhah 2), and in the Rambam chapter 2 of Hilkhot Bet Habechirah, it is written that man was created from the place of the *mizbeach*. The intent is that through the creation of man was made the *shitin* as in Sukkah page 49 and page 53. Therefore it was able to be sanctified even though there is no sanctity in the deep as we see from Yerushalmi chapter 1 of Bikkurim and study Zevahim page 24 that David sanctified it. And Tosafot in Pesahim page 67b, nevertheless the *shitin* were sanctified. And in Tosefta Sukkah.

This is the nature of repentance through the libations, "pour your heart like water" and tears are like the fountain of *shitin*. As in Eiruvin page 19, study that source. And to negate the opinion of the Tzidukkim and Baisussim, in order to make it public as in Yerushalmi Sukkah and study Sanhedrin page 38 the piece that starts with "Adam…" and what is written there and in Ketubot page 111 "as if he was buried under the *mizbeach*". Study it further. And this is the meaning of the *shitin*.

The Background:

This is one of the longer and more puzzling pieces of the Rogatchover's commentary on Bereshit. We will break it down step by step and uncover the main point he is innovating. Some of the subtle threads of this piece are highly ambiguous and I will therefore focus on the gist of it.

An intriguing question to ponder is, where exactly was the dust taken from with which Man was created? Does it matter? What possible significance can the geography have?

The Rambam[267] and the Yerushalmi[268] assert that man was created from the place of his atonement. Meaning, from the temple altar, on which sacrifices (*korbanot*) were brought. The formulation of this concept is framed as follows:

"Adam mimakom kapparaso nivra ve'halevai tehei lo amida"

"Man was created from the very place where his atonement comes from, and thus perhaps he will be able to endure."

Additionally we know that there were twin holes (the *shitin*) in the temple altar (the *mizbeach)* that descended into the depths of the earth. Into these twin holes were poured the libations (*nesachim*) of wine and water in the temple.

We also know that the twin holes were created in the six days of creation.[269]

With these facts in mind we can explain a serious halakhic discrepancy.

---

267   See Mishnah Torah Hilkhot Beit Habechira Chapter 2 halakhah 2:

ומסורת ביד הכול, שהמקום שבנה בו דויד ושלמה המזבח בגורן ארוונה—הוא המקום שבנה בו אברהם המזבח ועקד עליו

יצחק, והוא המקום שבנה בו נוח כשיצא מן התיבה, והוא המזבח שהקריב עליו קין והבל. ובו הקריב אדם הראשון כשנברא קרבן, ומשם נברא; אמרו חכמים, אדם ממקום כפרתו נברא

"It is universally accepted that the place on which David and Solomon built the Altar... is the location where Abraham built the Altar on which he prepared Isaac for sacrifice.

Noah built [an altar] on that location when he left the ark. It was also [the place] of the Altar on which Cain and Abel brought sacrifices. Similarly, Adam, the first man, offered a sacrifice there and was created at that very spot, as our Sages said: "Man was created from the place where he [would find] atonement."

268   The Talmud Yerushalmi says (Nazir Chapter 7 halakhah 2):

אמר ר' יודה בן :זי: מלא תרווד אחד נטל הקב"ה ממקום המזבח וברא בו

אדם הראשון, אמר: הלואי ייברא ממקום המזבח ותהא לו עמידה

"One jarful of earth G-d took from the place of the *mizbeach* and created Man with it. G-d said, 'Perhaps if I create Man from the place of the *mizbeach*, he will endure.'"

269   Sukkah 49a:

אמר רבה בר בר חנה אמר ר' יוחנן: שיתין משֹשת ימי בראשית

נבראו,

"Rabbah the son of Chana said in the name of Reb Yohanan,'the shitin were created in the six days of creation.'"

The law is[270] that there is no concept of ownership in the depths of the earth.

However the Talmud (24a) assumes[271] as a matter of course, that the temple courtyard has sanctity that descends into the depths, and is not just holy on the surface.

The question that arises from this is the following:

If indeed there is no halakhic basis or precedent for proprietary rights that are below the surface of the earth then we must ask, how can the temple floor have been sanctified upon the building and completion of it? There simply is no legal or religious mechanism for acquiring ownership of sub-surface land.

The answer to this is lies in a clever twist by the Rogatchover in the Tosefta which states in Sukkah Chapter 3 halakhah 4:

שני ספלים של כסף היו בראשו של מזבח אחד של מים ואחד של יין

ומנוקבין כמין שני חוטמין דקין שבהן יורדין

ונבלעין בתוכו שנאמר בקדש הסך שעשה לו המקום שיבלע בקדושה

---

270   Talmud Yerushalmi Bikkurim Chapter 1 halakhah 1:

המוכר שביל לחבירו מקום דריסה הוא מכר או עד התהום מכה. אין תימר מקום דריסה מכר מביא וקורא אין תימר עד התהום מכר לא יביא אף עיקר. מספק מביא ואינו קורא. רבנין פשיטא לון שמכר עד התהום

"One who sells a path that runs through his field to his fellow- has he sold only the place of treading [i.e. the surface], or has he sold even the depths [of that strip of land]?

The difference would be whether the buyer can build on that path or make holes in the ground. If he bought all the earth to the depths, he could. If he only purchased the surface he cannot.

271

בעי ר' אמי נעקרה האבן ועמד במקומה מהו י מאי קא מיבעיא ליה
כי קדיש רצפה עליונה קדיש, או דילמא עד לארעית דתהומא קדיש. ותיבעי ליה
כל העזרה כולה
לעולם פשיטא ליה דעד ארעית
דתהומא קדיש והכי קמיבעיא, דרך שירות בכך או אין דרך שירות בבד

"Reb Ami asked, 'if a stone in the temple courtyard was uprooted and a Kohen performed the service while standing on that loose stone, what is the law?' What is he asking- if his question is whether only the floor of the courtyard was sanctified or whether the sanctity descended into the depths, then let him frame the question as pertaining to the whole courtyard! **Rather it is obvious that the sanctity of the temple descends past the surface into the deep... and his question is merely whether this is considered an acceptable form of service.**"

"There were two jugs of silver on the top of the altar. One contained water and one contained wine. There were two holes that descended like two thin nostrils through which the libations were poured and absorbed into. As it says "pour in holiness" i.e. G-d made that the libations should descend in holiness."

The Rogatchover is suggesting the following. Instead of interpreting the Tosefta as saying

שעשה לו המקום שיבלע בקדושה

that they made a place for the libations to be poured in holiness. Instead he interprets it as referencing G-d who is often referred to as *Hamakom* or "the place" and thus the Tosefta is saying that G-d made the twin-holes

שעשה לו המקום

in order

שיבלע בקדושה

that the twin holes have sanctity.

When did G-d make the twin holes? Well, we know that Man was created with dust taken from the area of the courtyard and the altar of the temple. That being the case, perhaps the twin holes were created when G-d scooped earth from the land. The twin holes then were essentially the remaining cavern that was formed by G-d digging up earth for the creation of Man. If that is the case, then we can understand how this sub-surface area became holy, since it was G-d Himself that sculpted it. This is what the Tosefta is conveying, that G-d himself formed and thus sanctified the sub-surface area of the twin holes and the temple.

* * *

Bereshit 2:19

Overview:

The Rogatchover discusses the significance of the naming process of the animals by Adam.

וַיִּצֶר יְהוָה אֱלֹהִים מִן-הָאֲדָמָה, כָּל-חַיַּת הַשָּׂדֶה וְאֵת כָּל-עוֹף הַשָּׁמַיִם, וַיָּבֵא אֶל-הָאָדָם, לִרְאוֹת מַה-יִּקְרָא-לוֹ; וְכֹל אֲשֶׁר יִקְרָא-לוֹ הָאָדָם נֶפֶשׁ חַיָּה, הוּא שְׁמוֹ.

"And out of the ground the Lord G-d formed every beast of the field and every bird of the air; and brought them to man to see what he would call them; **and whatever man would call every living creature, that was to be its name.**"

The Rogatchover:

"I already wrote concerning this that each species has a unique trait that is not found in any other animal and on this [trait], Adam conferred its name. Study Torat Kohanim Parshat Bechukosai regarding [the verse]' I will destroy marauding animals'.

And [Adam also called them names] to acquire them; study Kidushin page 22b '*korah lah*'. And study what is written in Tosafot Hulin 66b if he gave names to the fish or not. And study Sanhedrin 59b.

The practical consequence of this is that if the unique trait changes the animal no longer has this name. And study Torat Kohanim Parshat Bechukosai regarding marauding animals, study it well.

The snake's unique trait is explained in Bechorot 8b regarding a desire to cohabitate with no need for existence and in Hebrew this is called *nachash*. This is the understanding in the Yerushalmi in Pe'ah that the snake has no benefit from its bite at all, and study what Tosafot writes in Bava Kama 16a."

The Background:

What does it mean that Adam called the animals' names? Were they arbitrary? What was his decision making process? And what were the consequences of his allocation of names?

In fact it was a most precise process. Each name that was given was to illustrate the unique quality of that specific animal. And its uniqueness was embedded in the name. How and where in the name, the specific quality is illustrated is not known to us. Thus it clearly took tremendous wisdom and sensitivity to understand what quality is epitomized in each animal. This is why in the rabbinic literature we find that *Adam* was greatly praised for naming the animals.

A ramification of this is that if an animal's unique quality changes somehow, then its name would also change and the former species would be effectively extinct. So if a deer's intrinsic unique element metamorphosed into something else, the species of deer would be considered extinct. It would be a different animal and thus would have a different name since its name is a description of its unique qualities.

According to this we can shed light on a piece of Torat Kohanim[272] (Parshat Bechukosai Perek 1):

On the verse (in Parshat Bechukosai), *ve'hishbati chaya ra'ah* ("and I will destroy all marauding animals"), there is a dispute amongst the rabbis. Rabbi Yehudah interprets this literally, that in the times of Moshiach G-d will physically remove all species of marauding animals from the world. Rabbi Shimon says G-d will just destroy and remove the marauding tendency and nature from these species but they will physically remain extant in the world.

What is the central point that the dispute hinges on? From our vantage point we can see that Rabbi Shimon is of the opinion that as soon as the nature and qualities of these animals are changed then these animals have already been destroyed since their name would change thus fulfilling the Biblical promise. Whereas Rabbi Yehudah holds that an animal is not defined by its qualities and that even if the nature of a beast is changed that very beast is seen as maintaining its existence and retaining its name albet in a slightly different manner.[273]

---

272   פ"א פרק ב: ר' יהודה אומר: מעבירן מן העולם. ר' שמעון אומר: משביתן
שלא יזיקו. אמר ר"ש: אימתי הוא שבהו של מקום, בזמן שאין מזיקים, או בזמן
שיש מזיקים ואין מזיקים—אמור: בזמן שיש מזיקים ואין מזיקים.

273   See Mefaneach Tzfunot Perek 1, Siman 9, Oit 2 for a more complex and involved analysis of this dispute in which the argument revolves around quality versus quantity. Rabbi Yehudah holds that quantity is the dominant factor and therefore even if the quality of the animal changes we cannot say

Another thing that was accomplished by Adam allocating names to all the animals was that he thereby acquired them for himself.[274]

The Talmud (Kidushin 34a) explains that one can acquire ownership of an animal by calling its name. *Keitzad be'meshicha? Korah lah shem ve'hee ba'ah.*

"How does one use the ownership mechanism of drawing (*meshicha*)? You call the animal by its name and it comes toward you."

Why does one acquire an animal merely through calling its name without any need for action?

It is because the name of a species is not just an arbitrary sound that society has agreed to use for a certain animal. Rather it is the very essence of the animal itself. Therefore one can acquire it in this manner.

What about the creatures of the sea, were they also brought to Adam to be named and thus acquired?

Regarding this there are two opinions. Tosafot in Hulin 66b[275] asks how our Sages know that "*kol sheyesh lo kaskeses yesh lo snapir*"—'any fish that has scales has fins' and is therefore Kosher. Tosafot answers that perhaps they knew from Adam since he saw all the creatures of the sea when he gave them names. Others dispute this since the verse does not mention fish.[276]

---

that it is an entirely new species and that the Biblical promise has been fulfilled. Whereas Rabbi Shimon holds that quality is the dominant element and therefore as soon as the quality of the animal has changed it is utterly extinct and what stands before us is an absolutely new creature.

274   This gives new meaning to the fact that time and time again, regarding the animals the Torah states "*ve'kivshua*" that Adam should conquer them. This conquering was accomplished via the process of naming in which Adam actually acquired the animals.

275   S.v. *kol sheyesh lo:*

"וא"ת, מנין היה להם זה

לחכמים ... וליכא למימר מאדם, שקרא להם שמות קים להו הכי, שמסר לדורות כך

שהם טמאין, שכן הוא הכיר את כולם—דהא לא משמע במקרא שקרא שמות אלא

לבהמות ולעופות... בדגים מיהא לא אשכחן. וי"ל, מ,כל אשר יקרא לו האדם'

יש לרבות אפי' דגים ואיכא למימר דמאדם קים להו

276   It just says in verse 20, "And man gave names to all cattle and to the fowl of the air, and to every beast of the field". The first opinion answers that

Either way the question remains, were the fish acquired by Adam as well?

The Rogatchover explains that in truth, there is no capability of assuming ownership (a *kinyan*) of fish through calling its name (i.e. *meshicha*). We see in various places in Torah[277] that one does not acquire ownership of fish that were merely trapped in the water without being taken by the one who set the traps. In essence, these fish are still halakhically ownerless; however the Sages instituted a decree that these fish do belong to the one who set the traps in order to maintain peace and order. If one does not acquire fish (by Biblically law) even when they are trapped in one's traps, then that certainly is the case where one merely called them by name. One would not affect ownership over them until one actually took them by hand.

The sections in this piece about the snake will be explained in their primary location which is…

* * *

Bereshit 3:1

Overview:

The Rogatchover explains the essential nature of the snake.

וְהַנָּחָשׁ, הָיָה עָרוּם, מִכֹּל חַיַּת הַשָּׂדֶה, אֲשֶׁר עָשָׂה יְהוָה אֱלֹהִים

"Now **the serpent** was more cunning than any beast of the field which the Lord G-d had made…

The Rogatchover:

Study Bechorot 8b that the snake is one who desires excesses. Even when the female is pregnant she wills still have relations with the male, study there. And study Hulin 49b that the snake is an aberration and study Avodah Zara 43a.

---

fish are hinted to in the extra words "<u>and</u> whatever man would call them" in verse 19.

277   See Gitin 59a, Sanhedrin 25a and Mishnah Torah Hilkhot Zechiya Umatana Chapter 1 halakhah 2 and the commentaries.

The Background:

In the last piece we explored the idea that every species has a unique quality which defines it and on which Adam conferred a descriptive name. Although we are not informed of the unique quality of all the animals, the Rogatchover posits that we can indeed know the snake's quality. We see this from the Talmud in Bechorot 8b:[278]

"The Emperor once asked R. Yehoshua ben Chananya:

How long is the period of gestation and birth of a serpent?

He replied to him: Seven years.

But did not the Sages of the Athenian school couple a male serpent with a female and they gave birth in three years?

He replied to him: Those had already been pregnant for four years.

But did they not have sexual contact? [The implication being that since we know animals never have sexual relations when they're already pregnant, clearly the snake was not pregnant.]

He replied to him: **Serpents have sexual intercourse in the same manner as human beings.** [In other words, even when they're pregnant.]"

278

א"ל קיסר לר' יהושע בן חנניא: נחש לכמה מיעבר ומוליד ? א"ל: לשב שני.

זהא סבי דבי אתונא ארבעינהו ואוליד לתלת? הנהו מיעברי הוו מעיקרא ד' שנין

והא קמשמשי שמושי

אינהו נמי משמשי כאדם

"The Emperor once asked R. Yehoshua en. Chanania: 'How long is the period of gestation and birth of a serpent'? He replied to him: 'Seven years'. '

But did not the Sages of the Athenian school couple a male serpent with a female and they gave birth in three years'?

'Those had already been pregnant for four years'.

'But did they not have sexual contact'?

'Serpents have sexual intercourse in the same manner as human beings.'"

We see from this Gemara that snakes have an appetite for sexual relations that are not strictly necessary for their survival since the female is already pregnant.

This fits nicely with the Yerushalmi in Pe'ah[279] (Chapter 1 halakhah 1) that denigrates the snake for biting people even though it gets no benefit from it? All other animals kill to eat but the snake kills just for the pleasure of it. This idea is even brought into play amidst a legal discussion in the Talmud[280] concerning what is considered a normal natural attack by an animal. In an intriguing teaching, the Talmud states that all the animals come and accuse the snake of hurting others without deriving any actual benefit from its attacks.

In all these instances we see the same fundamental point. The snake engages in activities that survival and nature do not dictate or mandate it to do, yet it engages in them anyways, notwithstanding its lack of benefit from it.

The Rogatchover in another context[281] equates this quality of the snake as paralleling the quality of the Satan, the evil inclination.

279

אמר ר' שמואל בר נחמן אומרים ל נחש. . . מה הנייה, לך שאת

נושך י אריה טורף ואוכל זאב טורף ואוכל, את מה הנייה, יש לך

"Said Rabbi Shmuel bar Nachman: We say to the snake- what benefit do you receive from biting people? The lion bites and eats, the wolf bites and eats.... yet you bite and get no benefit from it!"

280   See Taanit 5a:

שנתקבצו כל החיות אצל הנחש ואומרות לו: מה הנאה יש לך י מ"מ כיון

דאורחיה בהכי הוי כמו רגל ופטור ברה"ר

"All the animals gang up on the snake and say" what possible benefit can you get [from your bite]?" Nonetheless it is considered a usual natural attack for a snake and thus the owner is not liable for its damages in the public area as per the rules of regel."

281   Tsafnat Paneah Hilkhot Trumot Chapter 3 halakhah 1:

וזהו גדר שטן

מתאוה לדברים שאינם לקיומו של עולם וזהו נחש וכמבואר

בבכורות דף ח / ע"ב, דהוא לבדו מין שיש לו תאוה, לדברים שאין בהם קיום

העולם והוא שפיתה לחוה, והטיל בה זוהמא, ור"ל שנתן בה גדר תאוה, לדברים

שאין בהם קיום

"This is the nature of the Satan. He desires things that are not necessary for the continuance of the world, and this is the same idea as the snake as we see in Bechorot 8b that it alone has the desire for things not necessary for its survival. This is what the snake did to Chava and inserted his influence into her. In other

Sin is at its core, an action that does not promote the continuance of the world and is not necessary. This is the influence and behavior that the snake introduced Chava to during the sin of eating from the tree of knowledge; to desire unnecessary excesses.

* * *

Bereshit 3:6

Overview:

וַתֵּרֶא הָאִשָּׁה כִּי טוֹב הָעֵץ לְמַאֲכָל וְכִי תַאֲוָה-הוּא לָעֵינַיִם, וְנֶחְמָד הָעֵץ לְהַשְׂכִּיל, וַתִּקַּח מִפִּרְיוֹ, וַתֹּאכַל; וַתִּתֵּן גַּם-לְאִישָׁהּ עִמָּהּ, וַיֹּאכַל

And when the woman saw that the tree was good for food, and that it was a delight to the eyes, and that the tree was to be desired to make one wise, she took of its fruit and ate; and she gave also to her husband with her, and he ate.

The Rogatchover:

It says in the Midrash that she was gripped by the sickness of *bulmes* and became deathly ill until her eyes lit up, study Yoma page 83a study it well. First one needs to eat bread and then different types of sweets, look there. This is the language of the verse "it was good for food" and then "it was a delight to the eyes" and then it allowed one to discern between good and bad.

If so it was dangerous. Nevertheless what caused *bulmes* to grip her? It was through that she instigated her own evil inclination, study Nidah 13b, regarding one who self-instigates sexual arousal…

This is the category of one who is careless in the beginning even though later they are not in control, study Ketubot 53a regarding this and 54a. And study Tosafot in Bava Kama 41 s.v. "*kegon shekafatz*".

---

words the snake introduced her to the idea of desiring excesses and things that do not promote the continuance of the world."

Study Tosafot there regarding this and study Bava Metzia 93b "*harei holichon*" …and this is not the place to elaborate concerning this.

The Background:

In the verse that describes the appearance of the tree of knowledge and how Eve perceived the tree there are several perplexing adjectives.

1. It states "the tree was good to eat".
2. It states "it was a delight (or desire) to the eyes"
3. It states "the tree was to be desired to make one wise". What form of wisdom did it confer on the one who eats from it? In 2:9 it states "and the tree of **the knowledge of good and evil**".

All three descriptions are flowery and somewhat ambiguous terms to describe a tree. Why was it necessary to state each one? And what is the connection between the three?

The Rogatchover develops the idea that Eve was stricken by an ancient sickness called *bulmes* discussed in the Talmud. All three of these descriptions are used in the Talmud when describing the sickness or cure.

What was the nature of this sickness? It was a terrible hunger that gripped the person and if they were not immediately fed whatever they desired, they would die. Therefore the Talmud[282] (Yoma 83a in the Mishnah) states that we can and must feed them even non-kosher foods.

Additionally the person's eyes would darken and only once they were fed whatever food they desired, would their eyes light up. Once the eyes would light up it was known that the worst was

---

282

מי שאחזו בולמוס מאכילין אותו אפילו דברים טמאים עד שיאורו עיניו

"One who is gripped by bulmes we must feed them even non-kosher items until their eyes light up".

over. Therefore they would need to be fed sweet foods,[283] since according to the Talmud sweet foods light up a person's eyes.

What does it mean that the person's eyes lit up and which form of light was this? The Talmud[284] explains that it means having the awareness to distinguish between good and bad.

If so, applying this information to the story of Eve in the garden, we can see that Eve was gripped by the deathly sickness of *bulmes* and she desired to eat from the tree of knowledge to satiate and cure the illness. This is why it says that the tree was "a delight to the eyes" and "it was desired to make one wise" since these both are essential ingredients in the cure for *bulmes*. The sick person must eat sweet foods, which would include fruits that have natural sugars, and would have to eat until their eyes lit up, meaning until they have the awareness to distinguish between good and bad. The tree of knowledge performed both functions admirably since it was a "delight to the eyes" and also a repository of the "knowledge of good and evil", both necessary parts of the cure.

That being the case, what did she do wrong? We saw from the Talmud that one who is gripped by *bulmes* is fed whatever they want since they will die if not fed their hearts desire. All the laws of the Torah and directives of G-d are placed on hold to save someone's life, so why was G-d upset at her? Was not she on solid legal and moral ground when eating from the tree of knowledge?

The answer lies in a Talmudic and halakhic principle about self-control and personal responsibility. The principle is called *techilato be'pshiya ve'sofo be'ones* or "the beginning was careless-

---

283

מי שאחזו בולמוס מאכילין אותו דבש וכל מיני מתיקה.

שהדבש וכל מיני מתיקה מאירין מאור עיניו של אדם . . . אמר אביי לא שנו אלא

לאחר אכילה, אבל קודם אכילה אכילה מגרר גריר

"One who is gripped by bulmes we feed them honey and all sorts of sweets because honey and sweets light up the eyes of a person. Abaye said, this only applies after the initial feeding in which their eyes start to light up....but if we feed them sweets right away it only makes the sickness stronger."

284   In Yoma ibid:

מנין היו יודעין שהאירו עיניו ו משיבחין בין טוב לרע

"How did they know that his eyes lit up? Once he was able to distinguish between good and bad".

ness and the end was involuntary". This means that even if what occurred in the end was beyond your control and involuntary, nonetheless you are legally and morally responsible if the beginning was with your consent and control.

The Talmud rules in accordance with this principle in several places. Concerning a woman who committed adultery[285] and concerning a woman who was raped.[286]

Another classic example of this is the case of a *shomer chinam* or free caretaker. A free caretaker is one who is watching your possessions for free, as a favor. If something beyond their control, say theft, should happen to your possessions they are exempt. If however the beginning of the problem was due to their inadequate care and attention, such as leaving the doors unlocked, then even if the thieves come and steal the possessions, something which is beyond the caretaker's capability to guard from, nonetheless they are liable since they were careless in the beginning by leaving the doors unlocked.

In our story, concerning Eve, once she was stricken by *bulmes*, it was within her rights to eat from the tree; but the catalyst for her *bulmes* was voluntary and when she was in control.[287] There-

---

285   See Ketubot 23a:

אמר רב חסדא זינתה אין לה מזונות אמר רב יוסף כיחלה ופירכסה אין לה מזונות מאן דאמר זינתה כל שכן כיחלה ופירכסה מאן דאמר כיחלה ופירכסה אבל זינתה אית לה מאי טעמא יצר אנסה

R. Chisda ruled: If she played the harlot she is not entitled to maintenance. R. Joseph ruled: If she painted her eyes or dyed her hair she is not entitled to maintenance. He who ruled: 'If she played the harlot' would even more so deprive her of maintenance if she paints her eyes or dyes her hair. He, however, who ruled: 'If she painted her eyes or dyed her hair' would allow her maintenance if she played the harlot. What is the reason?—**Her passions have overpowered her.**

286   See Ketubot 51b:

דאמר רבא: כל שתחלתה באונס וסוף ברצון אפילו היא

אומרת: הניחו לו, שאלמלא נזקק לה היא שוכרתו—מותרת. מאי טעמא? יצר

אלבשא

For Rava said, any case that was begun with force and ended with desire, even if the woman says [regarding the rapist] " Let him be, if he were not forcing himself upon me I would go hire him" [i.e. her desire was aroused during the rape] she would still be permitted to her husband since she was overcome by her desire.

287   Although the Rogatchover does not explain where we see a voluntary carelessness in the verses, perhaps it was her extended and lengthy conversation with the snake. This symbolized a sort of self-instigation and voluntary

fore she was liable since it was a case of *techilato be'pshiya ve'sofo be'ones,* "the beginning was carelessness and the end was involuntary".

* * *

Bereshit 3:15

Overview:

Shows the curse on the snake reflected in the legal system.

וְאֵיבָה אָשִׁית, בֵּינְךָ וּבֵין הָאִשָּׁה, וּבֵין זַרְעֲךָ, וּבֵין זַרְעָהּ

And I will put enmity between you and the woman, and between your offspring and her offspring

The Rogatchover:

This is the difference to what was taught in Sanhedrin 2a and 15b that a snake does not require a court. The Rambam also rules this way in Hilkhot Sanhedrin, just that it is enough to have one.

The Background:

G-d curses the snake that there will be hatred between his species and women forever.

The Rogatchover clarifies where we see this curse reflected in the halakhic legal system. The Talmud explains[288] that wild animals that killed someone are put to death and adjudicated by a court of twenty three as is the standard for any case that can result

---

engagement with the forbidden tree which later caused her to fall sick with *bulmes.*

288   See Sanhedrin 2a:

הזאב והארי הדוב והנמר והברדלס והנחש מיתתן בעשרים ושלשה. ר׳

אליעזר אומר: כל הקודם להורגן זכה. ד׳ עקיבא אומר: מיתתן בעשרים ושלשה.

"The wolf, the lion, the leopard, the cheetah and the snake are adjudicated by a court of twenty three. Rabbi Eliezer says they do not require adjudication; rather whoever sees them may kill them on the spot. Rabbi Akiva says, they require a court of twenty three."

in capital punishments. Rabbi Akiva[289] disagreed with this and ruled that for a snake anyone can immediately kill it since the presumption is that it will strike a person unprovoked.

The Rambam[290] codifies Rabbi Akiva's opinion in law.

Bereshit 3:21

Overview:

Discusses the significance of man's clothes that were made by G-d.

וַיַּעַשׂ יְהוָה אֱלֹהִים לְאָדָם וּלְאִשְׁתּוֹ, כָּתְנוֹת עוֹר—וַיַּלְבִּשֵׁם

And the Lord G-d made for Adam and for his wife garments of skins, and clothed them

The Rogatchover:

Here it chose "and G-d made" because this was the completion of man and he became entrenched in nature. Like the opinion in Nidah 25a that it means actual skin and before this man had no skin. For this comes from semen as in Nidah 31a and concerning this is the dispute whether skin is susceptible to impurity or not, study Nidah 55a if this is part of the essence of man or just an external protective layer. Study the Gemara there and study Tosefta Berakhot (Chapter 2) and the Yerushalmi Nidah Chap-

---

289   See Sanhedrin 15b:

ר' עקיבא היינו תנא קמא איכא ביניייהו: נחש

290   See Hilkhot Sanhedrin Chapter 5 halakhah 2:

אין דנין דיני נפשות בפחות מעשרים ושלשה שהן סנהדרי קטנה בין דיני נפשות של אדם בין דיני נפשות של בהמה לפיכך אין דנין שור הנסקל ולא הבהמה הנרבעת או הרובע אלא בבית דין של עשרים ושלשה אפילו ארי ודוב וברדלס שהן בני תרבות ויש להן בעלים שהמיתו מיתתן בעשרים ושלשה אבל נחש שהמית אחד הורג אותו

"Cases involving capital punishment may not be judged by a court with less than twenty three judges, i.e., a minor Sanhedrin. This applies not only to instances where humans are judged with regard to capital punishment, but also when animals face such judgment. Therefore an ox which is stoned to death and an animal used in bestial sexual practices is condemned to death only by a court of twenty three judges. Even when a lion, a bear, or a cheetah that have been domesticated and which have owners, kill a human, they are executed based on the judgment of a court of twenty three. When, however, a snake kills a human, even one ordinary person may kill him."

ter 3 regarding the fact that Adam was not created naked, rather in darkness and clouds.

And this is not possible with a man created from earth. Study Bechorot 7b, regarding this. At a minimum this was the final completion and this is the meaning if "And G-d made". And this is also the dispute in Sotah 14a if from wool or from linen, study that source.

The Background:

The verse states that G-d made clothes for man. The word *va'yaas*, that G-d "made" can be understood as representing a completion and ending of a constructive act.[291] Thus the Rogatchover asserts that the skins that G-d made for man here, were in fact the actual skin of the body and not external garments. Therefore the word *va'yaas* is used since this was the final act in constructing man and man was thus completed.

The Talmud states[292] that this skin is only existent with those who were fully formed by G-d. This has application to various childbirth laws such as if a fetus is lacking skin we know that there was no real formation of a body. We see that skin is the final end act of the formation of man.

However we can still ask, whether skin is an essential core component of man such as the internal organs, or if it is merely a sort of natural coat and sack to protect us from the elements and to contain all the blood and organs respectively.

This question has halakhic repercussions as well. There is a question in the field of Hilkhot Tumah[293] (the laws of ritual purity and impurity), whether the skin of a dead corpse conveys impurity or not. Amongst the technical legal discussion it emerg-

---

291   See Rashi to Bereshit 1:7 and the Ramban there.

292   Nidah 25a:

ויעש ה' אלקים לאדם ולאשתו כתנות עור

וילבישם' מלמד, שאין הקב"ה עושה עור לאדם אלא א"כ נוצר

"And the Lord G-d made for Adam and for his wife garments of skins, and clothed them, teaches that the Holy One, blessed be He, makes no skin for man before he is formed".

And in Tosafot s.v. "She'ein"..

293   See Nidah 55a.

es that the one of the opinions perceives the essential function of the skin to be of a protective nature. The Rogatchover posits that this legal dispute revolves around one's understanding of the essence of the skin of a person. If skin is external and merely a protective layer surrounding the body then essentially it not a core component of the body and thus should be considered foreign to the dead corpse and thus would not make a person impure. If skin is a core component and integral to man then it is to be considered essential to the body and would indeed make one impure.

The Tosefta in Berakhot[294] and the Yerushalmi in Nidah[295] state that man was not created naked but rather clothed by G-d. The form of clothing this took was the enclosing of the fetus in the placenta. However Adam was created from dust and did not gestate in a placenta?

The Talmud in Bechorot[296] understands that the placenta is not considered to be from the mother or from the baby, which is why even if both the mother and baby die during childbirth, the placenta remains pure, since it is not considered to be from

---

294   Chapter 2 halakhah 14:

כשברא הקב״יה את האדם לא בראו ערום, שנאמר: בשומי ענן,

לבושו וערפל חתולתו', ,ענן לבושו' זה השפיר, וערפל חתולתו' זה השליא—הרי

שהיתה מטפחת של בגד ושל עור חגורה לו על מתניו הרי זה קורא [קריאת שמען

"The Rabbis said that it is not praiseworthy for a person to be sitting naked, because the Holy One Blessed Be He did not create man naked as it says, "I clothed him in a cloud and [made] mist his shroud." (Iyov 38:9)"Clothed him in a cloud" that [refers to] the sack of the fetus, "and [made] mist his shroud" that [refers to] the placenta."

295   Chapter 3 halakhah 3:

שאין שפיר אלא באדם בלבד, הדא היא דכתיב: בשומי ענן לבושר

וערפל חת ׳-תו', לבושו' זה השפיר, וערפל חתולתו' זו השליא

296   7b:

אמר רב הונא: עור הבא כנגד פניו של חמור מותר. מאי טעמאי פירשא

בעלמא הוא. אמר ליה רב חסדא: תניא ׳מסיייע לך, עור הבא כנגד פניו של אדם

בין חי בין מת טהור, מאי לאו בין הוא הי ואמו היה בין הוא מת ואמו מתה

"R. Huna: The skin which is over the face of an ass at birth is permitted to be eaten.

What is the reason?—It is a mere secretion [but no real skin]. Said R. Chisda to him. There is a [Baraita] taught which supports you: A skin which is over the face of a man, whether alive or dead, is clean. Now, does not this mean whether both the offspring and its mother are alive, or whether both the offspring and its mother are dead?"

either of them. Additionally one can actually eat the placenta since it is not considered to be the flesh of the mother or the baby. The Rogatchover brings this source and the implication seems to be that this aligns with his earlier statement about G-d creating man already clothed. Since man was not created naked as we saw in the Tosefta and the Yerushalmi, and this form of clothing was the placenta and birth-sack, the fact that halakhah understands the placenta to be neither of the mother nor of the fetus, supports his contention that the placenta is a divinely fashioned wardrobe for man.

This whole discussion can be related to the dispute between Rav and Shmuel[297] whether the garments were wool or linen. If they were wool, then they came from the skin of sheep, which would compute into the perspective that the skin of man is an internal essential ingredient. If however, it came from linen, then we are dealing with the perspective that skin is an external protective layer of the human body.

✳ ✳ ✳

Bereshit 4:1-4:4

Overview:

The Rogatchover sheds light on a shocking Gemara.

וְהָאָדָם, יָדַע אֶת-חַוָּה אִשְׁתּוֹ; וַתַּהַר, וַתֵּלֶד אֶת-קַיִן, וַתֹּאמֶר, קָנִיתִי אִישׁ אֶת-יְהוָה. ב וַתֹּסֶף לָלֶדֶת, אֶת-אָחִיו אֶת-הָבֶל; וַיְהִי-הֶבֶל, רֹעֵה צֹאן, וְקַיִן, הָיָה עֹבֵד אֲדָמָה. ג וַיְהִי, מִקֵּץ יָמִים; וַיָּבֵא קַיִן מִפְּרִי הָאֲדָמָה, מִנְחָה—לַיהוָה. ד וְהֶבֶל הֵבִיא גַם-הוּא מִבְּכֹרוֹת צֹאנוֹ, וּמֵחֶלְבֵהֶן; וַיִּשַׁע יְהוָה, אֶל-הֶבֶל וְאֶל-מִנְחָתוֹ. ה וְאֶל-קַיִן וְאֶל-מִנְחָתוֹ, לֹא שָׁעָה

And the man knew Eve his wife; and she conceived and bore Cain, and said: 'I have gotten a man with the help of the Lord'. **2** And again she bore his brother Abel. And Abel was a keeper of sheep, but Cain was a tiller of the ground. **3** And in

---

297   Sotah 14a:

כתנות עוד רב ושמואל. חד אמר: דבר הבא מן העור,

וחד אמר: דבר שהעור נהנה ממנו

"Garments of skin. Rav and Shmuel argued concerning this. One said it means something which comes from skin (i.e. wool). The other said it means something that skin enjoys feeling (i.e. linen)."

process of time it came to pass, that Cain brought of the fruit of the ground an offering unto the Lord. 4 And Abel, he also brought of the firstlings of his flock and of the fat thereof. And the Lord had respect unto Abel and to his offering;5 but unto Cain and to his offering He had not respect...

The Rogatchover:

This was until the birth of Sheit, until that time there was no system of nature i.e. a system of natural continuity. Rather during all the days of Hevel there was only a system of miracles and after the murder of Hevel it was the opposite until the birth of Sheit. Such as witchcraft and the children of *tohu* and adultery. And study Eiruvin 18b and all the days of Hevel there was no nature only miracles. This is what is stated in Torat Kohanim Parshat Shemini "kimei olam", this is Hevel concerning which there is no *avodah zara* i.e. nature and study Sanhedrin 38b what is written there.

The Background:

The Talmud[298] states that Adam fathered demons of various kinds until he gave birth to a child who was in his own image i.e. human.

The Torat Kohanim states[299] that in the days of Hevel (Abel) there was no idol worship. The Rogatchover is abstracting the

---

298   Eiruvin 18b:

ואמר ר׳ ירמיה בן אלעזר: כל אותן השנים שהיה אדם הראשון בנידוי

הוליד רוחץ ושידין ולילין, שנאמר: ,ויחי אדם שלשים ומאת שגה ויולד בדמותי

כצלמו׳ מכלל דעד האידנא לאו כצלמו אוליד

"R. Yirmiyahu ben Elazar further stated: In all those years during which Adam was under the ban [i.e. the 130 years after his expulsion from the Garden of Eden] he begot ghosts and male demons and female demons, for it is said in Scripture:' And Adam lived a hundred and thirty years and begot a son in his own likeness, after his own image',- from which it follows that until that time he did not beget after his own image.

299   Parshat Shemini halakhah 31:

ועל אותו שעה הוא אומר ,וערבה לה׳ מנחת

יהודה וירושלים כימי עולם וכשנים קדמוניות׳ ,כימי עולם׳ כימי משה ,וכשנים

קדמוניות׳ כשני שלמה. רבי אומר: ,כימי עולם׳ כימי נח ,וכשנים קדמוניות׳ כשנות

הבל, שלא היתד עבודה זרה בעולם.

Rebbi said: it says 'and it will be pleasing to G-d the mincha of Yehudah and Yerushalayim as in the days of old and the primordial years'. The 'days of old'

concept of idolatry to symbolize the workings of nature and the pure years of Hevel as being a time in which the concept of nature, i.e. a natural continuity to the workings of the world, was not existent. Rather the world lived in a purely miracle state of direct divine influence on the workings of the world.

As such the Talmud's shocking assertion that Adam begat all forms of demons can be understood as consonant with this theme. In other words Adam begat demons during the years after Hevel was killed until Sheit (Seth) was born. Demons are associated with idolatry, which in turn is a metaphor for nature. As such the Talmud is stating that Adam after the killing of Hevel was living in a time of pure nature without any direct divine influence until Sheit was born.

∗ ∗ ∗

Bereshit 5:1

Overview:

The Rogatchover deepens the message and relevancy of this verse.

זֶה סֵפֶר, תּוֹלְדֹת אָדָם: בְּיוֹם, בְּרֹא אֱלֹהִים אָדָם, בִּדְמוּת אֱלֹהִים, עָשָׂה אֹתוֹ

This is the book of the generations of Adam. In the day that G-d created man, in the likeness of G-d He made him.

The Rogatchover:

Look in the Yerushalmi Nedarim Chapter 9 'regarding the great principle in Torah of loving your fellow as yourself as the Rambam writes in the Moreh, that all existence that occurred then is forever. So too with the individual man as it is with the species of Man. And study Bava Basra 9 and the Hagahot Maimon that thing written is not temporary rather every single second it is a new existence.

The Background:

refers to the days of Noach and the 'primordial years' refers to the days of Hevel during which there was no concept of avodah zara yet in the world.

The Talmud Yerushlami[300] brings the famous teaching of Rabbi Akiva 'And you shall love your fellow as yourself' this is a central principle in Torah. However in the Yerushalmi there is another opinion. Ben Azai said 'this is the book of the generation of man' is an even greater principle'.

Ben Azai's point is that loving your fellow as yourself is not as central as the intent underlying our verse in 4:1. This is because the verse ends with 'In the day that G-d created man, in the likeness of G-d He made him'. If we love our fellow because we recognize that every person is created with the dignity and honor that G-d possesses we will have even more love and camaraderie then if we just focused on the directive to love our fellow as ourself.

The Rogatchover then brings in another facet of this verse that adds relevance and impact to this verse's assertion that all of mankind is created in G-d's image.

Anything that is written in Torah has an eternal vibrancy to it. Partly due to it having been written and partly due to its having been written in the Torah. We find this reflected in halakhah in that we understand written documents to have an eternal and constant relevancy and application. Any sale that was documented is considered to be known to all, *shtar yesh la kala,* and any document is considered to be constantly active and operational[301] unless proven otherwise, as we see in the halakhot of property disputation and protestation, *chazakah and ma'cha'ah.* This concept it must be stressed, goes further then just saying that a document has constant relevance. Halakhah views the written word as an active and current message. Therefore the halakhah is that a document stating ownership of land is consid-

---

300   Nedarim Chapter 9 halakhah 4:

ואהבת לרעך כמוך. רבי עקיבה אומר זהו כלל גדול בתורה. בן עזאי אומר (בראשית ה) זה ספר תולדות אדם זה כלל גדול מזה

301   See the Hagahot Maimon Hilkhot Toen Ve'nitan 15:7:

דכיון שהשטר בידו חשיב מחאה
בכל שעה

And Tsafnat Paneah Trumot page 120:

כיון דכתיב
בתורה הוי דבר במשך ופועל תמיד

ered to be constantly "voicing" its proof which is why squatters cannot take over the land.[302]

As such this verse which proclaims 'this is the book of man' and the assertion of the divine dignity embedded in Man is constantly true in an active and current way. As the Rogatchover writes:[303]

שכל שכתיב בתורה הדבר הוי נצחי, ולא

רק מה שהיה

---

302   See Bava Basra 38b Tosafot s.v. "vetzarich".
303   Mahadura Tinyana 16b.

Made in the USA
Middletown, DE
11 December 2014